INTERMEDIATE
Teacher's Guide

INTERMEDIATE
Teacher's Guide

Center for the
Ministry of Teaching

MOREHOUSE PUBLISHING

© 1994 By Virginia Theological Seminary and Morehouse Publishing

Revised edition, 2000

All rights reserved. No part of this book may be reproduced, stored in a retrieval system, or transmitted in any form or by any means, electronic, mechanical, photocopying, recording, or otherwise, without the written permission of the publisher.

Developed by
Virginia Theological Seminary
Center for the Ministry of Teaching
3737 Seminary Road
Alexandria, VA 22304

Published by
Morehouse Publishing
P.O. Box 1321
Harrisburg, PA 17105
Morehouse Publishing is a division of *The Morehouse Group*.

Locke E. Bowman Jr., Editor-in-Chief

Amelia J. Gearey, Ph.D., Associate Editor

The Rev. George G. Kroupa III, Associate Editor

Judith W. Seaver, Ph.D., Managing Editor (1990-1996)

Dorothy S. Linthicum, Managing Editor (current)

Consultants for the Cross Year, Intermediate
    The Rev. William L. Evans, Alexandria, VA
    The Rev. David A. Scott, Ph.D., Virginia Theological Seminary
    The Rev. Benjamin E.K. Speare_Hardy II, Columbus, GA
    Jackie H. Stanley, Chapel Hill, NC
    The Rev. Anne O. Weatherholt, Boonsboro, MD

Community Times, student newspaper, designed by Jan E. Moffatt.
    Art by Bobbi Tull and Jan E. Moffatt, Alexandria, VA

Symbol Card art and Chalice Year Treasurebook design by Jan E. Moffatt.

For additional copies, contact:

MOREHOUSE PUBLISHING

Toll Free: 1-800-877-0012   Fax: 717-541-8128
www.morehousegroup.com
ISBN: 0-8192-6032-0

Printed in the United States of America
06 05 04 03   9 8 7 6 5 4

CONTENTS

BACKGROUND FOR TEACHERS
   The Teaching Ministry in Episcopal Churches 1
   Understanding Intermediate-Age Students 9
   Using the Curriculum 15
   Teaching Strategies and Resources 19

UNIT I: PROPHECY
   Letter to Parent 33
   Session 1. The Mission of the Prophets 35
   Session 2. Amos: Prophet of Justice 39
   Session 3. Isaiah: Messiah Will Come 43
   Session 4. Micah Spoke for God 47
   Session 5. Jeremiah: Prophet of Faith 51
   Session 6. Ezekiel: Seer of Visions 55
   Session 7. Isaiah Proclaims a Message of Light 59
   Session 8. Centuries of Prophecy 63
   Session 9. Honoring the Saints 67

UNIT II: PARABLES OF PROMISE
   Letter to Parent 71
   Session 1. A New Creation 73
   Session 2. Preparing the Way 77
   Session 3. The Genealogy of Jesus 81
   Session 4. The Messiah is Born 85
   Session 5. Flight into Egypt 89
   Session 6. Parable of the Sower 93
   Session 7. Parable of the Vineyard Workers 97
   Session 8. Parables of Treasure 101
   Session 9. The House upon a Rock 105

UNIT III: EUCHARIST: SHARED LIFE

    Letter to Parent 109
    Session 1. Gathering for Liturgy 111
    Session 2. The Word of God 115
    Session 3. Offering the Gifts 119
    Session 4. The Great Thanksgiving 123
    Session 5. Going Forth into the World 127
    Session 6. Holy Week Begins 131
    Session 7. The Passion of Christ 135
    Session 8. The Resurrection of Christ 139
    Session 9. Breakfast by the Sea 143

UNIT IV: THE CATECHISM

    Letter to Parent 147
    Session 1. The New Covenant 149
    Session 2. The Trinity 153
    Session 3. The Church 157
    Session 4. The Creeds 161
    Session 5. Sin and Redemption 165
    Session 6. Prayer and Worship 169
    Session 7. Ministry 173
    Session 8. Christian Hope 177
    Session 9. Celebrating Pentecost 181

FOUNDATION PAPER 185

BACKGROUND FOR TEACHERS

THE TEACHING MINISTRY IN EPISCOPAL CHURCHES

In the words of the Baptismal Covenant, we promise to "continue in the apostles' teaching and fellowship, in the breaking of bread, and in the prayers" (*The Book of Common Prayer*, p. 304). Holy Eucharist, the central act of worship for Christians, unites us with Jesus. Again and again as we partake of this sacrament, we remember and celebrate the life and ministry of Jesus Christ.

We are called to follow Jesus, the Son of God, who lived among us as teacher, preacher, and healer. Through his powerful example, Christians have come to understand that teaching is fundamental to our faith.

No precise definition or set of rules governs teaching in the Church. For all ages, as teachers and learners come to know one another, a special relationship develops. What transpires between them becomes a kind of "spiritual staff of life"—organic, dynamic, wonderful, and meaningful.

The *Children's Charter for the Church*, developed by the Office of Children's Ministries and a number of dioceses, calls for three responses to the children in our care: Nurture of the Child—to treasure each child as a gift from God; Ministry to the Child—to recognize and foster children's spirituality and unique gifts; and Ministry of the Child—to appreciate children's abilities and readiness to represent Christ and his church. All three responses will have an impact on relationships between teachers and students.

Teaching Is a Ministry

All Christians are teachers. Our daily lives bear witness to what we believe and treasure. Students and teachers in the church share a singular experience that goes beyond the facts and strategies of the moment. Every encounter between teachers and students is important—a possibility for connection and meaning. Teaching is a ministry involving:

• *Hospitality*—Teachers and learners share time and activity. There is a mutual sense of satisfaction in being together at this time and in this place.

• *Presence*—Teachers and students listen to and care about each other. Not only do we hear each other speaking, but also we feel the underlying emotion, tuned in to the meaning of conversations.

• *Participation*—Teachers and learners engage each other in a mutual spirit of inquiry, an interactive relationship. Roles are flexible.

• *Imagination*—For teachers and students, the choreography of the "dance of learning" is nourished by spirit and grace. Teaching and learning change those who teach and those who learn.

Christian formation is a lifelong process. Often the metaphors of journey or pilgrimage are used to describe these formations. The facts of our faith will be encountered again and again. From this perspective, intermediate-age students are just beginning a lifetime quest. Consider, for example, how—over the course of a lifetime—we renew our acquaintance with the stories of the nativity and Passion of Jesus Christ. The details become familiar, but the emotional power of the events touches us again and again. Age and experience enrich us with new meaning.

A Tool for Teachers

The aim of the Episcopal Children's Curriculum (ECC) is to sustain and strengthen the ministry of teaching in the Episcopal Church. The Curriculum's focus on classroom-based efforts does not deny the importance of other Christian education in a local congregation. It does reflect an intentional decision to affirm the act of teaching and spotlight the respective roles of teachers and learners.

The Curriculum is a tool for teachers. It serves as a resource to help teachers formulate answers to three pivotal questions:

- *What do I teach?*

The Curriculum offers a reasonable embodiment of the "data of our faith." Teachers using the materials are expected to pursue actively an adult-level understanding of the content of the session outlines, taking seriously their own roles as learners.

- *Whom do I teach?*

At every age level, teachers are challenged to adapt to both the developmental characteristics of the group as well as the particular interests of each individual. The ECC addresses issues of developmental differences from two important perspectives. Content is approached differently at each of the three age levels—preschool/kindergarten, primary, and intermediate. Then, within each session outline at every age level, provision is made in activity suggestions for varying degrees of skill and learning styles among students.

- *How do I teach?*

The Curriculum was written for teachers by teachers. Workability is essential. Options and guidelines to help teachers make adjustments to fit local circumstances are invaluable. In addition to a variety of activity suggestions for every session, there are practical comments and specific tips to guide learning.

It is hoped that teachers who use the ECC will be nurtured, inspired, and enriched personally as they prepare to teach and learn, and reflect on their efforts.

Teachers will find that the session outlines in this guide provide support and structure for the inexperienced, and challenge and flexibility for the more confident. It is highly recommended that every teacher have access to a Bible (NRSV), *The Book of Common Prayer*, and *The Hymnal 1982*. The *Access Bible* (NRSV) provides commentary, study tips, maps, and a concordance. At every age level, teachers can expect to find support for their preparation and planning. Every Intermediate session outline includes the following:

- *Unit Introduction*, to show how the sessions relate to the Unit theme. This is presented in a letter format that can be reproduced for parents/guardians of students in the class.
  - *Focus* statement, to state the concepts along with objectives.
  - *Getting Ready*, to provide factual background and personal inspiration.
  - *Teaching Tip*, to offer useful information about working with this age group.
  - *Teacher's Assessment*, to prompt thinking back over the session.
  - *Looking Ahead*, to preview upcoming concepts.

The Episcopal Perspective

The theological foundation of the Episcopal Children's Curriculum is set forth in a *Foundation Paper* (January 1990). This document is reproduced on the last pages of this Teacher's Guide. Teachers are urged to read the complete statement. Repeated below are the first few lines:

"The aim of Christian education in Episcopal Church parishes and congregations is to assist every member in living out the covenant made in Holy Baptism (BCP, p. 304). Hence the common ministry of teachers and learners focuses on matters of both faith and practice."

Baptism confers full participation in the Episcopal Church. The ECC sets forth a framework for helping all who teach and learn to grow in their understanding of the meaning of sacramental experiences. At every age, we are people of faith whose lives offer legitimate testimony to our baptismal promises. At every baptism, we are called to renew our commitment to these promises, in an unending, ever-enlarging circle of affirmation and action.

In describing ECC, these terms are key: "biblically based" and "liturgically oriented." The Curriculum is designed to follow the Bible in ways understood by young students. But the presence of biblical material does not mark the ECC as distinctively Episcopal. Like all Christians, we look to Holy Scripture for the content of our faith and practice. We view the Bible as the written Word of God.

Our Episcopal liturgy, set forth in *The Book of Common Prayer* and supported by *The Hymnal 1982*, invites each of us to enter into a relationship with God's Word. The three-year cycle of the Eucharistic Lectionary (appointed readings) and the seasons of the Church Year provide the pattern for worship. For Episcopalians, the Lectionary cycle ensures two things—fullness and context. Every year we hear the biblical witness to our salvation history.

Liturgy, defined as "the work of the people," brings us together as a congregation. We are invited to be active, not passive. In a deeply personal way, we encounter God's Word. We listen, seeking to hear God speaking to us through Scripture. As we hear—at whatever level of understanding—we are touched, informed, instructed, healed, and transformed. The liturgy provides a structure for this life-changing encounter. It is worship that establishes the "Episcopal" affirmation of Scripture.

Conscious of this role of liturgy, the editors and writers of the ECC have structured classroom experiences based on the general pattern of our Episcopal liturgy. We come together; we hear the Word, along with an explanation; and we go forth to live in the world. In ways appropriate for each age level, the Curriculum sessions prescribe a parallel pattern. At the intermediate-age level, the three essential activities are titled: Gathering, Introducing the Story, and Going Forth.

Students are encouraged through exposure and experience to learn words and actions for participation in worship and liturgy. The illustrations used in the ECC are specifically appropriate for Episcopalians. Clergy, churches, liturgical actions, text, and language are all used and portrayed as young people in Episcopal settings are most likely to experience them.

Selections from *The Book of Common Prayer* are incorporated into every session. Collects, prayers, and thanksgivings are included in every session. The music used in the ECC is found in *The Hymnal 1982*, and frequently appears also in the children's hymnal, *We Sing of God*. As students learn or listen on the *Children Sing!* tape to the suggested hymns, they will be acquiring words and melodies to help them participate in the Church's worship.

The Episcopal Children's Curriculum

The Curriculum uses a cumulative framework of age levels, years, units, and sessions. The three age levels of the Curriculum are Preschool/Kindergarten, Primary, and Intermediate. At each age level, there are three separate years of material. A total of nine years' worth of material is provided—three years at each of the three age levels.

Within each age level, the three years of material are designated by symbols linked to the Sacrament theme of each year: Shell (Baptism); Chalice (Eucharist); Cross (Worship).

Unit I	Unit II	Unit III	Unit IV
Old Testament Themes	New Testament Themes	Sacraments —Baptism —Eucharist —Worship	Church Themes

The use of symbols to identify years at each age level is a deliberate attempt to move away from a designation (such as grades or numbers) that would signal a particular order for the sequence of the years of material at each age level. Symbols also avoid confusion with the A, B, or C designations for Lectionary years.

The content of the Episcopal Children's Curriculum focuses on four areas: Old Testament (Hebrew Scriptures), New Testament, Sacraments, and the Church. The basic building block of the Curriculum is the Unit. Each year's 36 sessions of Curriculum materials are written in four Units of nine sessions each, representing the four areas.

The organization is intended to be sequential, cumulative, and consistent over the scope of the Curriculum. In the overall ECC framework, the content focus broadens and deepens as students advance through the Curriculum. A child beginning the Episcopal Children's Curriculum at the age of three, and proceeding forward for nine years will revisit Unit themes but will not actually repeat any material. Each level is a blend of the familiar and the new.

The accompanying three age-level charts provide an overview of the Unit themes within an age level, and help to explain how each of the four content areas unfold. We can see how the students are immersed, over and over, in the content of our faith and practice in ways most appropriate for their age levels. The approaches to teaching are different at each level.

Preschool/Kindergarten — Stories

🐚	Creation	Jesus: Son of God	Baptism: Belonging	We Are the Church
🏆	Promise	Jesus: Storyteller	Eucharist: Sacred Meal	The Church Prays
✝	Shepherd	Jesus: Teacher	Worship: Environment	The Church Sings

Preschool/Kindergarten. Written for three- through five-year-olds, this level of the Curriculum emphasizes the telling of stories as the principal experience for teaching and learning. Children this age come to know about their world primarily through stories. The Old Testament thread focuses on the stories of key figures in the Bible. Unit II tells stories of Jesus' birth and ministry. Unit III looks at Sacraments through stories of personal participation and experience. Unit IV recounts stories of the early Church.

Primary — People in Relationship

🐚	Pentateuch	Jesus: Healer Son of God	Baptism: People in Covenant	The Church in the New Testament
🏆	Judges/Kings	People in Parables	Eucharist: People Communion	The Church in the Prayer Book
✝	Stories	Sermon on the Mount	Worship: People in Community	Saints of the Church

Primary. Planned for children in Grades 1-3, the Curriculum continues the emphasis on stories with particular attention paid to people and relationships. The goal is to make the people of the Bible and the Church come alive for young learners. This is consistent with a belief that the Christian faith is nurtured through relationships. Each of the themes involves a revisiting and expansion of the stories first encountered at the Preschool/Kindergarten level. The Unit I, Old Testament sessions all focus on specific people, their families, their actions, and the events in their lives. In Unit II, we look more broadly and deeply at Jesus' life among us, the people he taught, preached to, and healed. The Sacrament Units consider people in relationship to the sacrament and to one another. The Church Units (IV) emphasize people—stories from the early Church in the Bible, the Church at prayer, and the lives of saints.

Background

Intermediate — Symbols

🐚	Covenant	Miracles	Baptism: New Life	The Apostle Paul
⏳	Prophesy	Parables of Promise	Eucharist: Shared Life	The Catechism
✝	Psalms & Wisdom	The Reign of God	Worship	Church History

Intermediate. Students in Grades 4-6 are able to use and understand symbols for ideas and events they encounter. The stories, people, and relationships first met at earlier levels are recalled and examined through the increasing complexity of their perspective on the world. The Old Testament Units focus on the concepts of covenant, prophecy, and psalms, and wisdom. Jesus' life and ministry are approached through miracles, parables, and the coming of God's kingdom. The Sacraments are examined in relationship to living out the gospel and creeds, and in Unit IV, Church history refers to the figures, events, and traditions of the Church both throughout history and today.

Themes and the Calendar

The Unit organization of the Episcopal Children's Curriculum allows considerable flexibility for scheduling in local congregations. All sessions within a Unit are undated. Sessions within each Unit develop the thematic focus. However, there is an explicit connection to the liturgical Church Year in the measured patterns of sessions within Units. Attention to major feast days is balanced with thematic development. In an important way, the Curriculum is seasonally compatible with our liturgy. Calendars for each year are available in the spring. Contact Morehouse or the Center for the Ministry of Teaching to receive one.

Scheduling Units and Sessions

The four Units are most appropriately used during specified Church Seasons. The chart below displays the pattern of seasonal connections for each Unit. Across all years and all age levels of the Curriculum, a clear, consistent pattern of Unit/Session connections to the Church Year has been preserved. Note that examples in the chart below are from the Intermediate Level—Chalice Year. The Unit titles are from this Teacher's Guide.

Unit Title Intermediate Chalice Year	I Covenant	II Miracles	III Baptism: New Life	IV The Apostle Paul
Church Calendar	Late Weeks after Pentecost	Advent/Christmas/Epiphany	Lent/Easter	Easter/Early Weeks after Easter
Probable Months	September-November	December-February	February-April	April-May
Session Detail	#1-8—Old Testament Themes #9—All Saints	#1-4—Advent/Christmas #5—Epiphany #6-9—New Testament Themes	#1-5—Sacramental Themes #6-9—Lent, Holy Week Easter	#1-8—Church Themes #9—Pentecost

Background

In order to take advantage of the thematic and liturgical sessions, church school leaders and teachers should plan a schedule that fits both their particular congregation's calendar and the yearly fluctuations in the liturgical calendar. Factors affecting scheduling variations are:
- different starting dates for local church schools;
- substitution of other parish activities for church school;
- rotation of class sessions with chapel or worship;
- and the yearly variations in the lectionary cycle that result in an "early" or "late" Easter, affecting the lengths of the periods after the Epiphany and after the Day of Pentecost.

Within any given Unit of nine sessions, some sessions should be coordinated with the current Church Year calendar. Other sessions can be more flexibly scheduled. It is expected that users will rearrange the numerical order of sessions within a Unit to accomplish scheduling requirements. Referring to the session patterns in the chart above, consider the scheduling decisions to be made within each Unit.

Unit I—Old Testament Themes. Designed to be used during the period from September (start of church school) through November (but not into Advent), Unit I coincides with the late Sundays after Pentecost. The nine sessions should be scheduled for use during this time period.

In those places where church school begins the first Sunday in September and meets weekly without interruption until Advent, the first Unit may need to be spread out over 13 or 14 weeks. Enough suggestions are provided in any session outline to make it possible to expand the activities over two class meetings. Teachers can choose which sessions to extend or, if need be, to combine as local needs demand.

Session 9 is always an All Saints' session. Depending on the local schedule, teachers could plan to use this session on the Sunday nearest to All Saints', the week before, or perhaps the week after if no classes are held on that principal feast day. The other eight sessions of the Unit can precede or follow the All Saints' session.

Unit II—New Testament Themes. Sessions 1-4 are for Advent/Christmas and Session 5 is an Epiphany session. Teachers should look at the focus statements for these sessions and match the most appropriate ones with the available dates for class meetings. Many congregations have traditions of plays, pageants, and other seasonal events that take precedence over focused class work at this time of year. Teachers may see a need to combine or compress material from Sessions 1-5.

Sessions 6-9 of Unit II are developed around the theme in the Unit title. These sessions will likely be used during the Epiphany season (January-February). Once again, the calendar can result in a long or short Epiphany season, requiring teachers to adjust sessions accordingly. Another option is to consider "borrowing" the first or second sessions from Unit III.

Unit III—Sacrament Themes. Schedule this Unit for use during Lent, Holy Week, Easter, and for one session into the Easter season. The sacramental focus of each year's material (Shell—Baptism; Chalice—Eucharist; Cross—Worship) is developed fully in Sessions 1-5. The material in Sessions 6-9 extends the year's specific sacramental focus, in connection to the liturgical events surrounding Easter.

Use the outlines related to sacraments in Sessions 1-7 before Easter Day, mainly during the weeks of Lent. Session 8 can be used for classes that meet on Easter Day or the next class meeting. Session 9 is for the early Easter season.

Extend, combine, or compress session outlines to fit the calendar for your congregation.

Unit IV—Church Themes. Plan to begin this Unit during the latter weeks of the Easter season and into the weeks after Pentecost. Sessions 1-8 focus on church history and traditions. The themes for this Unit are: Shell Year—Bible; Chalice Year—*The Book of Common Prayer*; Cross Year—*The Hymnal 1982*. Session 9 is always about the Feast of Pentecost. Plan to use it on the most appropriate date for your classes, even if it means interrupting the order of the other eight sessions.

The Intermediate Curriculum Materials

The Episcopal Children's Curriculum provides materials for both teachers and students. At each age level of the Curriculum, distinctive materials for students are designed to appeal particularly to that age group. Teachers' materials, while similar in format and function across age levels, reflect noticeably the changing characteristics of the classroom situation at each age level. At the Intermediate level, five different pieces of material are available.

For Directors
- *Director's Guide*
    Provides a comprehensive overview of all levels and years of the curriculum.

For Teachers
- *Teacher's Guide* (this volume)
    Contains 36 sessions of material organized into the four Units of the year. The Intermediate Chalice Year Units are: Unit I. Prophecy; Unit II. Parables of Promise; Unit III. Eucharist: Shared Life; and Unit IV. The Catechism. The Teacher's Background includes helpful general descriptive material and suggestions for additional resources.
- *Supplemental Guide (Intermediate)*
    Provides additional activities and alternative approaches for teaching at this age level.
- *Teacher's Packet* (posters and patterns)
    Offers 24 large sheets of color posters, black-and-white pictures, instructions, and patterns mentioned in the session outlines. Intended as a classroom resource.
- *Music Tapes*
    Contains all the music for each year recorded by a children's choir.

The Guide, Supplemental Guide, Packet, and Music Tapes are sufficient for an entire year and can be reused. We recommend that congregations have one Teacher's Guide for each teacher along with one Supplemental Guide, one set of Music Tapes, and one Teacher's Packet for each class group.

For Students
- *Community Times* (student newspaper—36 issues, one for each session)
    Carries the content for every session. Numerous references are made to material from the newspaper throughout the activity suggestions in each session outline. We strongly recommend that a set of 36 newspapers be purchased for each teacher and made available for each student in the class group. In an attractive, colorful format, each newspaper has a mix-

ture of feature stories, news articles, illustrations, puzzles, memory tasks, Scripture, maps, and more—all tailored to support a particular session. Feature stories are used in the Introducing the Story section.
- *Symbol Cards* (one to correspond to each of the 36 sessions)
  Appeal to students of this age and can be the beginning of a collection. These are small, full-color cards. Each has a symbol illustration, a Scripture verse, and an explanation on the back. They are designed to be collectible, shared with parents, and even traded. Across the three years of the Intermediate level, students can accumulate 108 symbol cards.
- *Chalice Year Treasurebook* (one book for the year)
  Serves as a student resource and reference book. Each year's *Treasurebook* has four parts that correspond to the four Unit themes of that year. Session outlines suggest ways to encourage student reading. The books will also be useful for teachers' preparation.

The student materials are intended to be distributed for personal use by students. As noted above, we consider it helpful for all students to have copies of the newspapers. The set of 36 symbol cards and the *Chalice Year Treasurebook* have the potential to provide important bridges between classroom and family/home. If at all possible, congregations should plan to purchase cards and books to give to each student.

UNDERSTANDING INTERMEDIATE-AGE STUDENTS

Who are the children we teach? The key to understanding intermediate-age students—ages nine, ten, and eleven—lies in a respect for children as individuals. This respect, accompanied by the knowledge of the differences among us, shapes all our efforts as teachers.

Look closely at any group of intermediates, and it is apparent on physical appearances alone that there is considerable diversity in the group. Reflect on the impact of the different social and ethnic backgrounds, economic circumstances, educational opportunities, skills and interests, and it becomes clear that general descriptions do not reflect the variety of social and cultural diversity among children of the same chronological age. Teaching children requires that we see them as individuals. There are, however, many sources of information to help us understand more about students in this age group.

Developmental theory offers insight for teaching. Educators look primarily to such theories for help in understanding the growth and development of children in the areas of physical, emotional, social, moral, and faith development. However, no single viewpoint is adequate by itself.

Experience of teachers themselves can contribute reliable information, including memories of their own journeys as students and participants in the educational process.

Theory and experience contribute to a multi-dimensional perspective on the lives and learning experiences of children. This blend of insights will be especially helpful in church school settings.

Theory

Developmental theories help us see the expected patterns of change from birth through maturity. All theories of development hold that increasing maturity brings a general increase in the complexity of behavior. Children move from being centered on the self to social interaction with others. Whether or not a theory uses ages or stages, the emphasis is on general expectations. No theory will predict the behavior of an individual child.

Most of the mainstream theories were formulated without particular regard for gender. Today, we have a much greater sensitivity to the differences in development of boys and girls. (See Carol Gilligan, *In a Different Voice*.)

Ages and Stages. Ages are convenient ways of classifying behaviors that change as the student matures. A six-month-old can sit up; a six-year-old can skip; a nine-year-old can throw a ball accurately. With maturity, the range of different behaviors within an age group increases: Many two-year-olds can say a few words, but eleven-year-olds can vary from the ability to speak several languages to functional illiteracy. There are numerous books that describe the physical growth and behaviors of children in this manner.

Thinking. The Swiss psychologist Jean Piaget has helped us understand that children simply do not think in the same way adults think. Using cognitive stages, loosely associated with chronological ages, Piaget has identified the ways of knowing that we pass through from birth (sensory motor learning) through about age eleven (symbolic learning). According to Piaget, children ages nine to eleven are capable of increasingly complex thought processes and are no longer limited by what they can see, hear, or touch. They can think about situations from more than one perspective, deal with several ideas at once, and think across time—past, present, and future. Around age eleven they begin to think abstractly—that is they think about thoughts and ideas.

Understanding the ways in which children think is useful for teachers. However, cognitive theories do not specify what we should have children think about. And, perhaps more critically, Piaget's stages of knowing do not uniformly apply to children growing up in different socio-cultural environments. Many people feel that the variety of life experiences dramatically change the ages at which the various types of thinking abilities emerge. In relation to teaching in church schools, cognitive functioning has no direct relation to the development of faith. It only helps us understand how children think about the stories we teach.

Social context. During the intermediate years, children increase their social group of family, friends, and community. Personal interests dictate much of what children are likely to do and who they will encounter. Influence on the child moves from the parents to peers and others.

Erik Erikson's work suggests a view of development that interweaves the power of social interaction with ongoing biological maturity. According to Erikson, at each of eight stages of life a psychosocial crisis must be resolved in order for development to proceed normally. The dominant concern of intermediate-age children is that of industry versus inferiority. Children achieve competence as they focus on work that requires skill. It is a period of cooperation, competition, and learning information. All children have gifts to succeed and all have a sense of failure at some point in their development. Helping children to discover their gifts and deal with their struggles of inferiority is a major task of the teacher of this age student.

Lawrence Kohlberg and Carol Gilligan have given us ways to think about the moral development of children. With maturation, experience, and expanding ways of thinking, children and adults approach and resolve moral issues in more complex ways.

Each of these theorists has given us a broader view of the complicated process of development. While none of them specifically addresses the growth of religious thought, their work has been the basis for those theorists who have explored faith development.

New Ways of Approaching the Educational Process

In recent years, researchers have begun to explore the learning process within the classroom. How teachers teach and how students learn have come into a sharper focus.

Learning Styles. Some researchers have concentrated on the different ways individuals take in information and process it in order to learn. Auditory, visual, and kinesthetic learning styles are those most easily identified in classrooms. Auditory learners are those who listen carefully and are better able to retain what they hear. Since this is the dominant teaching style in many classrooms, auditory learners perform well. Visual learners must be able to connect what they are learning either with real pictures or ones they create in their imagination. Pictures and objects that students can see strengthen the educational experience for this type of learner. Kinesthetic learners need to be able to use their bodies to move, touch, or manipulate items related to ideas in order to fully remember what they learn.

All students use some form of all three styles in the early years of learning; later one style becomes more dominant based on school and other experiences. Teaching that incorporates a variety of opportunities to see, hear, and touch will be more successful and enjoyable for both teachers and students.

Multiple Intelligences is another approach to the classroom experience developed by Howard Gardner. Gardner has proposed that humans have eight different ability areas, or intelligences. Since most educational materials and experiences focus on only two, many students are left out of or are not using their potential for learning. Teachers who provide activities that enhance the different intelligences are able to engage more students in the learning process more of the time.

The eight intelligences are Linguistic (Word Smart), Logical-Mathematical (Number Smart), Musical, Visual-Spatial (Picture Smart), Bodily-Kinesthetic (Body Smart), Intrapersonal (Self-Smart), Interpersonal (People Smart), and Natural or (Nature Smart). Each of the intelligences can provide an entry way into the learning experience for different students. Using the biblical story of Noah, linguistic students would write poems; mathematical students could measure the ark and build a scale model; musical students could write a song; visual students would paint pictures; bodily-kinesthetic students would dance the story; interpersonal students would interview each other about the experience of being on the ark; intrapersonal students would reflect on their own feelings about the story and perhaps compose a prayer; and natural students would be concerned about the species of animals that were brought on board.

Using the multiple intelligences in the classroom provides all individuals with an entry point into a particular story. For most classrooms, time and space don't permit all eight intelligences to be in operation at one time. However, keeping the variety of experiences in mind as we plan for teaching and learning can help to make church school more exciting and meaningful for all involved.

Developmental Resources
Ames, Louise Bates & Carol Chase Haber. *Your eight-year-old.* New York: Delacorte Press, 1989.

Ames, Louise Bates & Carol Chase Haber. *Your nine-year-old*. New York: Delacorte Press, 1990.

Ames, Louise Bates, Ilg, Frances L., & Stanley M. Baker. *Your ten to fourteen-year-old*. New York: Delacorte Press, 1988.

Armstrong, Thomas. *Multiple intelligences in the classroom*. Alexandria, VA: Association for Supervision and Curriculum Development, 1994.

Coles, Robert. *The call of stories: Teaching and the moral imagination*. Boston: Houghton Mifflin, 1989.

Coles, Robert. *The moral life of children*. Boston: Atlantic Monthly Press, 1986.

Coles, Robert. *The spiritual life of children*. Boston: Houghton Mifflin, 1990.

Crain, William C. *Theories of development: Concepts and applications*. (3rd ed.) Englewood Cliffs: Prentice-Hall, 1992.

Elkind, David. *The hurried child*. Reading: Addison-Wesley, 1981.

Erikson, Erik H. *Childhood and society*. (2nd ed.) New York: W. W. Norton, 1963.

Gardner, Howard. *Multiple intelligences: the theory in practice*. New York: Basic Books, 1993.

Gilligan, Carol. *In a different voice*. Cambridge: Harvard University Press, 1982.

Hashway, Robert M. *Cognitive styles: a primer to the literature*. San Francisco: EM Text, 1992.

Kuhmerker, Lisa with Uwe Gielen & Richard L. Hayes. *The Kohlberg legacy for the helping professions*. Birmingham: R.E.P., 1991.

Lewis, Anne Chambers. *Learning styles: putting research and common sense into practice*. Arlington, VA: American Association of School Administrators, 1991.

Medrich, Elliott A. et al. *The serious business of growing up: Children's lives outside school*. Berkeley: University of California Press, 1982.

Singer, Dorothy G. & Tracey A. Revenson. *A Piaget primer: How a child thinks*. New York: Plume/New American Library, 1978.

Faith in the Classroom

Faith is a gift from God.
Children are people of faith.

These two premises underlie all that we say and do in church school classrooms. They are also basic to the Children's Charter. It is faith that gives church school its unique mission. We do not teach faith. We hope that our work as teachers will nurture faith in the hearts and minds of our students.

Structure of Faith

Knowing that faith is personal, understanding the structure of faith, and realizing that faith changes over time are important concepts for teachers. Knowledge of the faith process will help teachers interpret the actions and responses of their students.

According to James Fowler's formulation, intermediate-age students are literalists looking primarily to others for the concepts and beliefs of their faith. Another educator, John Westerhoff, uses the image of concentric rings to portray how faith grows and matures within the web of relationships in a faith community. In this latter model, the beginnings of faith come from meaningful experience and belonging to a faith community.

Content of Faith

Faith derives its content from the Holy Scriptures and the preserved traditions of the Church. Episcopalians also turn to The Baptismal Covenant for guidance on the content of our faith and practice. In this Covenant, the first three questions and responses (the "faith" questions) incorporate belief statements found in the Apostles' Creed. The second part of the Covenant (the five "practice" or "action" questions) lays out standards for a Christian life. At every age, people of faith—children included—share responses to the questions of the Covenant. We have a marvelous opportunity to nurture the faith of intermediate-age students and to strengthen their ties to the Church.

Intermediates and The Baptismal Covenant

By drawing on information from developmental and faith theories and observing children's lives, we can use the questions of The Baptismal Covenant as a structure for a composite description of the faith and practice of a "typical" intermediate-age student.

Faith: Threefold Affirmation

Do you believe in God the Father? Intermediates perceive God as the supreme being and creator. Generally confident in their relationships and competent with their daily tasks, they are more appreciative and less awestruck by God's power than they were in earlier childhood. Characteristically, they have a comfortable "I and Thou" relationship with God.

Do you believe in Jesus Christ, the Son of God? Jesus is known as a teacher, leader, and authority figure. Students of intermediate-age accept Jesus' relationship with God—Son and Father, child and parent—but do not yet fully appreciate the far-reaching theological implications of his divinity and humanity. They know that Jesus was loved and hated, and they can identify the actions and feelings of his friends and disciples. Most are quite interested in the details and facts of Jesus' life and have a sense of the sequence of events in his ministry.

Do you believe in God the Holy Spirit? Images of the dove and the wind are seen as plausible manifestations of the Holy Spirit. For students who are regular participants in a faith community, expressions of personal spirituality may begin through prayer or conversation with trusted adults.

Practice: Five Questions About Living

Will you continue in the apostles' teaching and fellowship, in the breaking of bread, and in the prayers? Regular and full inclusion in the sacramental life and worship of the congregation is essential for intermediate students. Faith is nurtured through interactive participation in the corporate liturgical life of the Church. Their contributions as choir singers, acolytes, junior altar guild members, and ushers are genuinely helpful. To parents and friends they will readily acknowledge ties to their church and communicate a sense of satisfaction from taking part in group activities.

Will you persevere in resisting evil, and, whenever you fall into sin, repent and return to the Lord? Students at this age are aware of right and wrong, fairness and injustice, good and evil. They may be fiercely unyielding regarding the boundaries between any two sides of an issue. Firm judgments about where someone else stands are candidly advanced. Nine-, ten-, and eleven-year-olds are social creatures, engaged in many activities. Hence, the opportunities to offend others arise fairly often. Their words can be vicious, and their actions wounding. Trying something new, making mistakes along the way, and even failing, are a part of gaining new skills. Forgiving and forgiveness are practiced realities among friends and families.

Will you proclaim by word and example the Good News of God in Jesus Christ?

Background

Many students this age enjoy reading Bible stories. They are involved with Scripture, and can be very active within their local church community. Within this sphere they may be aware of the Christian example of their words and actions.

Will you seek and serve Christ in all persons, loving your neighbor as yourself? Service to others is a feasible option for intermediate-age students. It can be a natural outgrowth of participating in community-wide activities. Their stamina, skills, and social astuteness combine to make them willing workers. A growing sense of responsibility to others stems from fulfilling commitments for chores, homework, and practicing with teams or performance groups. Best friends, strong group loyalties, and self-sorting into boys' groups and girls' groups characterize this age. These factors will at times set limits on intermediates' ability to embrace "all" persons with love, as the Covenant requires.

Will you strive for justice and peace among all people, and respect the dignity of every human being? Global awareness is a positive by-product of the television and Internet age. Knowing and seeing people all over the world is the first step. The daily images of people in all parts of the world, the ordinary and the not so ordinary, strengthen students' understanding that people everywhere are more alike than different.

Resources on Faith

Aleshire, Daniel O. *Faithcare.* Philadelphia: Westminster Press, 1988.
Berryman, Jerome W. *Godly play.* San Francisco: Harper & Row, 1991.
Coles, Robert. *The spiritual life of children.* Boston: Houghton Mifflin, 1990.
Dykstra, Craig & Sharon Parks, eds. *Faith development and Fowler.* Birmingham: Religious Education Press, 1986.
Fowler, James W. *Stages of faith.* New York: Harper & Row, 1981.
Hyde, Kenneth E. *Religion in childhood and adolescence.* Birmingham: Religious Education Press, 1990.
Sawyers, Lindell, ed. *Faith and families.* Philadelphia: Geneva Press, 1986.
Stokes, Kenneth. *Faith is a verb.* Mystic: Twenty-Third Publications, 1989.
Westerhoff, John H., III. *Will our children have faith?* New York: Seabury Press, 1976.

Episcopal Resources

The Book of Common Prayer. New York: The Church Hymnal Corporation, 1979.
The Book of Occasional Services. (2nd. ed.) New York: The Church Hymnal Corporation, 1988.
Booty, John E. *What makes us Episcopalians?* Wilton: Morehouse-Barlow, 1982.
Children in the Eucharist. New York: Episcopal Church Center, undated.
Called to teach and learn: A catechetical guide for the Episcopal Church. New York: The Episcopal Church Center, 1994.
The Hymnal 1982. New York: The Church Hymnal Corporation, 1985.
Lesser feasts and fasts. New York: The Church Hymnal Corporation, 1991.
Lift every voice and sing II: An African-American hymnal. New York: The Church Hymnal Corporation, 1993.
Molrine, Charlotte N. & Ronald C. Molrine. *Encountering Christ.* Harrisburg: Morehouse, 2000.
Prichard, Robert W. *History of the Episcopal Church.* Harrisburg: Morehouse, 1991.
Roth, Robert N., & Nancy L. Roth, eds. *We sing of God.* New York: The Church Hymnal Corporation, 1989.
Sydnor, William. *More than words.* San Francisco: Harper & Row, 1990.

The story of Anglicanism: Part 1-Ancient and medieval foundations; Part 2-Reformation and its consequences; Part 3-Creating a global family. Westlake Village, CA: Cathedral Films and Video, undated.

The story of the Episcopal Church: Part 1-From Jamestown to Revolution; Part 2-The call to mission. Westlake Village, CA: Cathedral Films and Video, undated.

Wall, John S. *A new dictionary for Episcopalians.* San Francisco: Harper & Row, 1985.

Westerhoff, John H. *A people called Episcopalians.* Atlanta: St Bartholomew's Episcopal Church, 1993.

Wonder, love, and praise: a supplement to The Hymnal, 1982. New York: Church Publishing, 1997.

USING THE CURRICULUM

The three age levels of the Episcopal Children's Curriculum correspond to traditional school groupings for children: Preschool/Kindergarten (ages 3-5); Primary (Grades 1-3); and Intermediate (Grades 4-6). The Curriculum supports both single-grade and broadly graded class groups.

Church schools with small numbers of children may wish to group students of similar ages together in broadly graded classes to correspond to the three levels of the Curriculum. Students could stay in each broadly graded group for three years, progressing through the Shell, Chalice, and Cross year materials for that group. When a student moves into the next age group, another set of Shell, Chalice, and Cross material is offered. While content themes are always a blend of the familiar and the new, no material is ever exactly repeated.

Where numbers and circumstances permit, church schools may be organized into nine single-grade groups (ages three years through Grade 6). In this situation, each class group can be assigned a different level and year of the Curriculum—beginning with Preschool Shell for three-year-old children and ending with Intermediate Cross for Grade 6. As students move through the grades, they will encounter new material each year.

Mixed-Age Groups

For many congregations, the decision about church school groupings cannot always be neatly handled. There may be only a few families with children of church school age. Or a growing parish or mission may find that the numbers of children are unevenly distributed across age levels—with many preschoolers and only two or three learners in Grades 4-6. Mixed-age groups are a practical necessity in these situations.

When a class group spans one or more age levels of the Curriculum, which level should be used? Consider both the teacher and learners in making the decision. Count and group the learners. The most desirable groupings for mixed ages combine children whose developmental capacities and learning styles are similar. If most are preschool-, primary-, or intermediate-age, purchase the ECC Level that matches the developmental/age level of the majority of the group. If this does not result in a clear-cut decision, consider choosing the Primary Level materials and adapting them for preschoolers and intermediates. Remember that most teachers will find it less complicated to simplify material for younger learners than to locate and design more sophisticated activities for older learners.

Mixed-age groups offer special opportunities as well as challenges for both teachers and learners. Two key concepts for teachers to consider when working with children of varied ages in the same group are:

- **the learners' emerging skills and capabilities:**

Students themselves are aware of the varying levels of skill present among the groups to which they belong. Teachers can set the tone in a group by recognizing the value of every learner's effort and contribution. Teachers who praise learners truthfully affirm for children the value of their work. The message to be conveyed is simple: It is quite all right to be growing and trying and learning in different ways.

When teaching, think about how the youngest and oldest within the group handle various activities. Note the wide variations in the students' interests and gifts. With this range in mind, plan varied approaches to the class meetings. Ask: What is likely to have maximum appeal with this particular group?

For example, an art activity may appeal to all ages if there is latitude for process, product, and interpretation. Placemats can provide preschoolers with a canvas for fingerpainting; primary-age learners with a project/product they can take home and use at dinner with their families; and intermediates with a doodle page on which to add symbols, phrases, or pictures they have created.

- **the necessity for family-style social interaction:**

Probably the most effective approach for handling group interaction for students of widely varying ages is to assist them in learning to be helpful to one another. At times, older children can assume leadership roles—sharing their skills with younger ones. At other times, they will work individually, or rotate personal time with teachers. Give-and-take with siblings and parents provides a familiar and accessible model for managing group living in small, mixed-age groups.

Intergenerational Groups

Under the label Intergenerational Activities, church educators and program planners have rediscovered the virtues of "one-room" education. Potluck suppers, hymn-sings, Pentecost parties, storytimes, movie showings, greening the church, meal preparation for soup kitchens, house repairs, and outings for senior citizens—all these invite the participation of people of all ages.

For small congregations, intergenerational activities offer a workable solution to the question of allocating leaders' time and resources, and the sometimes perplexing problems of meeting the needs of varied groups of learners. Large parishes, where age-group numbers dictate closely graded classes, may have to work hard to replicate the cross-age and cross-community linkages that occur naturally in small parishes. Meticulously planned, intergenerational activities at regularly scheduled intervals can foster a very desirable sense of community in large parishes.

Celebrations of major feast days and special parish days are most successful when all ages are involved in the activities. The seasonal liturgical plan of the Episcopal Children's Curriculum is compatible with congregational plans for intergenerational celebrations. Within each Unit, the session outlines that are keyed to principal feast days and celebrations contain activity suggestions that can be adapted and incorporated easily into intergenerational programs. Each year's material, at all age levels of the Curriculum, includes one or more sessions targeted for use at particular points in the Church Year: All Saints (1), Advent/Christmas (4), Epiphany (1), Lent/Holy Week (3), Easter (2), and Pentecost (1). See the Intermediate Supplemental Guide for suggestions for intergenerational activities.

Intergenerational Resources

Carey, Diana & Judy Large. *Festivals, family and food.* Gloucestershire, England: Hawthorne Press, 1982.

Griggs, Donald, & Patricia Griggs. *Generations learning together.* Nashville: Abingdon, 1981.

Nelson, Gertrud Mueller. *To dance with God: Family ritual and community celebration.* New York: Paulist Press, 1986.

Westerhoff, John H., III. *A pilgrim people.* San Francisco: Harper & Row, 1984.

White, James W. *Intergenerational religious education.* Birmingham: Religious Education Press, 1988.

Williams, Mel, & Mary Ann Britain. *Christian education in family clusters.* Valley Forge: Judson, 1982.

Planning Intermediate Class Sessions

Planning sets the stage for teaching and learning. In preparation for meeting with students, teachers need to *select* a set of activities, and then put these activities into an *order* for each class meeting. The session outlines of the Intermediate level of the Episcopal Children's Curriculum offer three sets of activity categories that can be used to compose a class session. These are:

Teacher Supports—five sections directed at helping teachers prepare.

Essential Activities—Gathering, Introducing the Story, and Going Forth are the three core experiences for each session.

Optional Activities—about ten different suggestions of activities teachers may choose to do in a given session. *No teacher or class is expected to use every optional activity in any session outline. The emphasis is on choice.*

The following illustration shows the overall relationship of the Intermediate activities. The three essential activities are shown in green type. Flexibility and adaptability are evident. Time estimates are included to aid in choosing activities to fit class needs. (Teachers who have used either the Preschool/Kindergarten or Primary materials will notice certain similarities in the design of session outlines and specification of session categories.)

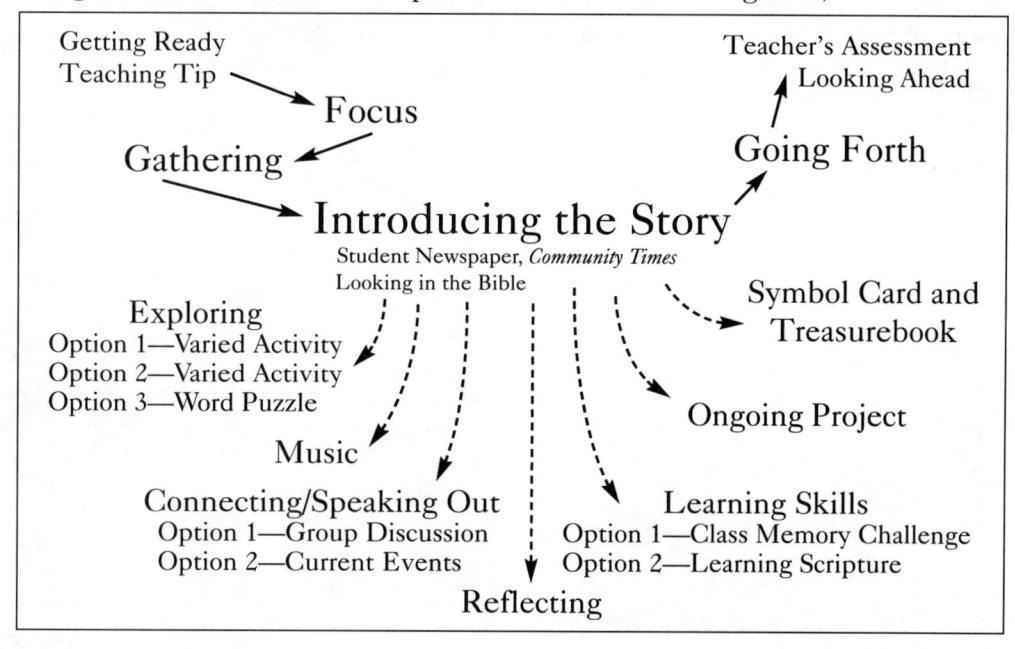

```
Getting Ready                                    Teacher's Assessment
Teaching Tip                                      Looking Ahead
              ↘ Focus
                                                 Going Forth
  Gathering ←
              ↘ Introducing the Story
                  Student Newspaper, Community Times
                  Looking in the Bible
                                              Symbol Card and
  Exploring                                    Treasurebook
  Option 1—Varied Activity
  Option 2—Varied Activity
  Option 3—Word Puzzle
                                              Ongoing Project
        Music
  Connecting/Speaking Out           Learning Skills
  Option 1—Group Discussion         Option 1—Class Memory Challenge
  Option 2—Current Events           Option 2—Learning Scripture
                    Reflecting
```

Background

Composing a Session

Church school sessions in congregations across the country vary greatly in length—typically ranging from 20 minutes to 90 minutes or more. The ECC was designed with a "core" of just three essential activities to accommodate this time variation. At the Intermediate level, for example, the core steps are called Gathering, Introducing the Story, and Going Forth. Classes with 20-minute sessions can expect to accomplish these, and not much more. Teachers of classes with longer meeting times may choose from a variety of additional activities offered in each session outline.

The session categories function as the building blocks for planning. There is no single "right" way to plan a class session. Teachers can construct an activity/time schedule for each class session that fits the time available, builds on their own skills, and meets students' needs and interests. Activity blocks for the sessions can be selected and sequenced in a variety of ways. All the examples given below are based on use of the three essential categories.

Illustration 1. A way to proceed when session time is short and time schedules are tight. A different optional activity may be chosen for each session—thus providing a variety of ways over a period of time to examine the session themes.

Gathering, Introducing the Story, Exploring (Option 1), and Going Forth

Illustration 2. This plan balances active and quiet activities, and gives students both directed and imaginative ways to approach themes.

Gathering, Music, Introducing the Story, Exploring (Option 2), Exploring (Option 3), Reflecting, and Going Forth.

Illustration 3. This is a full class session with a number of different types of activities and a comfortable flow for the session.

Gathering, Introducing the Story (incorporating questions from Connecting/Speaking Out), Exploring (Option 1), Exploring (Option 2), Music, Reflecting, Ongoing Project, Going Forth.

Illustration 4. This two-session plan illustrates how the material from one session outline can be extended over two class meetings. Fluctuations in the Church Year calendar may require teachers to extend or compress the nine sessions of a Unit in order to accommodate the current calendar.

First session. Gathering, Introducing the Story, Exploring (any option), Going Forth.

Second session. Connecting/Speaking Out, Exploring, Ongoing Project, Going Forth.

> **Centers**
>
> One approach to using the options in each session is to arrange the classroom into Learning Centers. Learning Centers are planned activities where all instructions and materials for a specific subject are provided for students to work independently or with others. Intermediate students particularly enjoy this opportunity to work with others and the change from traditional classroom activities. The advantage to Learning Centers is the chance to use more of the activities provided during one time period.
>
> To begin, review the options in the session and choose the ones you think will interest the students you work with. Decide on the key concept for each option and ask what the student needs to find out. Design the learning task with clear directions and enticing titles. Choose the number of centers needed for the size of the group. Enough choices should be available to permit the last arriving student to choose among at least three options. Provide a list of the centers for the students to help them keep track of which ones they have completed.
>
> Learning Centers have optimum impact when the class period begins and ends with a group time. Introducing the Story could be followed by time in the centers and a gathering for the Closing activity.

Supplies

The Episcopal Children's Curriculum assumes that teachers will have access to a reasonable variety of standard supplies—including pencils and markers, paper of various kinds, paints, tape and glue, modeling materials, "elegant junk," miscellaneous office supplies, and tools such as scissors and staplers.

Activity suggestions in the session outlines describe the materials needed and how they are to be used for a given activity. A list of materials is provided in the Director's Guide.

TEACHING STRATEGIES AND RESOURCES

Organized church school and other classroom-based activities are indispensable for students. The particular challenge for teachers working with intermediate-age students is to balance the pragmatic requirements of teaching preparation with the swiftly moving reality of classroom activity. Respecting the individuality of students, and honoring their genuine capabilities as leaders means sharing *authority* and tolerating *ambiguity*. What does it mean to be a teacher in a church school classroom for intermediates?

Teacher and Student Roles

Five broad areas of competency characterize teachers in the Church. A summary of these universal functions follows, with descriptions tailored specifically to the nuances of classroom situations.

Teachers orchestrate learning. *Students are dependent on teachers for the provision of materials, sufficient opportunities for choices, and orderly management of learning situations.*

In the classroom, the teacher sets the stage. Teachers are responsible for preparing themselves, the room, the materials, the session plans. Clearly, there is an element of control in this function of a teacher, but with preparation, planning, and structure comes the freedom to focus on students.

Teachers facilitate classroom activities through interactive planning with students. Intermediate-age students will be able to exercise leadership roles in choosing and implementing projects. Students' interests will strongly affect the direction of discussions.

Teachers understand their students. *Students deserve attention, affirming experiences, and reasonable challenges.* To nurture and guide the faith journey of another person demands a personal relationship. Bonds of trust, respect, and affection grow when caring and understanding prevail.

Appropriate sources of information for teachers of intermediate-age students include developmental theory, thoughtful observation of local community culture, sensitive appraisal of popular trends, and a sympathetic openness to each child.

Teachers are interpreters. *Students can expect honest answers to their questions—including the response, "I don't know."* In classroom situations, what students talk about, question, explore, and wonder about reflects their teachers' ability to mediate and interpret faith and heritage. Often the simplest of questions can evoke profound discussion.

Intermediate-age students can be intensely interested in wrestling with ethical issues. As teachers and students engage in conversations of faith, they are sharing feelings and values as well as words and facts. In a very real sense, teachers expose their beliefs when they engage in conversation with learners.

Intermediates' increasing skills enable them to be critical thinkers, although most still work best with concrete ideas. They are many-sided thinkers, able to handle dimensions, perspectives, possibilities, and conditions. Teachers have a responsibility to be equally open and flexible.

Teachers are links with the Christian community. *Students come to know and trust a community of adults.* Fourth, fifth, and sixth graders spend much of their time with close age-mates. Peers are a dominant force in the life of most intermediates. Parents, other family members, and neighbors increasingly occupy a background role. Teachers function as a bridge between the familiar early childhood world of home and family and the beckoning allure of various church, school, and community groups.

Teaching in church school is an opportunity to make an enduring friendship with a group of boys and girls. It is a chance to cross generations in friendship, and meet the friends of one's own children. Having taught a group of children, a teacher can continue to observe their growth and involvement in the church. Over the years, students can come to know and be known by an ever-increasing number of adult members of the congregation.

Teachers are part of a team of ministers. *Students' experiences will include many teachers in many different settings.* Teachers, especially volunteers in church schools, may work in teams to share time and talents. Teachers also work in partnership with parents, clergy, and church staff in helping to guide the faith journeys of students. The perspective of a teaching team is not confined to what happens in a particular classroom, but includes all the programs and events in the church. Teachers, therefore, do not work alone or in a vacuum.

Adults make church school happen. Critical decisions on time, schedule, budget, space, and program policy define the Christian education classroom-based program in a local congregation. When teachers work with students they are transmitting the particular vision of a particular congregation. Meaningful classroom experiences are most likely to occur when intermediate-age students are included in congregational worship and programs. They can serve as acolytes, ushers, choir members, bellringers, and in other capacities. Full participation in the congregation sets the stage for classroom-based explanations.

Teaching Resources

Bowman, Locke E., Jr. *Teaching for Christian hearts, souls, and minds.* San Francisco: Harper & Row, 1990.

Cohen, Elizabeth G. *Designing groupwork: Strategies for the heterogeneous classroom.* New York: Teachers College Press, 1986.

Furnish, Dorothy Jean. *Experiencing the Bible with children.* Nashville: Abingdon, 1990.

Gobbel, A. Roger & Gertrude G. Gobbel. *The Bible: A child's playground.* Philadelphia: Fortress, 1986.

Katz, Lilian G. & Sylvia C. Chard. *Engaging children's minds: The project approach.* Norwood: Ablex, 1989.

Harris, Maria. *Teaching and religious imagination.* San Francisco: Harper & Row, 1987.

Pritchard, Gretchen Wolff. *Offering the Gospel to children.* Boston: Cowley, 1992.

Ratcliff, Donald E., ed. *Handbook of children's religious education.* Birmingham: Religious Education Press, 1992.

Strategies for Essential Categories

Gathering   Introducing the Story   Going Forth

These three categories are the core experiences of the Episcopal Children's Curriculum at the Intermediate level. The conceptual integrity of the Curriculum is best preserved by consistent use of these core experiences.

Throughout all levels of the Curriculum, students are introduced to and given opportunities for practical rehearsal of the words and actions of the church. Teachers come to appreciate the combined power of *ritual* and *word* as they pursue the goals of awakening and nurturing faith in young students.

Gathering

Planned in two parts to provide a dependable structure to begin each session, the initial Gathering activities are orderly, of short duration, and designed to entice the interest of the group. When all students are present, the group deliberately shifts to a more formal mode for an opening ritual. The teacher leads the group in prayer using a designated Collect from *The Book of Common Prayer.* A student lector then introduces and reads a Scripture selection (NRSV) keyed to the session theme. This two-step process of Gathering follows our congregational pattern of coming together for worship and hearing the Word.

The goal of the Gathering activity is to make holy the coming together of teachers and students. We acknowledge that when Christians are together, it is a special time. Teachers will find their confidence grows through the use of Gathering rituals and may be surprised at the energy with which students enter into such activities.

Hospitality and welcome. Teachers should view the Gathering activity as an occasion for offering hospitality and conversation. Words and gestures can communicate a sense of welcome and pleasure at being in this particular company. This opening informal time is prime time for "community-building." At every session, use students' names, introduce and re-introduce them, and inquire about activities and events in their lives. Try to connect students with one another, just as a good host/hostess would do at a party. Do not assume that all students share the same neighborhoods and schools. Best friend pairs and tightly knit groups will be more inclusive of others when their teacher models hospitality.

Since all groups require time to gather, slowly or quickly reaching the expected class size, the first part of the Gathering is an activity that anticipates in modest form the theme of the session. This activity helps students "settle in" and encourages students' interest and involvement.

Participation. Praying and hearing the Word are central components of our worship. The second, more formal part of the Gathering activity for intermediates provides for direct involvement of students. The teacher calls the group to prayer saying, "Let us pray." A relevant Collect from *The Book of Common Prayer*, or other appropriate prayer is used. (In time, older students may choose to take turns at calling the group to prayer and reading the selected Collect.) Next, a "student lector" reads from the Bible. The suggested Collect and the NRSV version of the suggested passage appear in the Teacher's Guide in every session outline.

Teachers can take some simple steps to enhance an attitude of reverence at the Gathering. Consider obtaining a special "class Bible" to be used for the readings. Mark the reading each week with a ribbon, direct the reader to a particular spot in the room, and post responses on large paper until all have memorized the words. Teachers should expect that fourth- through sixth- grade students will vary in their ability (or desire) to read aloud. Respect students' feelings. Ask for volunteers, or provide support with paired readings if necessary. In some situations it may be possible to schedule "student lectors" several sessions ahead, giving them ample time to practice. Encourage students to regard these class readings as a privilege. Perfection is not the only acceptable result; teachers should make it clear that all worthy efforts are to be praised.

Introducing the Story

This is the heart of the session for teachers and students. The goal is to engage the student's interest in the story. Students are asked to locate key passages in the Bible and respond critically to questions. This provides the group a communal base of information for subsequent session activities. The expectation is that both teachers and students will be mutually engaged with the material during this time. Each session outline proposes a creative strategy for teachers and students to employ. Practical suggestions are offered, including interactive storytelling, role plays and dramas, guided discussions, group interviews, reports, projects, and presentations. Articles and illustrations in the student newspaper, **Community Times,** are considered indispensable for this work. Wherever possible, all students and teachers should have their own copies of each session's issue. All subsequent, optional activity categories are keyed to both the Focus statement and the material explored in *Introducing the Story*.

Community Times, the Chalice Year Intermediate student newspaper, helps students to examine the stories or concepts introduced in the sessions in a fresh way. The stories are written as if reporters had interviewed the participants directly. Issues or other significant information are presented for the student to think about and explore. Memory Challenges include the "First Song of Isaiah," parables of Jesus, the Nicene Creed, and outline of *The Book of Common Prayer*. There are also opportunities for learning Scripture verses. A puzzle that reinforces the vocabulary for the theme is included. Original artwork, maps, and diagrams are used to enhance the students' understanding.

The colorful, attractive design of the paper is matched to students' interests and reading levels. The newspapers serve as an important bridge linking church school classroom and family activities. It is beneficial for all students working with the ECC to have copies of the newspaper. Activities frequently refer to material from the newspaper.

Activity suggestions for Introducing the Story assume that teachers and students will interact with one another. Consider each session's suggestion not as a fixed recipe for what to do but as a set of ingredients to prepare and set out. Prepare yourself, prepare your classroom, and expect the students to produce a dynamic, spirited exchange of views and roles.

Consider very carefully how to proceed. Either begin with the content or with students' experiences. This fundamental strategy decision will determine the shape of the learning experience for students and teachers. Use these two strategies as patterns of working.

Telling. The emphasis is on the content, or subject matter, of the session. The most familiar approach is for teachers to "tell" students about the subject, emphasizing the important details. Telling does not always mean the teacher lectures and students listen. Clever telling strategies might involve illustrations, dramas, and conversations. Teachers are responsible for identifying the scope of content. Students follow with questions. Projects and activities allow them to explore and create as they examine and apply the content to their daily experiences. This *deductive* strategy is efficient and precisely targeted. It begins at a specific point and ends by opening out to broader involvement.

Discovering. Students begin to approach the session's content through observation and investigation. Inquiry, speculation, and experimentation characterize these early activities. With guidelines and teacher support, the students look for ways to generalize and to form tentative conclusions. Together, students and teachers narrow their efforts to focus on the "key" discovery. This *inductive* strategy is free-formed and casts a wide net. It begins with an array of data and ends by clarifying a specific idea.

Teachers and students compose anew the learning process in every encounter they have. Teachers will find it helpful to visualize the shape of the process, selecting those "moves" and "resources" that seem best for their particular students.

STORYTELLING

Storytelling is a principal action in the teaching ministry. As part of the Introducing the Story activities at the Intermediate level, teachers will frequently employ storytelling techniques as a means of weaving together presentations and discussions. Indispensable ingredients for effective storytelling are:

Telling skills. Some "telling" skills to practice:

- *Inviting your listeners.* Suspend ordinary time and enter a special place together. Consider the setting—the gathering place, the mood—the sights and smells; and the expectations—the ritual invitation to open the imagination and join together on a story journey.
- *Knowing the facts and order of a story.* Storytellers shape their stories, pacing and punctuating to captivate their listeners. Imagine a shape for every story, and let that shape guide the telling. Listeners expect a beginning, a middle, and an end.
- *Describing people, places, and events from the "eye" of your imagination.* As the story unfolds, describe these details so that the listeners will "see" them just as you do: faces, ways of speaking, clothing, towns, roads, interiors of houses, and the like.
- *Capturing the climax or high point of an event in words that evoke a response from listeners.* Consider gestures and facial expressions that will best serve your intent. Convey reactions of joy, sorrow, surprise, or disappointment with specially chosen words and phrases.

Knowledge of the Bible. Session outlines give an orderly presentation of thematic material, noting highlights to emphasize. Teachers are urged to read the Bible. Instinctively, storytellers share their personal beliefs and understandings; this is what makes stories such a powerful tool for transmitting the Christian heritage. Biblical stories are for a lifetime, truly multi-generational. The students in your class will hear them again and again, listening with new awareness and broader life experience each time.

Presentation/Storytelling Resources
Bausch, William J. *Storytelling: Imagination and faith.* Mystic: Twenty-Third Publications, 1984.
Griggs, Patricia. *Using storytelling in Christian education.* Nashville: Abingdon Press, 1981.
Maguire, Jack. *Creative storytelling.* New York: McGraw-Hill, 1985.
Mellon, Nancy. *Storytelling and the art of imagination.* Rockport: Element, 1992.
Moore, Robin. *Awakening the hidden storyteller.* Boston: Shambhala, 1991.
Russell, Joseph P. *Sharing our Biblical story.* Rev. Ed. Wilton: Morehouse-Barlow, 1988.
Ward, Elaine M. *The art of storytelling.* Brea: Educational Ministries, 1990.

Bible Study Resources for Adults
Bach, Alice & Cheryl J.Exum. *Miriam's well: Stories about women in the Bible.* New York: Delacorte, 1991.
Bach, Alice & Cheryl J. Exum. *Moses' ark.* New York: Delacorte, 1989
Brownrigg, Ronald. *Who's who in the New Testament.* New York: Oxford University Press, 1993.
Charpentier, Etienne. *How to read the New Testament.* New York: Crossroad, 1989.
Charpentier, Etienne. *How to read the Old Testament.* New York: Crossroad, 1989.
Comay, Joan. *Who's who in the Old Testament.* New York: Oxford University Press, 1993.
Donovan, John Britt. *The family book of Bible stories.* Wilton: Morehouse, 1986.
Heller, Marc. *Does God have a big toe?* New York: HarperCollins, 1989.
Jesus and His times. Pleasantville: Reader's Digest Association, 1987.
Roberts, Jenny. *Bible facts.* New York: Dorset Press, 1990.
Sayers, Dorothy L. *The man born to be king.* London: Victor Gollangz Ltd., 1969.
Teringo, J. Robert. *The land and people Jesus knew.* Minneapolis: Bethany House, 1985.
Williams, Michael E., series ed. *The storyteller's companion to the Bible (Multi-volume series).* Nashville: Abingdon, 1992-1995.
Woodrow, Martin & Sanders, E. P. *People from the Bible.* Wilton: Morehouse Publishing, 1987.

Going Forth

For each Unit, a selection from the Prayers of the People in *The Book of Common Prayer* is used for the closing. *Going Forth* is a ritual closing to mark the end of time teachers and students spend together. Students are given an opportunity to add their own prayers, petitions, or intercessions at this time. Occasionally, a prayer of intercession or thanksgiving from one of the activities may also be added. This simple dismissal models the conclusion of our Episcopal worship, signifying the fact that it is time to leave this place of explanation and exploration and re-enter the world as practicing Christians.

Without careful attention, class sessions usually end in a swirl of chaos as students and their parents race to get coats, find take-home items, and leave quickly for services or home. A concluding ritual will help to provide a transition away from the classroom activity. Be deliberate about taking time for *Going Forth*, if necessary scheduling the closing ritual slightly before the actual time for leave-taking. Strive to make the Closing unhurried and reverent in tone.

Following the prayer suggested for the Unit, the dismissal is the familiar "Let us go forth in the name of Christ," to which the learners respond, "Thanks be to God."

Optional Session Categories: Activities and Resources

Exploring

This category offers three distinct options for students to become actively involved with the content presented in *Introducing the Story*. Suggested activities include art, drama, projects, and games for full group activities, individual projects, and word puzzles for independent or group use. All the activity options are self-contained, with no expectation of carryover into the next session. Access to standard supplies is assumed. Some patterns, diagrams, or instructions are included in the Teacher's Packet. The time estimates given in the Curriculum may need to be adjusted to reflect the work habits of particular classes.

These are guided opportunities to "do" something with the session content. The wide range of options is intended to help students experience the ideas and facts of the session in a variety of ways. Some of us learn best by looking, some of us by hearing, and some of us by doing. Play—the serious, yet magical business of making experiences our very own—is a necessary ingredient for learning at every age. We play with ideas, we role play feelings, and we can display responses. Still able to be captivated by the sensory pleasures of play, intermediates are readily engaged by art materials, costumes, and games.

What distinguishes activities for intermediates is the critical role language plays. Speaking, reading, and writing are genuine tools for exploring. They will take great satisfaction from group efforts as well as individual work.

Group Activities. The group is of tangible importance to intermediates. Belonging, being recognized as a group member, and knowing others are highly desirable social achievements. Teachers should recognize that group activity suggestions, for some students, may simply provide a common purpose, a good excuse for a group to form and work together. The activity needs to be relevant, but an equally compelling goal is building community among class members. Seek ways for students to assume responsibility for setting up, choosing alternatives or devising adaptations of an idea, supporting the ongoing work, and cleaning up after activities. Teachers can invite intermediates to be part of the planning and preparation in very real ways. Facilitate conversation during the activity. (Consider incorporating the conversation suggestions in *Connecting/Speaking Out*.) Observe how comfortably students relate to and work with one another. Use smaller groupings to ease shyness or defuse negative behaviors.

Individual Activities. Art projects and impressionistic activities are offered in many sessions. While the description presumes that students will work singly, teachers could adapt the suggestions for group work. Needed supplies are described; teachers are encouraged to substitute whatever available materials they deem suitable.

Every suggested activity has a purpose, and an explicit link to the themes presented earlier in the session. Encourage students to explore these connections through conversation and reflection at the start of the activity. Invite students to offer comments and thoughts as they work. When appropriate, provide a way for students to share their work.

Teachers can expect a very wide range of artistic ability among intermediate-age students. Meticulously detailed work will co-exist with passionate strokes of line and color. Students may be eager to speak about their efforts, or quite willing to write explanations about their work. For intermediates, thinking and talking about what has been expressed is an integral part of the act of creating.

Word Puzzles. The vocabulary of our faith can be encountered in print as well as in speaking. Many intermediate-age students enjoy working with words and ideas. They have the opportunity to think about concepts such as prophecy, justice, teaching, community, thanksgiving; names such as Isaiah, John the Baptist, Mary Magdalene; places such as Bethlehem and Jerusalem; and key events of Jesus' life—baptism, the Last Supper, footwashing, crucifixion, resurrection, ascension. Or, words such as these from *The Book of Common Prayer:* Liturgy, Morning Prayer, and Eucharist.

The student newspaper, *Community Times*, includes a word puzzle in every issue (typically appearing on the back page). The puzzles may be crosswords, word searches, word scrambles, acrostics, fill-in-the-blank, etc. Each puzzle has been created to highlight words representing key concepts or facts of the session.

Puzzles can be done in class independently, in pairs, or as a total group activity. Another option is to allow students to do the puzzles at home with family members. Teachers may establish a routine method for inserting the puzzle activity into class sessions, or vary its use session by session.

Music

The Episcopal Children's Curriculum introduces students to music that is part of our Episcopal heritage. The chosen hymns are consistent with session themes and/or the Church calendar. Hymns selected for emphasis in the Curriculum are ones students are likely to hear and sing in their corporate worship with their congregations. All appear in *The Hymnal 1982* and on the tape *Children Sing!* for the Intermediate Chalice Year. (Many can also be found in *We Sing of God*, a children's hymnal with Teacher's Guide available from The Church Hymnal Corporation.) In each session outline, brief suggestions are offered for introducing and singing the hymns or exploring aspects of the hymns' texts through projects and discussion.

Music is an elemental part of the language of faith. Consider the full meaning of the oft-quoted phrase, "Those who sing, pray twice."

We are blessed in the Episcopal Church with a wealth of great music as part of our liturgical tradition. *The Hymnal 1982* includes service music and hymns for congregational singing. The texts and settings are drawn from ancient and contemporary sources from around the world.

Appreciation and familiarity with this music is an uncomplicated, worthwhile goal for Christian education.

Intermediates and music. At this age level, it is likely that students will have had prior exposure to music in schools. They are capable of learning the words, the rhythmic structure, and the melody of a hymn or song. As singers, they can imitate and echo what they hear. In addition, many intermediates will be interested in reading music. Many will be highly motivated, enjoy performing, and achieve remarkable success during these years of musical study.

Pre-adolescents are big consumers of cassettes, compact discs, and music videos. These are also the years of judgments about personal musical abilities, exemplified by comments such as "I'm not a good singer." Even those who enjoy music may not fully participate because of peer pressure.

Music at church. Suggest to those who plan the liturgy that they include one or more of the hymns selected for emphasis during a Unit in worship services that the students attend. This may be easier with the seasonal hymn selections. (See the session plans for selected hymns.)

How can a "non-singing" teacher incorporate music in a group's classroom activities? The answer is two parts attitude and one part strategy. For attitude: Express your feelings in words and actions about the value of music, along with your pleasure in making music. For strategy: Get help—from your students and musicians in the congregation. A few specific tips:

- Remember that the line can be very blurred between singing, chanting, and saying the words of a hymn. It is not necessary to "sing a solo" to introduce a hymn in class. Saying words with feeling also communicates powerfully.
- If a hymn tune is unfamiliar, ask for help from a musician. Listen to the tape available for the Chalice Intermediate Year entitled *Children Sing!* Play it at home or in the car as you go about your daily activities. Let the tune creep into your memory. Share this recording with the class.
- Use some kind of "body language" to help you memorize words and rhythm. Working phrase-by-phrase, clap or tap the beat, or swing and sway with the words. Even with familiar hymns, this technique will entice you more fully into the music.
- Solicit help from your students. Maybe you have a "song leader"—someone who can start on pitch and carry a tune. Do you have anyone who plays an instrument? Affirm these skills and nurture student leadership.
- Pay close attention to the social interaction within your class, and the general atmosphere. With music activities, initially, try to match the emotional dynamic. For example, in a class of socially cohesive, eager talkers invite everyone to chant the words and clap the rhythm. Solicit discussion about the text. Or, if yours is a quiet class, hesitant and wary, let the music surround them first. Play recordings, read the text silently, softly whisper the words or tap the rhythm.

Music Resources. If at all possible, arrange to have a sufficient number of copies of *The Hymnal 1982* available for class use as well as one music cassette of *Children Sing!* for the Intermediate Chalice Year. The Church Hymnal Corporation has published a set of companion volumes to the hymnal that are designed for children's worship. The paperback hymnal, *We Sing of God: A Hymnal for Children* contains selected stanzas and refrains of hymns. A separate volume, *We Sing of God: Teacher's Guide* is a compendium of creative activity suggestions keyed to each hymn. Editors Robert and Nancy Roth share insight gained from their many years of singing with children.

> **Connecting/Speaking Out**
> Conversation is sparked by good questions. Two approaches to conversation are included in this category. Option 1, Group Discussion proposes questions intended to elicit students' opinions about the session's theme, the people, events, symbols, and concepts. Option 2, Current Events proposes questions aimed at helping students make connections between the themes of the session and their daily lives. Teachers may use either option singly or combined with another selected activity.

One insightful definition of teaching states that it is purposeful conversation. Throughout any classroom encounter, teachers and students should trade turns talking and listening. Within this framework, students may come to understand prayer itself as a conversation with God.

We need not hesitate to use the words of our faith with students. "Teachers in the church are aware that they must provide bridges between the Word of God (known to us in Jesus Christ, the Bible, and the Church) and the everyday life of learners." (The ECC Foundation Paper, 1990.) Throughout this Teacher's

Guide, stress is laid on the importance of language—and the need for language to be part of the transaction between teacher and learner.

Embedded in Scripture and liturgy, history, and tradition, the language and vocabulary of faith become part of our common experience.

Teachers use language to label, interpret, and convey meaning. The vocabulary of faith, the words students have available with which to talk about their faith, grows in direct relationship to exposure and practice. To teach the stories of our faith requires language.

Teachers can ask themselves, "Do we have an adequate command of the vocabulary of our faith tradition? Are we comfortable in using the language of Scripture and the Church in our teaching ministry?"

Intermediate-age students can be good conversationalists. Conversation is an elemental part of the nurture of faith for young students. The lively dynamic of conversation includes both speaking and listening. Through speaking and listening, the participants in a conversation use language to create a relationship within which one's thoughts, feelings, and values can be shared.

Some observations on conversation for intermediate-age students:

- The pattern of moves in intermediates' conversation is almost always a mutual duet; I talk and you listen, you talk and I listen; I talk and you listen, etc.
- The "pregnant pause" as someone gets ready to speak, and the silence of an active "inner conversation," are respected and occur routinely.
- Conversations are multi-directional. Students will talk directly to each other (listening to and commenting on each other's thoughts), perhaps temporarily bypassing any adults.
- Students expect conversation to be interactive. Good conversationalists talk *with* others, not *at* them.
- Conversation is purposeful.

Schedule class conversation time to minimize interruptions. For example, it is tough to start a discussion if class is over in five minutes and students are starting to get itchy about getting their things, meeting their families, and leaving. Plan sufficient time to allow the group to wait comfortably. Avoid pressing for pauses and silences to flow into words. Plan to "talk" in a location where all members of the group can easily make eye contact with and hear one another. Sitting in a circle or dividing a large group into several smaller groups are good strategies.

Intermediates need more than props or pictures to provide a sense of purpose for their conversations (although these can be helpful at times). Express through your voice a sense of invitation and welcome as you request students to join the conversation. Then invite student contributions almost immediately. Weave the purpose of the conversation into the early questions rather than announcing it like a master of ceremonies.

Another strategy for conversation is to tuck in the talking around activities. Working together on a project creates an encouraging mood for spontaneous conversation. Moments of cooperation are ripe for starting conversations.

Reflecting

Activity suggestions are fashioned to furnish a quiet time for students to make a personal, and perhaps private, response to material presented in the session. Students' responses may take the form of a journal entry, a prayer, an artistic response, or meditative thoughts. Each Unit follows a particular approach through its nine sessions. Sturdy envelopes, called, "Reflection Collections," are suggested to preserve students' work. Reflecting could be a regularly planned activity, or an occasional exercise.

Without imagination, learning may be reduced to sets of facts and fixed meanings. Students gain immeasurably from the opportunity

> to wonder and to wish . . .
> to muse and to mull . . .
> to puzzle and to probe . . .
> to contemplate and to cogitate . . .
> to speculate and to surmise . . .

Through private and personal reflection, students can "move into" a scene or "play with" an idea, engaging in quiet, inner conversation.

Reflecting suggestions provide guidance for teachers to kindle students' thoughts through absorbing descriptions, intriguing questions, conditional statements, or soothing, sensory-based meditations.

Teachers can consider following a three-stage process: a peaceful beginning, an engrossing reflection, and a gently guided closure.

In each Unit, various types of responses are suggested—writing, drawing, just thinking. Materials needed for students' responses should be set out *before* the guided portion of the reflection activity.

Pay careful attention to preserving and protecting the privacy of students' responses. This will communicate the intimate, absorbing possibilities of reflecting activities. Use large sturdy envelopes with clasps, accordion file folders, boxes, portfolio folders, and the like. The idea is to have something for each student that can be easily stored between sessions, and that offers some type of secure fastening for privacy. These "Reflection Collections" can be sent home at the end of each Unit or the year.

Learning Skills

The Bible, *The Book of Common Prayer*, and *The Hymnal 1982* are important books for Episcopalians. Bible study is integrated into session activities throughout the Curriculum. The options in this category are designed to focus on particular skills and understandings which will be most beneficial for students using these great books. Option 1, Class Memory Challenge presents suggestions for memorizing material suitable for a lifetime of practical use. Option 2, Learning Scripture presents selected verses related to the session themes for individual students to commit to memory over the course of the Unit.

In Proper 28, we pray: "Blessed Lord, who has caused all holy Scriptures to be written for our learning: Grant us . . . to hear them, read them, mark, learn, and inwardly digest them . . . ." (BCP, p. 236).

Intermediate-age students need some sense of how the Bible came to be. They are now able to grasp the historical time-frame for the events in the Old and New Testaments. Teachers need to speak aloud of their love of the Bible, articulating clearly that it is a treasure for us. Similarly, students can be expected to explain in their own words what the Bible and other books of our faith mean to them personally. The *Treasurebooks*, which accompany each year of the ECC Intermediate level, are written to convey a sense of the value Episcopalians place on the Bible, the Prayer Book, and the Hymnal.

Bible study is integrated into the essential activities of every session. Reading from the Bible, locating Scriptures, and interpreting passages are part of virtually every session's *Gathering* (a student lector reads a passage) and *Introducing the Story* (students locate passages and respond to questions). Throughout the Curriculum, material from *The Book of Common Prayer* and *The*

Hymnal 1982 is incorporated into the optional activities within each session, or in some cases, may be used at *Gathering* or as part of *Introducing the Story*.

The category *Learning Skills* focuses explicitly on memory skills. Skill expectations include:
- Bible—names and order of the 66 books, how to use appendices, and maps
- Prayer Book—names and location of the various offices, collects, sacramental liturgies, other services, prayers and thanksgivings, psalter, and other material
- Hymnal—location and types of service music, the sequence in which hymns appear, and the several indices for the book

At the Intermediate level of the Curriculum, Scripture passages have been taken from the New Revised Standard Version (NRSV) of the Bible. This translation offers the most contemporary language of any, and is likely to be what many students will hear as part of their congregational worship. Teachers should feel free to substitute other approved versions.

Memory Work

Now is a great time for memory work. Intermediate-age students are capable learners, eager to acquire skills that will extend their competence. Many are beginning to participate fully in the worship and community life of their local congregation. Many are enthusiastic attenders of various organized Christian education programs. Students are hearing and saying the texts of our faith from the Bible, *The Book of Common Prayer*, and *The Hymnal 1982* in worship and the classroom. Memorizing some of these texts is a natural next step.

The Episcopal Children's Curriculum, at the Intermediate level, introduces two types of memory tasks for students. In the category *Learning Skills: Option 1. Class Memory Challenge* students are offered four memory tasks—one for each Unit. For the Chalice Year these are: Unit I—"First Song of Isaiah;" Unit II—parables of Jesus; Unit III—The Nicene Creed; and, Unit IV—an outline of *The Book of Common Prayer*. These are all items that will be useful now and in the future. Suggestions in each session include tips for helping students learn the material, and ways to recognize those who have done so. This is a Class Memory Challenge, designed to be used as a total group activity.

A second, individual memory option is provided in *Option 2. Learning Scripture*. Inspirational Scripture verses were selected from each session's theme for students to memorize. One of these appears on the session symbol card. Instructions are provided in the session outlines to guide teachers in managing this project. Support material for both the Class Memory Challenge and Learning Scripture appears in each issue of the student newspaper, *Community Times*.

Ongoing Project

Explicitly intended to carry over from session to session, a cumulative class project offers students and teachers the opportunity for continuity and review across the Unit sessions. Typically, these continuing projects lend themselves to display or sharing with the entire congregation.

Each session in the Episcopal Children's Curriculum is designed to be discrete and self-contained.

Yet, for intermediate-age students in particular, there are excellent reasons for entertaining the possibility of an *Ongoing Project*. Students can become interested in a theme and handle complex projects. Cooperation among class members heightens the possibility that those who may have missed a session will still know what happened. Also, during some Units, or some seasons of the Church Year, students' attendance may be predictably steady. Of greatest significance, however, is the potential of substantial ongoing projects to tap the talent of intermediates. They can organize, plan, and carry out these projects. Let the group help to solve any problems of space, storage, or participation.

An ongoing project can also be used at the Gathering in each session. A classroom display of the previous pieces of the project can provide a quick review of previous sessions' themes.

Projects of the scope and scale suggested in this category offer an opportunity to reach out to the congregation. In the Chalice Year of the Intermediate level, suggested projects include a prophet's time line (Unit I), a display of seasonal symbols and interviews about Jesus' parables (Unit II), liturgy planning for a selected Sunday and an outline of the days from Palm Sunday through the second Sunday of Easter (Unit III), and a picture catechism book based on the Catechism in *The Book of Common Prayer* (Unit IV).

Teachers interested in using an ongoing project are advised to read through the descriptions for all nine sessions of the Unit. After the first, fully detailed description, each session's outline suggests a small piece of the project that teachers could reasonably be expected to accomplish in one session. If circumstances do not permit work on the ongoing project at every session, teachers could combine one or two of the small steps later. Similarly, the ongoing project can be started or stopped at several points.

Symbol Cards

One of the developmental milestones for intermediate-age students is their ability to understand symbols. Symbols are included in sessions throughout the Intermediate level of the Curriculum. Each session of the ECC is accompanied by a small, collectible card that includes an illustration of a Christian symbol, an explanation, and a Scripture passage.

Teachers are encouraged to devise appropriate ways to include the cards as part of their class activities. Cards can be used to conclude the session, handed out as part of the Going Forth activities. Cards can be used to stimulate conversation, as references for art projects, or simply cherished as a gift from the church to each student. Symbol Cards, the *Treasurebook*, and *Community Times* are concrete and desirable links between home and church.

Treasurebook

Intended for guided, independent reading, the *Treasurebook* provides support for the four Units. Intermediate students can read on their own to learn more about their faith.

In the *Chalice Year Treasurebook*, students can examine prophets (Unit I); Jesus and his parables (Unit II); Holy Eucharist (Unit III); The Catechism in *The Book of Common Prayer* (Unit IV).

At the end of the session, along with the symbol card description, a suggestion is given to guide students' independent reading, along with a question for students to think about. Teachers are encouraged to read appropriate *Treasurebook* sections as part of their personal preparation in *Getting Ready*.

Resource and Reference Books
A book about Jesus. New York: American Bible Society, 1991.
A few who dared to trust God. New York: American Bible Society, 1990.
Aaseng, Rolf E. (Annegert Fuchshuber, illus.) *Augsburg story Bible*. Minneapolis: Augsburg, 1992.
An illustrated history of the Church. (Ten volume series). Minneapolis: Winston Press, 1980.

Batchelor, Mary. *The children's Bible in 365 stories*. Batavia: Lion Publishing, 1985.

Beguerie, Philippe, & Claude Duchesneau. *How to understand the sacraments*. New York: Crossroad, 1991.

Bible for today's family: New Testament. New York: American Bible Society, 1991.

Billington, Rachel, & Barbara Brown. *The first miracles*. Grand Rapids: Eerdman, 1990.

DePaola, Tomie. *The miracles of Jesus*. New York: Holiday House, 1987.

DePaola, Tomie. *The parables of Jesus*. New York: Holiday House, 1987.

Dickinson, Peter. (Michael Foreman, illus.) *City of gold and other stories from the Old Testament*. Boston: Otter Books, 1992.

Dillenberger, Jane. *Image & spirit in sacred and secular art*. New York: Crossroad, 1990.

Dillenberger, Jane. *Style & content in Christian art*. New York: Crossroad, 1986.

Fluegelman, Andrew, ed. *The new games book*. Garden City: Dolphin Books, 1976.

Good news travels fast: The Acts of the Apostles. New York: American Bible Society, 1988.

Gregson, Bob. *The incredible indoor games book*. Carthage: Fearon Teacher Aids, 1982.

Griggs, Patricia. *Beginning Bible skills: Opening the Bible with children*. Nashville: Abingdon, 1986.

Halverson, Delia. *Teaching prayer in the classroom*. Nashville: Abingdon, 1989.

Hebblethwaite, Margaret. *My secret life: A friendship with God*. Harrisburg: Morehouse, 1991.

Keithahn, Mary Nelson. *Creative ideas for teaching: Learning through writing*. Brea: Educational Ministries, 1987.

L'Engle, Madeleine. *Ladder of angels*. New York: Seabury, 1979.

Luke tells the good news about Jesus. New York: American Bible Society, 1987.

Marchon, Blandine. (Claude & Denise Millet, illus.) *The Bible: The greatest stories*. Nashville: Abingdon, 1992.

Milord, Susan. *Hands around the world*. Charlotte: Williamson Publishing, 1992.

Prichard, Robert W. *The bat and the bishop*. Harrisburg: Morehouse, 1989.

Roth, Nancy L. *Praying: A book for children*. New York: The Church Hymnal Corp., 1991

Smith, Judy Gattis. *Teaching to wonder: Spiritual growth through imagination and movement*. Nashville: Abingdon, 1989.

Smith, Judy Gattis. *Teaching with music through the church year*. Nashville: Abingdon, 1979.

Sparks, Lee, ed. *Fun group games for children's ministry*. Loveland: Group Publishing, 1990.

Staeheli, Alice M. *Costuming the Christmas and Easter play: With ideas for other Biblical dramas*. Colorado Springs: Meriwether, 1988.

Stewig, John Warren. *Informal drama in the elementary language arts program*. New York: Teachers College, 1983.

Stoddard, Sandol. (Tony Chen, illus.) *The Doubleday illustrated children's Bible*. New York: Doubleday, 1983.

Stoddard, Sandol. (Rachel Isadora, illus.) *Prayers, praises, and thanksgivings*. New York: Dial, 1992.

The Taize picture Bible. Philadelphia: Fortress, 1968.

Turner, Philip. (Brian Wildsmith, illus.) *The Bible story*. Oxford: Oxford University Press, 1968.

Wiseman, Ann. *Making things: The handbook of creative discovery*. Boston: Little, Brown, 1973.

Note: The following letter is for teachers and parents of children in the Intermediate level of church school. These two pages can be reproduced or used as a model for a personalized letter.

Episcopal Children's Curriculum
Unit I: PROPHECY

Dear Parents and Guardians,

During the first Unit of the Intermediate Chalice Year, student will examine portions of prophetic writings from the Bible. We will help them understand that the Hebrew prophets of the Old Testament were passionate advocates for faith in God and for moral and social responsibility. Again and again, they called Israel and Judah back to worship and obedience.

Jesus and his disciples knew the writings of the prophets. When Jesus visited the synagogue in Nazareth, he read aloud from a scroll of the *Book of Isaiah* and declared his own ministry to be the fulfillment of the passage *(Luke 4:16-21)*.

In the *Book of Acts*, it is clear that Peter, Paul, and the other leaders of the early church devoted themselves to persuading people that Jesus was the Messiah of whom the prophets spoke. Paul, brought up in the Jewish faith, viewed himself as "set apart for the gospel of God, which was promised beforehand through the prophets in the holy scriptures" *(Romans 1:1)*.

In a very real sense, then, the Covenant we make in Holy Baptism has a clear relationship to the Hebrew prophets. Because of this relationship, Christians can benefit from learning about the history and message of that large section of the Bible from *Isaiah* through *Malachi*—nearly a third of the Old Testament.

Plan to spend some time talking to your student about what he or she is learning. You can do this by reading the Scripture identified below, discussing the Symbol Cards and *Community Times* sent home each week, and by reading together Part I of the *Chalice Year Treasurebook*, which includes information about the prophets.

Following is a more detailed overview of the Unit:

Session 1: "The Mission of the Prophets" introduces their ministry during a specific period of Hebrew history. Included are the stories of Elijah and Elisha—two early prophets who left no writings. The prophets throughout this period were fearless in warning God's people about wrongdoing, and were seldom popular. However, they also brought the good news that a Messiah would establish the reign of God. (*II Kings 2:8-12*)

Session 2: "Amos, Prophet of Justice" focuses on Amos, the shepherd of Tekoa who lived in the eighth century BCE. This short book is a reminder that God's people are to be sensitive to the poor, to work actively for justice in the world, and to remember that God cares for all people. Amos is called the "prophet of justice." (*Amos 2:6-7b; 5:21-24*)

Session 3: "Isaiah: Messiah Will Come" is about the prophet who wrote *Isaiah 1-39*, known as "First Isaiah." He described spiritual dangers inherent in wealth and power. Although from the upper class, he rejected wealth to warn the people about judgment and destruction. His descriptions of the coming Messiah are often quoted. (*Isaiah 9:2a-3a; 6*)

Session 4: "Micah Spoke for God" is the story of a farmer who denounced both Israel and Judah for wrongdoing. He identified with the peasant people and cried out against those who took advantage of them. He predicted that Jerusalem would be destroyed as a result of the people's sins. Micah also told of the coming of a Messiah. (*Micah 6:6-8*)

Session 5: "Jeremiah: Prophet of Faith" moves ahead about a century. Because Judah was on the border between Babylonia and Egypt, it became a satellite country of Babylonia. Eventually, Judah fell and Jerusalem was plundered. Throughout this period, Jeremiah spoke out fearlessly for God and was imprisoned for being a traitor. He continued to proclaim the coming of a Messiah. (*Jeremiah 1:4-10*)

Session 6: "Ezekiel: Seer of Visions" presents an unusual figure in Hebrew history who lived in comfort as an exile in Babylon. After experiencing several encounters with God, he became a prophet of doom. Like those before him, he declared that the sins of God's people brought their troubles. And yet, he still told about a time of new life for Judah. (*Ezekiel 37:1-11*, excerpts)

Session 7: "Isaiah Proclaims a Message of Light," taken from *Isaiah 40-55*, is called "Second Isaiah" because it was written nearly 200 years after the first part of *Isaiah*. The writing centers around four poems, called Servant Songs. The writer foresees a Suffering Servant from God who would bring salvation to God's people. Christians understand this to be Jesus Christ the Messiah. (*Isaiah 42:5-9*)

Session 8: "Centuries of Prophecy" looks at three of the twelve "Minor Prophets," from Hosea to Malachi. The selected prophets are Hosea, Joel, and Jonah. Students will be introduced to key concepts from these prophets' writings. The message of all the prophets is about God's faithfulness in reaching out in love to bring God's people back into a relationship with the Creator and Redeemer. (*Hosea 14:4-7*)

Session 9: "Honoring the Saints" is to be used in the week nearest All Saints' Day (November 1). The lesson will not interrupt the flow of the sessions because the Hebrew prophets are among the saints of God that we remember at the Church's celebration of this Principal Feast. (*Ephesians 1:17-18; 2:19-20*)

Yours in Christ,

Church School Teachers

PROPHECY
SESSION 1
THE MISSION OF THE PROPHETS

FOCUS

The word "prophet" is central to an understanding of Scripture. God called individuals to speak to the chosen people during each period of their history. The students should be able to locate writings of the prophets in their Bibles and distinguish between the "major" and "minor" prophets.

GETTING READY

In the Hebrew Scriptures (Old Testament), prophets are individuals who were recognized as persons who spoke for God. They offered counsel and stern warnings to kings and leaders who turned to false gods and lived in ways contrary to the law of Moses.

The prophets were sensitive to the presence of God in human history and they were frequent bearers of bad news for both Israel and Judah in times of disobedience. But they also proclaimed good news about the future and foretold the coming of a Messiah who would establish a new relationship between God and humanity.

Although many persons in the Old Testament are called prophets, including Moses and David, the most memorable group are Amos, Hosea, Micah, Jeremiah, Ezekiel, and First and Second Isaiah. They lived during a period spanning two centuries (around 750-550 BCE), and they can be linked on a timeline with various kings of Israel and Judah.

The words of these "literary" prophets are preserved in the Bible. Jeremiah, Ezekiel, and Isaiah are frequently called "major" prophets, but only because their writings are longer than the others. Although the 12 shorter prophetic books are often labeled "minor," their content is not less important.

The prophetic writers were preceded—about a century earlier—by two influential prophets: Elijah and Elisha. They left no writings, so we have only the record of their deeds, found in the books of *I Kings 17-19* and *II Kings 1-13*. Recalling the stories of these two men of God is a good way to set the stage for looking at the writings of their successors.

Almighty God, you proclaim your truth in every age by many voices: Direct, in our time, we pray, those who speak where many listen and write what many read; that they may do their part in making the heart of this people wise, its mind sound, and its will righteous; to the honor of Jesus Christ our Lord. *Amen.*
For those who Influence Public Opinion
The Book of Common Prayer, p. 827

TEACHING TIP

Intermediate-age students can be given an opportunity to serve as classroom lectors in the same way members of Episcopal congregations read Scripture at services of worship. All class members deserve a chance to prepare for this assignment. (See suggestions for Gathering in the Strategies section of the Teacher's Background.) Because students have a variety of reading abilities, do not insist that every student participate.

GATHERING

Ahead of time, cut apart and display the Prophets' TimeLine on Poster No. 2 in the Teacher's Packet. For this session, place the pictures of Elijah and Elisha under the ninth century. Their dates are uncertain, but Elijah's time was around 850 BCE, with Elisha following immediately afterward.

As students arrive, direct their attention to the two pictures. Ask: What seems to be happening in each picture? Have you heard of these names?

When everyone is present, say:

Let us pray. (Use the prayer "For those who

Influence Public Opinion," above, or a prayer of your own choosing.)

The chosen student lector reads from the class Bible (NRSV) portions of the story of Elijah's ascent into heaven:

A Reading from the Book of Second Kings, chapter 2, verses 8 through 12.

Then Elijah took his mantle and rolled it up, and struck the water; the water was parted to the one side and to the other, until (Elijah and Elisha) crossed on dry ground.

When they had crossed, Elijah said to Elisha, "Tell me what I may do for you, before I am taken from you." Elisha said, "Please let me inherit a double share of your spirit." He responded, "You have asked a hard thing; yet, if you see me as I am being taken from you, it will be granted you; if not, it will not." As they continued walking and talking, a chariot of fire and horses of fire separated the two of them, and Elijah ascended in a whirlwind into heaven. Elisha kept watching and crying out, "Father, father! The chariots of Israel and its horsemen!" But when he could no longer see him, he grasped his own clothes and tore them in two pieces.

Reader: The Word of the Lord.
Response: Thanks be to God.

INTRODUCING THE STORY
(Time: 10–20 minutes)

Begin by telling in your own words the story of Elijah challenging the prophets of Baal in Israel. As background, refer to the article on page 1 of the student newspaper *Community Times* (Unit I, Issue 1) and the biblical narrative in *I Kings 18*.

Invite the students to participate in the storytelling by assigning half to say "boo" every time you say the word Baal, and the others to say "yea" when they hear the word Elijah. Use the colorful words from the passage to help the students envision the action in the story.

Explain that Elijah is one of the early prophets in the Old Testament. These people were called by God to speak fearlessly to God's people when they did wrong. None of the prophets were especially popular. Sometimes they were persecuted for speaking the truth. The prophets not only told of bad news, they also told of a day when a Messiah would establish the reign of God.

Suggest that the students open their Bibles and mark the final page of the Old Testament with a finger or small slip of paper. Then direct the group to locate the beginning of the *Book of Isaiah*. (If they are all using the same Bible, you can give the page number.) Estimate how much of the Old Testament from *Isaiah* through *Malachi* is about the prophets—about one-third!

Explain that this section is called "The Prophets," and includes some of the most important insights into the Hebrews' understanding of God. Point out the distinction between the major and minor books. Major simply means longer and minor means shorter.

Look up the story of Elijah's ascension in the chariot of fire and horses and Elisha's parting the water in *II Kings 2:1-15*. Ask: How did Elisha feel when he was left alone? Have you ever been left, as Elisha was, to do a job that seemed impossible? What happened?

EXPLORING
(Time: 15–20 minutes)

Option 1. Elijah and the Prophets of Baal

Consider the dramatic contrasts in the story of Elijah's encounter with prophets of the false god Baal. On a chalkboard or large piece of newsprint, prepare a three-column chart like the following:

	Prophets of Baal	*Elijah*
Number of prophets:	450	1
Sacrificial animal:	bull	bull
Preparation for sacrifice:		
Length of time:		
Ceremony:		
Results:		

Using the Bible and the student newspaper, *Community Times* (Unit I, Issue 1), encourage students to continue filling in the contrasting information. For example, under "Preparation for sacrifice," enter "Cut in pieces, lay on wood," and other phrases that capture the scene. Note that Elijah called for water to be poured around the animal.

Assign parts and act out the drama. Discuss how to act out the scene in *I Kings 18*. How do the prophets of Baal "limp" around the altar? Encourage the group to have fun with this colorful story.

Option 2. Turn Books

Prepare a supply of small sheets of plain paper, 3 x 2½ inches in size (about one-half the size of a file card). Suggest that students use the paper sheets to prepare sketches of scenes in the stories of Elijah (confronting the prophets of Baal) and Elisha (receiving Elijah's mantle). They may work individually or in pairs to map out the number of sketches needed.

When the sketches are finished, staple them together in the upper left hand corner so that the pages can be turned quickly to provide "animation" for a retelling of the stories.

Practice telling the stories using the turn books. Arrange an appropriate time for students to tell the stories to another group in the church using their picture books.

Option 3. Unscrambling Sentences

Turn in the student newspaper, *Community Times*, Unit I, Issue 1, to the puzzle titled "Scrambled Sentences." This exercise can be completed by individuals, teams, or the whole group.

MUSIC
(Time: 10 minutes)

Introduce the one-stanza hymn, "God be in my head" *(The Hymnal 1982, 694)* by reading it or listening to the *Children Sing!* tape. Ask: In what ways do the words remind us of God's prophets? Why would the hymn be especially appropriate for Elijah?

CONNECTING/SPEAKING OUT
(Time: 15–20 minutes)

Option 1. Group Discussion

The Hebrew prophets were called to speak the truth when kings and leaders turned away from God. Elijah, for example, warned Ahab, king of Israel, that he had done wrong in allowing people to worship Baal. Ahab had even allowed Baal's followers to build a temple. When a severe drought came, causing crops to wither, Ahab blamed Elijah whom he called a "troubler."

Encourage the students to put themselves in the place of either Elijah or Elisha and imagine how it would feel to stand up for the truth of God in the face of people's rebellion and resentment. Ask: What would you be willing to stand up for? Environmental issues such as pollution or saving a forest? Political issues such as civil rights? School issues such as dress codes or other rules? How would it feel to go against people in authority? If no one listened, what would you do? How would it feel to be punished for speaking?

Option 2. Current Events

Clip articles from current newspapers, magazines, or other sources about current social problems (such as street crime, dishonest financial dealings, or damage to the environment). Ask the students to choose clippings and explain what the prophets might say about each issue.

Ask: Who are some modern-day prophets who speak out to warn us about our behavior and the way we treat others? What do these prophets tell us?

REFLECTING
(Time: 10 minutes)

Provide each student with an envelope approximately 9 x 12 inches in size. Label each one "My Reflections." The students may add their names and appropriate decorations to the envelopes. These are to be used for saving and storing personal reflections during this Unit. (This may be a planned activity within every session, or it could be done only occasionally. In either case, it is important to preserve what the students produce. Store the envelopes between sessions, and assure the class members that the reflections are private—for their eyes only. They may be taken home at the end of the Unit.)

Share aloud or write out some directions about the kinds of reflections that may be included. For this session, say something like the following:

Put yourselves in the roles of prophets. Who are some of the people you would like to speak with today? What would you want to say? Why? How would you let others know you had been listening to God?

Write down or illustrate your thoughts. At the end of your reflection, add a brief prayer in your own words.

LEARNING SKILLS
(Time: 10–15 minutes)

Option 1. Class Memory Challenge

During this Unit's study of Hebrew prophets, offer the students the challenge of memorizing "The First Song of Isaiah" *(The Book of Common Prayer, Canticle 9, p. 86; Isaiah 12:2-6)*. The passage is an affirmation of the saving power of God. The words are comforting to individuals in times of trial or doubt.

Display Poster No. 1 of the Canticle from the Teacher's Packet. To begin the memory task, ask the

Unit I. Prophecy—Session 1
Chalice Year Intermediate—Copyright © 2000 Virginia Theological Sminary and Morehouse Publishing

class members to work in pairs to repeat aloud to each other verse 1: "Surely, it is God who saves me; I will trust in him and not be afraid."

As an aid to recalling the verse, suggest that the students focus on these key words: "God . . . saves," and "I will trust."

Option 2. Learning Scripture

Invite the students to choose either of the following to be learned before the next class session: *II Kings 2:11b* or *Psalm 85:8* (in any version or translation). See "Learning Scripture" in the student newspaper, *Community Times*. The students may be encouraged to use their Bibles at home and work with friends or family members.

For each verse suggested in this Unit (in this and succeeding sessions), make a simple brown torch from construction paper. Write a single Scripture verse on each torch. As individuals report that they have memorized a verse, add a small orange, red, or yellow flame to the tip of the appropriate torch. The result should be a set of flaming torches by the end of the Unit.

ONGOING PROJECT
(Time: 5–10 minutes)

Explain that a collection of prophets' collages will be produced during the Unit. Decide on a place in the church to display this "parade of prophets" as it grows (or at the end of the Unit).

In each session, create a simple portrait for the prophet (a face or full figure), to be placed at the center of the collage. Use sheets of posterboard for the background and supply scissors and glue along with additional items such as construction paper, clipped pictures and headlines from magazines, yarn, and other materials. Scenes, symbols, and words can be glued in expanding circles around the central image.

For this session, invite the students to work together to prepare two collages—one to depict Elijah and the other, Elisha. Students may add actual words spoken by prophets.

SYMBOL CARD and TREASUREBOOK

Card 1 contains a flaming chariot symbol, a verse of Scripture, and an explanation on the back.

Ask the students to look at *Chalice Year Treasurebook*, Part I, Section 1 that includes a listing of all the prophets of the Old Testament in chronological order. Which are "minor" books of prophecy and which are "major"?

GOING FORTH

Gather the group for the dismissal. The teacher or a student will say:
>I ask your prayers for all who seek God, or a deeper knowledge of him.
>Pray that they may find and be found by him.
>*Silence*
>
>[Learners may add their petitions.]
>
>Praise God for those in every generation in whom Christ has been honored especially those whom we remember today.
>Pray that we may have grace to glorify Christ in our own day.
>>From The Prayers of the People
>>*The Book of Common Prayer*, p. 386

Teacher: Let us go forth in the name of Christ.
Students: Thanks be to God.

TEACHER'S ASSESSMENT

Recall the students' responses to questions about prophets and their mission. What characteristics of prophets seemed meaningful to the class members? Why? Think of ways to continue making the connection between the prophets and the students' own experiences with standing up for the truth.

LOOKING AHEAD

The next session will be devoted to Amos, a "prophet of justice." In preparation for teaching, define justice for yourself.

PROPHECY
SESSION 2
AMOS: PROPHET OF JUSTICE

FOCUS

Amos is among the earliest prophets whose words were recorded by later disciples. A shepherd, he is best known for proclaiming the judgment and righteousness of God. He stressed justice for the poor. The students should be able to identify Amos as a prophet of God's justice and to explain how his message relates to our world today.

GETTING READY

The prophecy of Amos came about a hundred years after Elisha (around 760 BCE). As the pioneer of prophetic writing, he set the stage for the other prophets whose words we have in the Old Testament.

He lived in the Judean village of Tekoa, about seven miles southeast of Bethlehem. He was a herder of sheep and also a "dresser (cultivator) of sycamore trees."

In Amos' time, the people of Israel to the north had become confident and prosperous, as a result of military victories that made them feel secure. Now able to live in luxury, the ruling classes had become very lax morally. Drunkenness, extravagant living, and sexual immorality were accepted casually. The worship of God had also grown superficial. Worst of all, the wealthy exploited poor people for whom injustice and oppression were now commonplace.

Amos grew certain that God had called him to issue stern warnings about the behavior of the people. He traveled twenty-five miles north to the temple at Bethel, and there he delivered his strong pronouncements of judgment. The following ideas are central to the *Book of Amos*:

a. There is only one God—the God who brought Israel out of bondage in Egypt and established her as a new nation.

b. God cares for all nations of the world and desires what is good for them.

c. God wants justice among people, not just ceremonial rites of sacrifice. The poor are in greatest need of just treatment.

d. Military preparedness will, in the end, be of no benefit to God's people.

e. God's will and intention are revealed to prophets, and God does not act without first telling appointed prophets what is about to happen.

Amos' words end on the theme of divine punishment. We cannot derive much comfort from the prophet's words, but we can be grateful for the way he calls us all to be sensitive to the plight of the poor. From Amos we hear the clear summons to work for justice in the world. It is a good message for intermediate-age students.

The entire *Book of Amos* is less than ten pages in our Bibles. As you prepare, read especially chapters 3-6 about woes for Israel and chapters 7-9 about symbolic visions. The most-quoted line is *Amos 5:24*.

Almighty and most merciful God, we remember before you all the poor and neglected persons whom it would be easy for us to forget: the homeless and the destitute, the old and the sick, and all who have none to care for them. Help us to heal those who are broken in body or spirit, and to turn their sorrow into joy. Grant this, Father, for the love of your Son, who for our sake became poor, Jesus Christ our Lord. *Amen.*

For the Poor and the Neglected
The Book of Common Prayer, p. 826

TEACHING TIP

Amos was not worried about what people thought about him. He and his successors were certain they had been called by God to speak the truth. These prophetic qualities may appeal to intermediate-age students who can be accurate critics of people around them. They notice unfairness, and they protest by expressing strong judgment. Help students be aware of the effect of their stern judgments. Underscore the need for expressing *compassion* as well.

GATHERING

Continue the Prophets' TimeLine, which is contained in the Teacher's Packet and was introduced in Session 1 of the Unit. Place the picture of Amos under the line at about 760 BCE.

As the students arrive, invite them to speculate about the picture. What is the man doing with the trees? Why are the sheep in the background?

When everyone is present, say:

Let us pray. (Use the prayer "For the Poor and the Neglected," above, or a prayer of your own choosing.)

The chosen student lector reads from the class Bible (NRSV):

A *Reading from the Book of Amos, chapter 2, verses 6 and 7b, and chapter 5, verses 21 through 24.*

Thus says the Lord:
For three transgressions of Israel,
  and for four, I will not revoke the punishment;
because they sell the righteous for silver,
  and the needy for a pair of sandals—
they who trample the head of the poor into the dust
  of the earth,
  and push the afflicted out of the way; . . .
(The Lord says), I hate, I despise your festivals,
  and I take no delight in your solemn assemblies.
Even though you offer me your burnt offerings
  and grain offerings, I will not accept them;
and the offerings of well-being of your fatted animals
  I will not look upon.
Take away from me the noise of your songs;
  I will not listen to the melody of your harps.
But let justice roll down like waters,
  and righteousness like an everflowing stream.

Reader: The Word of the Lord.
Response: Thanks be to God.

INTRODUCING THE STORY
(Time: 10–20 minutes)

Introduce the character of Amos by using information in Getting Ready (above) and from the article on page 1 of the student newspaper *Community Times* (Unit I, Issue 2). If possible, read the short book of *Amos* in preparation.

Include the way Amos described himself as a herdsman and dresser of sycamore trees who was called by God to prophesy to the people of Israel. Did any of the students guess this about Amos during the Gathering activity?

Although he came from a small rural community in Judea, he was called to deliver his message to the wealthy and overconfident people of Israel. People were troubled by his message that God would no longer accept their offerings until they obeyed God's commandments. He stunned the listeners as he spoke of sin and evil and the certainty of God's punishment.

Amos was a fierce champion of the poor and he called for God's justice to "roll down like waters, and righteousness like an everflowing stream" (*Amos 5:24*).

Amos used strong words that drew strong responses from the people. Ask the students to close their eyes and form pictures in their minds as you say the following words. Say each word aloud, pausing briefly between words, and at longer intervals after each grouping:

evil, sinners, transgressions (*longer pause*)
punishment, destruction (*longer pause*)
wailing, mourning (*longer pause*)

Encourage class members to share briefly any images or stories that were suggested by the words. How did the words make them feel?

Ask the students to turn to the *Book of Amos* in their Bibles. Call attention to the mixture of short prose introductions and longer passages of poetry. Invite them to find interesting phrases or images to share with the group.

EXPLORING
(Time: 15–20 minutes)

Option 1. Acting on Justice

Suggest that class members form small groups or teams to prepare skits that illustrate a need for justice or fairness among people. The scenes can be drawn from community or school life. Examples: a clique of students exclude others from their sports teams or parties; students are inconsiderate of a physically handicapped classmate; siblings in a family refuse to help do the chores.

Urge the students to include in their skits a person who plays the role of "prophet" and calls for justice and compassion.

Option 2. Art Project, 'River of Righteousness'

Drawing on the imagery of *Amos 5:24*, encourage the students to create a "river of righteousness" in a creative art project. Gather sheets of tissue in varying shades of blue and green, and cut them into uneven, spear-shaped strips. On a long piece of white background paper, paint a thin layer of white glue thinned with water. While this is still wet, place the tissue strips on it. The colors will bleed and blend and the result will be a "river."

As the river dries, students may gather appropriate pictures of people from various backgrounds to attach to the background paper. The finished product will portray people living together in harmony and justice—in accord with Amos' vision.

Option 3. Word Puzzle

Turn in the student newspaper, *Community Times*, Unit I, Issue 2, to the word puzzle, "Amos." Students may work alone, in pairs, or as a total group.

MUSIC
(Time: 10 minutes)

Continue listening to "God be in my head" *(The Hymnal 1982*, 694*)* on the *Children Sing!* tape. Notice the hymn's use of these words: head, eyes, mouth, and heart. Ask: If Amos had sung this hymn, what might he have been thinking? Seeing? Saying? Feeling?

CONNECTING/SPEAKING OUT
(Time: 15–20 minutes)

Option 1. Group Discussion

Ask the students to examine in their Bibles the words of Amos about God's judgment in the following visions:

Amos 7—locusts (verses 1-3); shower of fire (verses 4-6); plumb line (verses 7-9).

Amos 8—basket of fruit (verses 1-3).

Which vision(s) would the students describe as most severe? Why? If you were a prophet, what images would you use that people would understand today? What role would technology—including televisions, computers, video games—play in your visions?

Option 2. Current Events

Amos found Israel to be corrupt and he expressed his strong opposition to the injustice and immorality that he saw all around him. In the same way, we can become keenly aware of similar conditions in our own world. Clip and distribute to the class members several newspaper and magazine articles about contemporary issues calling for justice. Ask students to look at these briefly and describe the main problems they present.

Invite the students to think about persons or groups who feel "used" (exploited) by other people. Ask: How do you think it feels to be poor or homeless? to be a member of a minority group that does not enjoy privileges of the majority? to feel inferior to others in some way?

Encourage the class members to consider what it is like to speak out on behalf of people in need of justice. Ask: What would you say? Why? How do you think your words would be received?

REFLECTING
(Time: 10 minutes)

Suggest that the students put themselves in Amos' shoes. He is a shepherd, a simple person who has lived in a village all his life. He has gone on a journey to deliver a message from God at a temple in a large city. He knows that his words will not make him popular.

Suppose that Amos is keeping a journal of his feelings. What might he write down just before he leaves on his trip? while he is traveling? after he speaks?

Individuals may write or draw their reflections, adding a prayer that they have written. The sheets may be stored in envelopes as described in Session 1.

LEARNING SKILLS
(Time: 10–15 minutes)

Option 1. Class Memory Challenge

Invite the students to continue the task of memorizing *Isaiah 12:2-6*, in the form of Canticle 9, in *The Book of Common Prayer*, p. 86. See the suggestions in Session 1, and display Poster No. 1 from the Teacher's Packet.

Encourage the class members to repeat in unison the first verse of the Song. Introduce verse 2, noting the key words: "Lord . . . defense, . . . will be my Savior." Again, form pairs to repeat the verse aloud several times.

Option 2. Learning Scripture

Make torches for each new verse class members have learned from the previous session, adding flames for students as described in Session 1.

Invite the students to memorize *Amos 3:7* or *5:24* before the next class session. See "Learning Scripture" in the student newspaper, *Community Times*.

ONGOING PROJECT
(Time: 5–10 minutes)

Invite the class members to continue the project described in Session 1. Spend some time considering how to design the central image for Amos. What kinds of pictures and words might be added to the background for his poster?

Display the completed picture of Amos alongside the poster(s) for Elijah and Elisha.

SYMBOL CARD and TREASUREBOOK

Card 2 contains a shepherd's staff, a verse of Scripture, and an explanation on the back.

Ask the students to read *Chalice Year Treasurebook*, Part I, Section 2 about Amos. What do we remember best about him?

GOING FORTH

Gather the group for the dismissal. The teacher or a student will say:
> I ask your prayers for all who seek God, or a deeper knowledge of him.
> Pray that they may find and be found by him.
> *Silence*
> [Learners may add their petitions.]
> Praise God for those in every generation in whom Christ has been honored especially those whom we remember today.
> Pray that we may have grace to glorify Christ in our own day.
> From The Prayers of the People
> *The Book of Common Prayer*, p. 386

Teacher: Let us go forth in the name of Christ.
Students: Thanks be to God.

TEACHER'S ASSESSMENT

From your observations, how well did the students grasp the main themes in Amos' prophecies? What was their response to his severe judgments? In what ways are they able to relate the prophet's message to our own society?

LOOKING AHEAD

The next session is on the first part of the *Book of Isaiah*, usually called "First Isaiah." In contrast to Amos, this prophet offers a message of hope and predicts the coming of the Messiah. In preparation, leaf through *Isaiah 1-39*, paying special attention to the poetic passages and looking for any lines that may be familiar. How does Isaiah's style contrast with that of Amos?

PROPHECY
SESSION 3
ISAIAH: MESSIAH WILL COME

FOCUS

The *Book of Isaiah* was written by at least two prophets. The first Isaiah was called by God to speak to the people of Judah. He reminded them of the holiness of God and he spoke of the Messiah who would come to rule. The students should be able to describe Isaiah's call, to locate one or more passages he wrote, and to tell why we read his words particularly at Christmas.

GETTING READY

The *Book of Isaiah* is the work of at least two prophets. First Isaiah (chapters 1-39) was written by a wealthy man in the southern kingdom of Judah who prophesied for forty years (740-700 BCE). He was married to a woman whom he called a "prophetess," and they had two sons.

Young Isaiah may have read and studied the words of Amos, written twenty-five years before he received his own call to prophetic ministry. He had gone to the temple to mourn the death of a very successful king of Judah named Uzziah. While praying, he had a vision (chapter 6) in which God cleansed his lips and sent him out to speak a message of judgment and redemption. From this story comes the "Holy, holy, holy" (Sanctus) of Christian worship (verse 3).

Isaiah saw that wealth and power caused people to turn away from God and to put their trust in human leaders and false gods. He rejected his own background of privilege and devoted himself to warning kings and citizens that a day of judgment and destruction would come to them because of their corruption and unfaithfulness.

More than any other Hebrew prophet, Isaiah stressed the *holiness* of God. He also conceived of Jerusalem as the city of God's great love, a kind of mystical center of faith. He is known, too, for his doctrine of "the remnant"—the concept that, in every time of rebellion and unfaithfulness, God would save a remaining chosen group and bless them with new beginnings.

Most of all, we remember First Isaiah for his beautiful descriptions of a Messiah who would come to usher in a reign of God. See especially *Isaiah 9:6-7* and *11:6-9*. It is partly from Isaiah that the Church of New Testament times drew inspiration for its preaching of Jesus Christ as Messiah, Son of God and Redeemer of the world.

Isaiah's clear message embracing all that is good, defending the poor, and rejecting all forms of evil can have strong appeal for intermediate-age students.

> Almighty God, whose loving hand has given us all that we possess: Grant us grace that we may honor you with our substance, and, remembering the account which we must one day give, may be faithful stewards of your bounty, through Jesus Christ our Lord. *Amen.*
>
> For the Right Use of God's Gifts
> *The Book of Common Prayer,* p. 827

TEACHING TIP

Be sure to emphasize both parts of First Isaiah's message. At the same time he warned the people about the day of judgment, he also described the coming Messiah in words that inspire us today. Many of the messages we receive, especially from the media, are dark and gloomy. Help your students see the beauty in the world around them and the kindness of people in their lives.

GATHERING

Continue using the Prophets' TimeLine from the Teacher's Packet. Add the picture of Isaiah under the years 740-700 BCE.

Unit I. Prophecy—Session 3
Chalice Year Intermediate—Copyright © 2000 Virginia Theological Siminary and Morehouse Publishing

As the students arrive, direct their attention to the scene. Ask: Where does the man in the picture seem to be? What is the meaning of the box with the winged creatures? What is the angel doing? Why is the man pointing to his lips? Encourage students to guess the story behind the picture.

When everyone is present, say:

Let us pray. (Use the prayer "For the Right Use of God's Gifts," above, or a prayer of your own choosing.)

The chosen student lector reads from the class Bible (NRSV):

A Reading from the Book of Isaiah, chapter 9, verses 2b through 3a, and verse 6.

The people who walked in darkness have seen a great light;
    those who lived in a land of deep darkness—
    on them light has shined.
You have multiplied the nation, you have increased its joy;
    ....
For a child has been born for us, a son given to us;
    authority rests upon his shoulders;
    and he is named
    Wonderful Counselor, Mighty God,
    Everlasting Father, Prince of Peace.

Reader: The Word of the Lord.
Response: Thanks be to God.

INTRODUCING THE STORY
(Time: 10–20 minutes)

Begin by asking the students to recall times when they have felt especially close to God. Ask: Where were you? What had just happened? What do you think God may have been saying to you?

Allow this moment of reflection to be private. Assure students that they will not be asked to share their ideas aloud.

Ask several volunteers to share their ideas about the picture used for the Gathering activity. Find out how they identified the box (the arc of the covenant) and the actions of the angel and the man (First Isaiah).

In your own words, tell the story of First Isaiah using material from Getting Ready and the article on page 1 of the student newspaper, *Community Times* (Unit I, Issue 3), about his call to be a prophet.

Describe Isaiah's call that occurred the year King Uzziah died (*Isaiah 6:1-8*). Look again at the timeline picture and point to the characters as you tell the story. This was a time when Isaiah felt especially close to God. He began at once to give a message of warning to the people of Judah.

Explain that Isaiah's ministry lasted forty years and he focused on his own southern nation of Judah. It had also become wealthy, although not as much so as the northern kingdom of Israel.

Share highlights of Isaiah's prophetic message, drawing on your readings from his writings. Conclude by sharing the fact that Christians especially treasure Isaiah's prophecy of a Messiah who would come to bring God's reign.

Point out that Isaiah wrote "oracles" (predictions) in the form of poetry. Invite the students to locate the beginnings of oracles in *Isaiah 13, 15, 17, 19, 21, 22,* and *23*. In some Bibles that have printed subheads, other oracles may be identified.

EXPLORING
(Time: 15–20 minutes)

Option 1. Finding the Right Pieces

Divide the students into two groups. Give each group a piece of posterboard and markers. Ask the first group to draw a picture or create a collage of the things that Isaiah says God will take away (*Isaiah 3:18-24*). The second group will create a similar picture based on Isaiah's prophecies about the Messiah (*Isaiah 9:2-3, 6-7*). Encourage both groups to use lots of color and fill in most of the white space.

Put one poster on top of another and cut them in pieces to resemble a jigsaw puzzle. When you are finished, both posters should have similar-shaped pieces. Put all the pieces in a bag and mix them thoroughly. Dump them out on a large table or floor.

Invite the students to put the pieces back together again. When the puzzles are complete, talk about the difficulty of sorting out the pieces. Ask: What was the most difficult part of putting the puzzles back together? Do we sometimes get God's message mixed up with the messages we get from television or our music? How can we keep the right pieces of our lives together?

Option 2. Illustrating Scripture

Supply sheets of posterboard and a variety of media—such as yarn, pipe cleaners, thin sponges, various weights and colors of paper or tissue, and crayons and markers. Encourage class members to develop their own creative ways to illustrate one or more passages from *Isaiah*. Possible texts: *Isaiah 2:1-4* (mountain, swords into plowshares); *Isaiah 9:2b-3a* (darkness and light); *Isaiah 11:6-7* (wolf and lamb).

Option 3. Crossword Puzzle

Turn in the student newspaper, *Community Times*, Unit I, Issue 3, to the crossword puzzle, "Recalling Isaiah." The class members may work individually, in teams, or as a total group.

MUSIC
(Time: 10 minutes)

Introduce the hymn, "God is working his purpose out" *(The Hymnal 1982*, 534*)*. Read the stanzas and then listen to the hymn on the *Children Sing!* tape. Point out that the themes of this hymn are from the prophet Isaiah. The closing line of each stanza ("when the earth shall be filled with the glory of God as the waters cover the sea") is from *Isaiah 11:9*.

CONNECTING/SPEAKING OUT
(Time: 15–20 minutes)

Option 1. Group Discussion

Recall that Amos' prophecy ended on a note of punishment, causing many to question whether he had hope for God's reign in the future. His writing left us wondering whether he felt that God's will would always be thwarted by the sins of humankind.

Discuss the importance of having hope for the future. What is hope? Where do you look for it? When you are sad, who or where do you turn for help? Are there times you feel more hopeful than others? Where can we turn for a true sense of hope?

Point out that Isaiah introduced both compassion and hope in his writings. He foresaw a day in which a descendant of David would be Messiah—one sent to humankind to bring in the reign of God.

Option 2. Current Events

Isaiah gave stern warnings from God to King Ahaz *(Isaiah 7)*. He was fortunate to be able to speak these unpleasant truths without fear of being killed or put in prison. That was not the case for all the prophets.

Ask the students to name places in the world today where people can exercise freedom of speech without fearing punishment. Where is such freedom curtailed or lacking? How do the class members feel about their own freedom to speak the truth? Do they exercise that freedom?

REFLECTING
(Time: 10 minutes)

Suggest that the students imagine a person or group of people who are suffering or in trouble. Perhaps the problem is lack of good health care, homelessness, or hunger. What words of hope might Isaiah offer? What would he say to people in a position to offer money and help?

Next ask students to think about things they could say or do to help people who are suffering. Mention activities in the church designed to help others, such as coat drives, food baskets at holidays, or building projects. Ask: How could you be a part of helping those in need?

Encourage class members to write or draw their reflections. Would Isaiah's message be different for people today? Ask the group to end the reflection with a prayer in their own words. For privacy and safekeeping, store the sheets in envelopes as described in Session 1.

LEARNING SKILLS
(Time: 10-15 minutes)

Option 1. Class Memory Challenge

Continue to work on memorizing "The First Song of Isaiah," Canticle 9 (BCP, p. 86), as suggested in Session 1.

Invite the group to repeat, in unison, *Isaiah 1-2*, and introduce verse 3. Key words are "water" and "springs." Again, form pairs to assist each other in recalling the verse.

Option 2. Learning Scripture

If the class members have memorized verses given in the previous sessions, add torches and flames as described in Session 1. Remind the students that any verse cited during this Unit may be memorized at any time. The complete list of passages for the Unit appears in the student newspaper, *Community Times*, under "Learning Scripture."

Invite the students to memorize *Isaiah 6:3b, 9:2b*, and *11:6* before the next class session.

ONGOING PROJECT
(Time: 5–10 minutes)

Provide a sheet of posterboard and collage materials to encourage this ongoing project to continue, as described in Session 1. Design a central image for the prophet Isaiah and decide on other scenes and words to add to the background. Display the completed poster next to the picture of Amos.

SYMBOL CARD and TREASUREBOOK

Card 3 contains a saw for Isaiah, a verse of Scripture, and an explanation on the back.

Encourage the class members to read the outline of the structure of First Isaiah in Part I, Section 3 in the *Chalice Year Treasurebook*. How did God call this person to be a prophet? What was First Isaiah's message?

GOING FORTH

Gather the group for the dismissal. The teacher or a student will say:
> I ask your prayers for all who seek God, or a deeper knowledge of him.
> Pray that they may find and be found by him.
> *Silence*

[Learners may add their petitions.]

> Praise God for those in every generation in whom Christ has been honored especially those whom we remember today.
> Pray that we may have grace to glorify Christ in our own day.
>> From The Prayers of the People
>> *The Book of Common Prayer*, p. 386

Teacher: Let us go forth in the name of Christ.
Students: Thanks be to God.

TEACHER'S ASSESSMENT

What are the students likely to recall best from this session on First Isaiah? In what ways do the class members distinguish the prophets' messages from one another? Are students able to find one or more familiar passages in First Isaiah?

LOOKING AHEAD

The next session is on the prophet Micah, a follower of First Isaiah. He employs the literary device of a "lawsuit" in which God's people are on trial. Reflect on the contemporary world as you read the *Book of Micah*. Are his words relevant to our own time? Why, or why not?

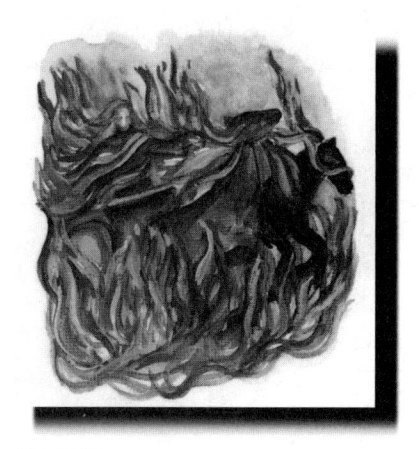

PROPHECY
SESSION 4
MICAH SPOKE FOR GOD

FOCUS

The prophet Micah spoke out against a wealthy ruling class that ignored the needs of the poor. We remember him for his summary of what God requires of us and because he told of the coming destruction of Jerusalem. The students should be able to state the main ideas in Micah's prophecy.

GETTING READY

Micah is believed to have been a follower of First Isaiah. He was a farmer from Moresheth, a small town twenty-five miles southwest of Jerusalem, and his prophecy occurred around 730 BCE. His prophecies denounced both Israel and Judah for their sins.

He identified with peasant people and cried out against those who took advantage of them. Nowhere in the Bible is there a stronger word of judgment than in *Micah 2:1-2:* "Alas for those who devise wickedness and evil deeds on their beds! When the morning dawns, they perform it, because it is in their power. They covet fields, and seize them; houses, and take them away; they oppress householder and house, people and their inheritance."

Isaiah and others had said that Jerusalem would be spared from destruction in the future, in spite of the people's disobedience. But Micah saw a different outcome. He said that God loves righteousness even more than the beloved temple. He predicted that Jerusalem, too, would fall. His words came true.

In *Micah 6:1-8*, Micah used the literary device of a "lawsuit," in which God is prosecutor and the people are the defendants. The passage ends with the prophet's famous summary of God's requirement: to act justly, to love kindness (mercy), and to walk humbly with God.

In *Micah 5:2*, the prophet speaks of a ruler who will one day come from Bethlehem. Christians have understood this to be a reference to Jesus Christ, the Messiah.

Micah's trust in God is his great strength. His dedication and fearless truth-telling is appealing to young people.

Eternal God, in whose perfect kingdom no sword is drawn but the sword of righteousness, no strength known but the strength of love: So mightily spread abroad your Spirit, that all peoples may be gathered under the banner of the Prince of Peace, as children of one Father; to whom be dominion and glory, now and for ever. *Amen.*

For Peace
The Book of Common Prayer, p. 815

TEACHING TIP

Intermediate-age students are aware of increasing number of lawsuits in our society. Conflicts that were once kept private are now openly discussed in a courtroom. Almost any day of the week, students can watch people argue about domestic squabbles on television courtroom shows. Emphasize the difference between issues in television courtrooms and those discussed in Micah's "lawsuit."

GATHERING

Add the picture of Micah (from the Teacher's Packet) to the Prophets' TimeLine. Place him near 730 BCE. As the students arrive, call their attention to the new addition and invite them to think about who the prophet might be.

When everyone is present, say:

Let us pray. (Use the prayer "For Peace," above, or a prayer of your own choosing.)

The chosen student lector reads from the class Bible (NRSV):

A Reading from the Book of Micah, chapter 6, verses 6 through 8.

> With what shall I come before the Lord,
>   and bow myself before God on high?
> Shall I come before him with burnt offerings,
>   with calves a year old?
> Will the Lord be pleased with thousands of rams,
>   with ten thousands of rivers of oil?
> Shall I give my firstborn for my transgression,
>   the fruit of my body for the sin of my soul?
> He has told you, O mortal, what is good;
>   and what does the Lord require of you
> but to do justice, and to love kindness,
>   and to walk humbly with your God?

Reader: The Word of the Lord.
Response: Thanks be to God.

INTRODUCING THE STORY
(Time: 10–20 minutes)

Begin by sharing the background of Micah, a small-town farmer who followed First Isaiah in condemning the exploitation of the poor by those who had wealth and power.

In preparation, read the article about Micah on page 1 of the student newspaper, *Community Times* (Unit I, Issue 4). During the Gathering activity, did anyone guess that Micah might have been a farmer? Based on their knowledge of other prophets they have studied in this Unit, did anyone figure out his basic message? As an example of this prophet's strong words of judgment, read aloud *Micah 2:1-2* (cited in Getting Ready, above).

Next describe the dramatic contrasts in *Micah 6:1-8*. In this passage, the prophet sets the stage by describing the Lord's "controversy" with the people of Israel. The controversy is presented as a lawsuit. In verses 1-2, the prophet introduces the courtroom scene. God is both prosecutor and judge. In verses 3-5, God presents the charge against the disobedient people. This is followed by Israel's defense (verses 6-7). The final verse is the prophet's report of the verdict.

Using either the Bible itself or the script provided in *Community Times*, p. 2, stage a reenactment of the lawsuit. One team of students can rehearse and present the charge, followed by a defense from a second team. One or more students can play the role of Micah to set the stage and give the ringing conclusion. Encourage the actors to portray the contrasting roles with feeling and emotion. Note that the defendants (Israel) ask a series of difficult questions: Does God want thousands of animals? Does God want rivers of oil? Does God want them to give up their children?

Point out that we also remember Micah for his prediction that the Messiah would be born in Bethlehem.

Ask the students to turn in their Bibles to *Micah 5:1-2*, to locate Micah's prediction of a Messiah who would come from Bethlehem. What kind of ruler did Micah and the Hebrews expect?

EXPLORING
(Time: 15–20 minutes)

Option 1. Despair and Hope

Divide the students into two groups. Assign the first group the task of making a list of things that cause disappointment and sadness in their lives, in the community, and in the world. For example: poor grades in school, betrayal by friends, homelessness, crime, wars, and natural disasters. Ask the second group to write "Do Justice," "Love Kindness," and "Walk Humbly With God" several times on separate pieces of 8 x 10 sheets of paper.

Ask a representative from the first group to write one of the things from the list they made. The other group must decide which of the three requirements will conquer the disappointment that is written. For example, if Group 1 writes "hunger," the other group could counter with "Do Justice." Continue with other words from the list made by Group 1 or until all the items are used. Talk about how God helps us counter sadness with hope.

Option 2. Micah Map

Make copies of the small outline map of the kingdoms of Israel and Judah, found on Poster No. 3 in the Teacher's Packet. Suggest that the class members work individually to add places and scenes from Micah's time (such as Moresheth and Jerusalem). Bring in several biblical maps that show the kingdoms of Israel and Judah. Students may want to draw miniature scenes to add to the map. For example, they could draw a small boat next to the Salt Sea or a group of nomads with camels in the desert areas east of the sea.

Option 3. Matching Exercise

Turn in the student newspaper, *Community Times*, Unit I, Issue 4, to "Match Micah's Words." Students may work alone, in pairs, or as a total group.

MUSIC
(Time: 10 minutes)

Sing "What does the Lord require" *(The Hymnal 1982,* 605*)* or listen to it on the *Children Sing!* tape. Call attention to the final line of each stanza that originated with the prophet Micah.

CONNECTING/SPEAKING OUT
(Time: 15–20 minutes)

Option 1. Group Discussion

Divide the class members into groups or teams to look up and discuss the following passages from *Micah*:
- *Micah 1:2-6.* What does the prophet say will happen to the nations of Israel and Judah? Why?
- *Micah 3:9-12.* What have the priests and prophets done? What does Micah predict about the future of Jerusalem?
- *Micah 4:1-5; 5:2.* What does Micah promise for the future? What will be different?

Ask the groups to report on what they discovered. Point out that Micah's judgments were severe, but he also offered a strong sense of hope for the people of God. Christians have understood *Micah 4-5* as prophecies of the coming of Jesus Christ.

Option 2. Current Events

Point out that Micah was a fierce defender of poor and defenseless people. Ask: Who are the individuals and groups who defend and assist the poor today? Find out how much the students know about individuals and agencies that help the poor.

Help class members identify different people who help the poor or those who need assistance. For example, public defenders help in the court system; churches, private agencies, and the government operate shelters for the homeless; individuals and religious groups feed the hungry at soup kitchens; health professionals donate their time at low-cost health clinics; and school groups and others fill food pantries.

Ask: Have you ever done something that helped the poor? What did you do? How did it make you feel?

REFLECTING
(Time: 10 minutes)

Ask the students to think about the Lord's three requirements of us in *Micah 6:8*. (If you did Option 1 in Exploring, refer to the list Group 2 made.) Invite the class to think about one thing they could do individually to meet each requirement. Ask: How can you be more fair to others? Who needs your kindness? What does it mean to walk humbly before God? What could you do to walk with God in this way?

Encourage students to write or draw their personal responses to the questions, then compose prayers of their own. For privacy's sake, they may place their work in individual envelopes labeled "My Reflections." (See Reflecting, Session 1.)

LEARNING SKILLS
(Time: 10–15 minutes)

Option 1. Class Memory Challenge

Continue memorizing "The First Song of Isaiah," Canticle 9 (BCP, p. 86), as introduced in Session 1. Use Poster No. 1 provided in the Teacher's Packet.

Begin by reciting, in unison, *Isaiah 12:1-3*. Then introduce verse 4. Suggest that students take turns being a narrator who says, "On that day you shall say," with the whole group responding, "Give thanks to the Lord and call upon his Name."

Option 2. Learning Scripture

Offer an opportunity for any students who have memorized verses suggested in previous sessions to add torches and flames as suggested in Session 1.

Remind the class members that any verse cited during this Unit may be memorized at any time. The complete list of passages for the Unit appears in the student newspaper, *Community Times*, under "Learning Scripture."

Invite the students to choose either of the following to be learned before the next class session: *Micah 4:5b* or *6:8b*.

ONGOING PROJECT
(Time: 5–10 minutes)

Add Micah to the prophets' parade, next to Isaiah. Prepare a central image of the prophet, to be placed in the center of a sheet of posterboard. Supply collage materials for creating scenes depicting Micah's message. (See Session 1 for a fuller description of this continuing project.)

SYMBOL CARD and TREASUREBOOK

Card 4 contains a trumpet (symbolizing the call for judgment), a verse of Scripture, and an explanation on the back.

Ask the students to read in *Chalice Year Treasurebook*, Part I, Section 4, about Micah's mission. What did he say God requires of us?

GOING FORTH

Gather the group for the dismissal. The teacher or a student will say:
> I ask your prayers for all who seek God, or a deeper knowledge of him.
> Pray that they may find and be found by him.
> *Silence*
>
> [Learners may add their petitions.]
>
> Praise God for those in every generation in whom Christ has been honored especially those whom we remember today.
> Pray that we may have grace to glorify Christ in our own day.
> From The Prayers of the People
> *The Book of Common Prayer*, p. 386

Teacher: Let us go forth in the name of Christ.
Students: Thanks be to God.

TEACHER'S ASSESSMENT

From your observations, do the students appear to be aware of the common themes in the prophets' writings? Are they able to put into their own words the contrasts between faithfulness and disobedience, judgment and hope, doom and restoration? Do these contrasts relate to the class members' own lives?

LOOKING AHEAD

The next session is on the prophet Jeremiah, sometimes called "the weeping prophet." What are some of the events and issues of our own time that cause you to weep? Where do you see signs of hope in the midst of sorrow?

PROPHECY
SESSION 5
JEREMIAH: PROPHET OF FAITH

FOCUS

The prophet Jeremiah spoke out for God through forty disastrous years, during which neighboring kingdoms struggled against one another and against Judah. The students should be able to tell the story of Jeremiah's life.

GETTING READY

Jeremiah was born between 645 and 640 BCE, in Anathoth, which was about an hour's walk northeast of Jerusalem. He received his call to be a prophet in 627 or 626. For forty years he spoke out for God as the people of Judah experienced invasion, threats, and loss of their homes and freedom. He shared the heartbreak of the people's captivity and wept when they suffered. But his prophecies were so unpopular that he was in constant danger.

Some of our present *Book of Jeremiah* was written by the prophet himself, part of it was dictated to a secretary named Baruch, and some of it was probably added by Baruch.

Jeremiah began his ministry as Judah faced possible invasion by Scythians, fierce marauders from the north who were ruthless to their enemies. More dangers followed. The Assyrians, a great world power, fell to the Babylonians (or Chaldeans) in 612. Then Babylon and Egypt wrestled for domination of the world. Judah was on the border between the two warring nations. Although Judah was dominated by Babylon, the kings of Judah continued to expect that Egypt would keep its promises to their nation.

Twice the Babylonians came to Jerusalem with armies to punish Judah for being disloyal. In the end, under King Nebuchadnezzar, Jerusalem was reduced to ruins.

Through all these years, Jeremiah was a faithful spokesman for God. He was not popular because he had denounced the errors and sins of the kings and people—a very unpleasant task. He was condemned as a traitor and held as a prisoner. Yet he continued to plead God's cause, and he foresaw a day when God would send a Messiah to establish a "new covenant" *(Jeremiah 31:31)*. His life was colorful, courageous, and his predictions dramatic.

Many of the events that occurred under various kings of Judah during the period when Jeremiah lived can be found in *II Kings 21-24*.

> O God our Father, whose Son forgave his enemies while he was suffering shame and death: Strengthen those who suffer for the sake of conscience; when they are accused, save them from speaking in hate; when they are rejected, save them from bitterness; when they are imprisoned, save them from despair; and to us your servants, give grace to respect their witness and to discern the truth, that our society may be cleansed and strengthened. This we ask for the sake of Jesus Christ, our merciful and righteous Judge. *Amen.*

For those who suffer for the sake of Conscience
The Book of Common Prayer, p. 823

TEACHING TIP

Intermediate-age students deal daily with authority figures (parents, teachers, coaches, and others). They may experience conflicts as they make choices about whose rules to follow. On occasion, they may be required to take a stand that is not popular. Look for opportunities to draw parallels. Students today, just like the Hebrews, are faced with the need to be truthful in word and deed.

GATHERING

Add to the Prophets' TimeLine the picture of Jeremiah from the Teacher's Packet. Dates for his prophecies are approximately 627-585 BCE. As the students arrive, invite them to wonder: What is the man wearing around his neck? Did someone make him wear it? If not, can you think of a reason he would put it on?

When everyone is present, say:

Let us pray. (Use the prayer "For those who suffer for the sake of Conscience," above, or a prayer of your own choosing.)

The chosen student lector reads from the class Bible (NRSV):

A Reading from the Book of Jeremiah, chapter 1, verses 4 through 10.

(Jeremiah said,) Now the word of the Lord came to me saying,
"Before I formed you in the womb I knew you,
 and before you were born I consecrated you;
 I appointed you a prophet to the nations."
Then I said, "Ah, Lord God! Truly I do not know how to speak,
for I am only a boy." But the Lord said to me,
 "Do not say, 'I am only a boy';
 for you shall go to all to whom I send you,
 and you shall speak whatever I command you,
 Do not be afraid of them,
 for I am with you to deliver you,
  says the Lord."
Then the Lord put out his hand and touched my mouth;
 and the Lord said to me,
 "Now I have put my words in your mouth.
 See, today I appoint you over nations
  and over kingdoms,
 to pluck up and to pull down,
 to destroy and to overthrow,
 to build and to plant."

Reader: The Word of the Lord.
Response: Thanks be to God.

INTRODUCING THE STORY
(Time: 10–20 minutes)

Begin by displaying the "Jeremiah Symbols" sheet from the Teacher's Packet, which includes a kettle boiling over, a blooming almond branch, a pot, a jug, figs, and a yoke.

Then summarize the story of Jeremiah's life, drawing on the material under Getting Ready (above) and the student newspaper, *Community Times* (Unit I, Issue 5). Include the following details and point to the appropriate symbols:

Jeremiah was quite young when he became a prophet, perhaps between thirteen and eighteen years of age. His father was a priest and also a landowner. Through more than forty years of difficult times, Jeremiah was a colorful figure who spoke and wrote to warn the people of God about impending invasion by other nations.

• Jeremiah's call from God came in two visions—a kettle boiling over, which stood for a threat from cruel invaders, and an almond branch, which was a sign that God would be with the young prophet to tear down what was evil and build up what was right *(Jeremiah 1:4-19)*.

• He went to a potter's house and saw a clay pot that was spoiled on the wheel. The potter then reworked it and made a good pot. Jeremiah saw this as a symbol that God could shape the future of Israel in the same way. He called on the people to turn from their evil ways to avoid the disaster of destruction *(Jeremiah 18:1-11)*.

• Jeremiah bought a clay jug and later broke it as a crowd looked on. He declared that, because of their disobedience, God would break their nation in the same way, and it would be beyond repair *(Jeremiah 19)*.

• The Lord showed Jeremiah two baskets of figs outside the temple. One basket contained ripe and good fruit; the other basket was filled with very bad, inedible figs. The prophet saw the good figs as the exiles who had been carried away from Judah and the bad figs as the king of Judah and his officials, who would suffer disgrace *(Jeremiah 24:1-10)*.

• Jeremiah put on a yoke and wore it in the streets. He declared that all nations would be placed under the yoke of the king of Babylon, including the people of Judah *(Jeremiah 27-28)*.

Note that Jeremiah has been called a weeping prophet. Ask the students to turn in their Bibles to *Jeremiah 13:15-17*. Why would Jeremiah weep bitterly?

EXPLORING
(Time: 15–20 minutes)

Option 1. Laws in Poetry

Even though the *Book of Jeremiah* is filled with dire warnings and consequences, it also contains wonderful images and poetry. As illustrated in his story, Jeremiah found many ways to get his message across.

If you have not already done so, spend a few minutes making a list of rules for the classroom to help students to respect the rights of others. For example, not talking while someone else is speaking, giving everyone a chance to share ideas, avoid hitting or shoving others.

Announce that the class has been called by God to be prophets. Divide the class rules among pairs or small groups of students. Ask the groups to rewrite the rules using colorful images and poetry. For example: When another speaks, you are to be silent like lambs.

After a brief time, share the rules by acting them out or reading them aloud to the entire group. Ask a volunteer to record the new rules as Baruch wrote the words of Jeremiah.

Option 2. Potters and Clay

Distribute copies of *Jeremiah 18:1-11* (the potter and the clay) or ask students to look up this prophecy in their Bibles. Supply a variety of art materials: molding clay, drawing paper, pencils, markers, crayons, posterboard, black or brown construction paper, glue, and scissors. Encourage the students to illustrate the passage. Suggestions: mold clay pots, draw and color the scene, or cut out silhouettes to be glued to a posterboard background.

Option 3. Word Puzzle

Turn in the student newspaper, *Community Times*, Unit I, Issue 5, to the word puzzle, "Jeremiah's Yoke." Students may work alone, in pairs, or as a total group.

MUSIC
(Time: 10 minutes)

Listen on the *Children Sing!* tape to "O praise ye the Lord! Praise him in the height" *(The Hymnal 1982, 432)* or read the stanzas aloud in unison. Point out that the hymn is based on *Psalms 148* and *150*. Ask: In what ways do the words remind us of the Hebrew prophets? Sing the first two stanzas.

CONNECTING/SPEAKING OUT
(Time: 15–20 minutes)

Option 1. Group Discussion

One of the suggested Old Testament passages to be read at the Ordination of a Deacon is *Jeremiah 1:4-9*. (See *The Book of Common Prayer*, p. 540.)

Ask the students to work in teams to read this passage (the call of Jeremiah). What is God asking Jeremiah to do? What kind of person is he expected to be?

Suggest that the group look at "The Examination" of a person who is to be ordained a deacon (BCP, p. 543). From this section, make a list of expectations of church deacons. For example, "serve all people, particularly the poor, the weak, the sick, and the lonely." Go back over the list and put a star by each item that is similar to the call of Jeremiah and the other prophets. How many similarities did you find?

Option 2. Current Events

Remind the students that Jeremiah was probably only a teenager when God called him to be a prophet. Jeremiah responded, "Ah, Lord God. Truly I do not know how to speak, for I am only a boy" *(Jeremiah 1:6)*. Are we too young to serve God? Why, or why not?

Ask the class how they would respond if God called them to do something difficult. Ask: What are your strengths? How could God use them? What are your weaknesses? How could God help you overcome them?

What ways can young people serve God and others? The media has reported stories about young people who earned money to buy blankets for the homeless or who meet weekly to make sandwiches for a soup kitchen. How are these acts a service to God? Invite the class to list other ways young people can minister to others.

REFLECTING
(Time: 10 minutes)

Invite the class members to imagine that they are Jeremiah during the days of King Hezekiah. People were angry at him and he was thrown into a cistern where he was left for many days. [Note: Be sure that class members know what a cistern is. A description and drawing is included on page 2 of the student newspaper, *Community Times*.] Ask: How would you feel about this turn of events? What would you say? What would you want to do to your captors? Would you change your message? Why, or why not?

Suggest that the students write or draw their reflections, adding prayers of their own composition. The sheets may then be placed in private envelopes, as described in Session 1.

LEARNING SKILLS
(Time: 10–15 minutes)

Option 1. Class Memory Challenge

Continue working on the task of memorizing "The First Song of Isaiah," Canticle 9 (BCP, p. 86), as suggested in Session 1.

Review *Isaiah 12:1-4* without the Teacher's Packet poster on display. Divide the class members into two groups and suggest they alternate in saying the verses (Group 1, verses 1 and 3, and Group 2, verses 2 and 4). Check the accuracy of the words, then reverse the process.

Introduce verse 5. Key words are "deeds" and "remember." Invite the students to suggest ways to involve everyone in committing the verse to memory.

Option 2. Learning Scripture

If class members have memorized verses suggested in previous sessions, add torches and flames as described in Session 1.

Invite the students to commit to memory one or both of the following: *Jeremiah 8:11* or *18:6b*. See "Learning Scripture" in the student newspaper, *Community Times*.

ONGOING PROJECT
(Time: 5-10 minutes)

Provide materials for continuing the series of collages on the prophets being studied in this Unit. See the description in Session 1. Decide on a way to design an image for Jeremiah (face or full figure) and place it in the middle of a sheet of posterboard. Develop scenes and symbols from Jeremiah's ministry to complete the project. Use the symbols from Poster No. 3 in the Teacher's Packet. Display it alongside Micah in the "parade."

SYMBOL CARD and TREASUREBOOK

Card 5 contains the symbol of clay on a potter's wheel, a verse of Scripture, and an explanation on the back.

Suggest that the students read a description of Jeremiah's four decades as a prophet in *Chalice Year Treasurebook*, Part I, Section 5. How did he dramatize his message? What were some of the trials he endured?

GOING FORTH

Gather the group for the dismissal. The teacher or a student will say:

> I ask your prayers for all who seek God, or a deeper knowledge of him.
> Pray that they may find and be found by him.
> *Silence*
>
> [Learners may add their petitions.]
>
> Praise God for those in every generation in whom Christ has been honored especially those whom we remember today.
> Pray that we may have grace to glorify Christ in our own day.
>
> From The Prayers of the People
> *The Book of Common Prayer*, p. 386

Teacher: Let us go forth in the name of Christ.
Students: Thanks be to God.

TEACHER'S ASSESSMENT

Consider the students' exploration of the prophet Jeremiah and his times. Were they able to gain a sense of what it meant to serve God as a prophet through forty years of national disaster and personal misery? Was it clear to the class members that Jeremiah was very close to God throughout his life?

LOOKING AHEAD

The next session is about the prophet Ezekiel, a seer of visions. What comes to mind when you hear the word "vision"? What role does the concept of "vision" play in your own life?

PROPHECY
SESSION 6
EZEKIEL: SEER OF VISIONS

FOCUS

Ezekiel was the most dramatic of the prophets. As a prophet in exile, he was very unpopular at first, but in their suffering the people were grateful for his presence. The students should be able to summarize the ministry of Ezekiel, citing one or more of his teachings.

GETTING READY

During the time of Jeremiah, a boy named Ezekiel grew up in Jerusalem where his father was a priest of the temple. Suddenly, great changes came into his life. In 587 BCE, the Chaldeans (Babylonians) seized the city and deported the best educated and wealthiest citizens. Ezekiel was among them, and he was never again able to return to his home.

In exile in Babylon, he was married and lived comfortably by the river Chebar. He seems to have had leisure time in this country that had become the commercial center of the world.

In 592, Ezekiel experienced a vision that is described in *Ezekiel 1:4-3:15*. This call of the prophet is like no other in the Bible. It included a strange creature with both human and animal parts, wheels within wheels, eyes, brilliant light, and great noise. A man sat on a throne that looked like sapphire. Ezekiel fell to the ground and heard the voice of God calling him to speak to his fellow exiles. He was given a scroll and asked to eat it. He did so and found it to be sweet like honey.

Again and again, Ezekiel experienced the Spirit and was struck dumb, lifted up, carried back and forth, and inspired to do many dramatic "signs."

The exiles believed that they would not be away from their homes very long—that there would be someone to deliver them from captivity. But Ezekiel knew they were wrong. He prophesied that the city of Jerusalem would be destroyed. His words came true in 587.

Like Micah and Jeremiah, Ezekiel told the people that their exile was due to their own sins and those of their forebears. He painted a very gloomy picture of their guilt and declared that everyone was personally responsible for the fate of the Hebrews.

In the end, Ezekiel was appreciated for his pastoral care. He did not leave his people without hope. He foretold a time when God would give Judah a new heart and a new spirit. He also had a famous vision of the "valley of dry bones" (*Ezekiel 37:1-14*).

Heavenly Father, whose blessed Son came not to be served but to serve: Bless all who, following in his steps, give themselves to the service of others; that with wisdom, patience, and courage, they may minister in his Name to the suffering, the friendless, and the needy; for the love of him who laid down his life for us, your Son our Savior Jesus Christ, who lives and reigns with you and the Holy Spirit, one God, for ever and ever. *Amen.*

For Social Service
The Book of Common Prayer, p. 260

TEACHING TIP

Intermediate-age students are intrigued by stories that invite them to use their imagination. They are able to understand fantasy and imagery. Capitalize on these traits to introduce the class to the images of Ezekiel's visions and prophesies.

GATHERING

Continue the Prophets' TimeLine. Poster No. 2 in the Teacher's Packet includes a picture of Ezekiel looking at dry bones in a valley—to be placed under the years 587-570 BCE. As the students arrive, invite them to reflect on what is happening in the scene. Where did the bones come from? What is the man doing?

When everyone is present, say:

Let us pray. (Use the Collect "For Social Service," above, or a prayer of your own choosing.)

The chosen student lector reads from the class Bible (NRSV):

A Reading from the Book of Ezekiel, chapter 37, excerpts from verses 1 through 11:

(Ezekiel said,) The hand of the Lord came upon me, and he brought me out by the spirit of the Lord and set me down in the middle of a valley; it was full of bones. He led me all around them; there were very many lying in the valley, and they were very dry. He said to me, "Mortal, can these bones live?" I answered, "O Lord God, you know." Then he said to me, "Prophesy to these bones, . . ."

So I prophesied as I had been commanded; and as I prophesied, suddenly there was a noise, a rattling, and the bones came together, bone to its bone. I looked, and there were sinews in them, and flesh had come upon them, and skin had covered them; but there was no breath in them. Then he said to me, "Prophesy to the breath, prophesy, mortal, and say to the breath: Thus says the Lord God: Come from the four winds, O breath, and breathe upon these slain, that they may live." I prophesied as he commanded me, and the breath came into them, and they lived, and stood on their feet, a vast multitude.

Then he said to me, "Mortal, these bones are the whole house of Israel. . . ."

Reader: The Word of the Lord.
Response: Thanks be to God.

INTRODUCING THE STORY
(Time: 10–20 minutes)

From the Teacher's Packet, display the classic art on Poster No. 4 showing a vision of Ezekiel. In your own words, tell the story of Ezekiel's call in *Ezekiel 1:4-3:15*.

Ask the students to work in teams as they read the first two chapters of *Ezekiel*. Suggest that each team make a list of things Ezekiel saw in his vision. What was the reason for this experience in his life?

Continue the story of Ezekiel by sharing one or more signs the prophet performed to illustrate disaster and punishment for both Israel and Judah. Refer to the stories in the student newspaper, *Community Times* (Unit 1, Issue 6) for background.

Among the signs Ezekiel performed that you may choose to include in your story are:

• He built a miniature brick city. *(Ezekiel 4:1-3)*
• He lay down on his left side 350 days (for Israel), then 40 days on his right side (for Judah); he was bound with cords and ate special rations. *(Ezekiel 4:4-16)*
• He cut off his hair with a sharp sword and divided it into three parts. *(Ekeziel 5)*
• He dug a hole in the side of his house and carried out the furniture on his back. *(Ezekiel 12:3-16)*
• He ate his bread with quaking and drank his water with trembling. *(Ezekiel 12:17-20)*
• He performed a sword dance to the accompaniment of a sharp, ringing song of death. *(Ezekiel 21:8-17)*

Conclude by pointing out that Ezekiel did not leave the people comfortless. He also spoke of a day when God would act to give them a new heart and a new spirit. The vision of the valley of dry bones in chapter 37 is a message of hope.

EXPLORING
(Time: 15–20 minutes)

Option 1. Charades of Ezekiel's Words

Divide the class members into teams and give each team a slip of paper containing a significant word found in the visions and prophecies of Ezekiel. Examples: scroll, wheels, chariot, sword, eagle, vine, bones, breath.

Ask each team in turn to act out its word(s), as in a charade. The other teams are to guess until they have named each word correctly. If additional words are needed, the students can choose them from the *Book of Ezekiel*.

Option 2. Creations from Ezekiel

Supply a variety of art materials (pipe cleaners, tissue, fabric, foils and papers, yarn, glue, markers, and the like). Suggest that the students create their own interpretations of scenes from the *Book of Ezekiel*—his call, signs, or visions.

Students, for example, may want to make a sculpture or drawing of the creatures in *Ezekiel 1*. Class members may want to work in teams—one group could work on the four faces on the head, while another could make the four wings. A third group could construct the body with straight legs and feet that look like a calf's foot.

For additional ideas, refer to the passages from Introducing the Story. You may wish to list the Scripture passages from this section on a chalkboard or piece of newsprint.

Display the creations in the classroom for the rest of the Unit.

Option 3. Crossword Puzzle

Turn in the student newspaper, *Community Times*, Unit I, Issue 6, to the circular crossword puzzle, "Ezekiel's Wheel." Students may work independently, in pairs, or as a group.

MUSIC
(Time: 10 minutes)

Lead the students in singing the traditional song, "Dem bones, dem bones, dem dry bones." The words are provided in the student newspaper, *Community Times*. Or sing instead "Ezekiel Saw De Wheel" *(Lift Every Voice and Sing II, 224)*. The students may add motions to go with the phrases.

CONNECTING/SPEAKING OUT
(Time: 15–20 minutes)

Option 1. Group Discussion

Ask the students to summarize, in their own words, what they regard as memorable about the prophet Ezekiel. Discuss:

What makes Ezekiel so unusual? How would you describe him?

Ezekiel was one of many people held captive in Babylonia. How do you think you would have felt if you had been one of his fellow captives listening to his stern prophecies?

Think about a time you were being punished for something you did that was wrong. How did you feel about the punishment? What if someone—a sibling or another person in your family—told you that you deserved even more punishment? How would you feel about that person? Do you think the people liked Ezekiel?

Focus on the vision of the valley of the dry bones *(Ezekiel 37:1-14)*. Ask: Why do you think bones are used to represent Israel? Describe the stages of the bones' return to life (sinew, flesh, skin, and finally breath). What does this gradual process suggest?

Option 2. Current Events

We remember Ezekiel for two aspects of his ministry and message: 1.) He was a prophet of doom, reminding the people of their own sins and those of their ancestors in Israel. 2.) He offered a message of hope and new life for the people in their captivity. Discuss:

Who are some of the people in our own time who speak out like prophets to warn of sins and failures? For example, Archbishop Desmond Tutu in South Africa feared for his life and his family when he spoke out against the injustices of apartheid. Martin Luther King, Jr., who called for peaceful demonstrations to end the evils of segregation, was killed by a sniper. (You may wish to bring in several books or articles about people who are prophets today.)

Who are the people in our world and in our lives who offer messages of comfort and hope? Mother Teresa, for example, called on people throughout the world to care for the poorest of the poor. How do we respond to this kind of message? Which would you rather be, a prophet or a caregiver?

REFLECTING
(Time: 10 minutes)

Encourage the students to imagine what it would be like to have an extraordinary vision like the one in which God called Ezekiel. *(Ezekiel 1, 2, and 3:1-15)*. For seven days afterward, Ezekiel was overwhelmed.

Ask: How would you respond to a vision like the one Ezekiel had? Would you ask someone to help you understand what it meant? What could God call you to do? If you were a prophet at your school or with a group of your friends or teammates, what message would God want you to deliver?

Students may write or draw their reflections, adding prayers of their own. The sheets may be added to the private envelopes as described in Session 1.

LEARNING SKILLS
(Time: 10–15 minutes)

Option 1. Class Memory Challenge

Work on the continuing task of memorizing "The First Song of Isaiah," Canticle 9 (BCP, p. 86). Use the poster provided in the Teacher's Packet. Ask each student to say *Isaiah 12:6* aloud, either to a partner or in a group. The key words are "sing . . . praises of the Lord."

When the class members are confident that they have mastered the verse, form two groups to recite verses 1-6 antiphonally, as follows: Group 1, verses 1, 3, and 5; Group 2, verses 2, 4, and 6. Reverse the process and repeat.

Option 2. Learning Scripture

Add torches and flames as suggested in Session 1 for students who have memorized verses suggested in previous sessions.

Invite the students to memorize before the next class session one or both of the following: *Ezekiel 1:15, 16c,* or *37:4.* See "Learning Scripture" in the newspaper, *Community Times.*

ONGOING PROJECT
(Time: 5-10 minutes)

Invite the students to continue working on the poster parade of prophets as described in Session 1. Design a center circle to include an image for Ezekiel and use collage materials to create surrounding scenes. You can use artwork from the Exploring activity or scenes from Introducing the Story. Label the finished product and place it next to Jeremiah. Can this project be shared with the congregation in an accessible location?

SYMBOL CARD and TREASUREBOOK

Card 6 contains a wheel for Ezekiel, a verse of Scripture, and an explanation on the back.

Ask the class members to read in *Chalice Year Treasurebook*, Part I, Section 6, about the prophet Ezekiel. Which of his famous visions do we remember best?

GOING FORTH

Gather the group for the dismissal. The teacher or a student will say:

> I ask your prayers for all who seek God, or a deeper knowledge of him.
> Pray that they may find and be found by him.
> *Silence*
>
> [Learners may add their petitions.]
> Praise God for those in every generation in whom Christ has been honored especially those whom we remember today.
> Pray that we may have grace to glorify Christ in our own day.
>
> From The Prayers of the People
> *The Book of Common Prayer*, p. 386

Teacher: Let us go forth in the name of Christ.
Students: Thanks be to God.

TEACHER'S ASSESSMENT

What were the students' prevailing reactions to the scenes from the life of the prophet Ezekiel? Were they able to appreciate his ministry (prophetic judgment and pastoral concern)? As you reflect on this Unit's study, which prophets have seemed to have the greatest appeal for the class members?

LOOKING AHEAD

The next session is on *Isaiah 40-55* (Second Isaiah), particularly the four suffering servant songs. In what sense do we understand Jesus Christ to be a "suffering servant"?

PROPHECY
SESSION 7
ISAIAH PROCLAIMS A MESSAGE OF LIGHT

FOCUS

The *Book of Isaiah* is believed to be the work of at least two writers. Second Isaiah wrote *Isaiah 40-55* and possibly more. He lived in the time of the exile in Babylon and we remember him for the message of hope in his four Servant Songs. The students should be able to explain why Second Isaiah's words are especially treasured by Christians.

GETTING READY

For twenty years after Ezekiel's last prophecy in 570 BCE, nothing happened to change the situation of God's people in Babylon. Then a new and hopeful development occurred: Cyrus became king of Persia in 550. Within four years he had begun to march into northern Babylon. The Jewish people saw this as a sign of hope. So did some of the Babylonians themselves.

The Persian conquest continued until, in 539 BCE, the city of Babylon fell. Cyrus was now in charge and the exiles began to hope that he would permit them to return to their homeland.

In Session 3 of this Unit, we looked at *Isaiah 1-39*, which dates from 740-700 BCE—a period long before the Babylonian exile. The writings in *Isaiah 40-55* in the *Book of Isaiah* are clearly from the period of Cyrus, two centuries after the earlier chapters. Nearly all biblical scholars agree that this second section is best called "Second Isaiah." What is not clear is how to date *Isaiah 56-66*, which is sometimes attributed to a third writer; other scholars believe it is a collection from a variety of writers.

What makes Second Isaiah very important is the strong note of hope and newness which the writer foresees for the future. He writes about a Suffering Servant who would come to bring salvation to the people.

Intermediate-age learners can learn to appreciate four poems (Servant Songs) that are especially meaningful for Christians. The early Church believed these passages described the crucified and risen Jesus Christ, the long-awaited Messiah, who fulfilled the vision of Second Isaiah.

The four songs are *Isaiah 42:1-9; 49:1-13; 50:4-9;* and *52:13-53:12.*

O God, you declare your almighty power chiefly in showing mercy and pity: Grant us the fullness of your grace, that we, running to obtain your promises, may become partakers of your heavenly treasure; through Jesus Christ our Lord, who lives and reigns with you and the Holy Spirit, one God, for ever and ever. *Amen.*

Proper 21
The Book of Common Prayer, p. 234

TEACHING TIP

The words of hope expressed in Second Isaiah in the Servant Songs were written about 500 years before Jesus was born. Intermediate-age students are beginning to experience periods of waiting in their lives—to be teenagers, to drive a car, to live on their own, for example. They can begin to understand how the waiting period for the Messiah was filled with frustration, eagerness, hope, and even anger. They can find comfort in the words of hope found in Second Isaiah as they await new experiences in their lives.

GATHERING

Add the picture of Second Isaiah from Poster No. 2 in the Teacher's Packet to the ongoing Prophets' TimeLine. The approximate date for this portion of prophecy is 540 BCE. As the students arrive, invite them to consider why the name Isaiah appears twice on the line. Also point out the bird in the timeline picture. What does a bird usually symbolize? Why did the artist include a bird in this scene?

When everyone is present, say:

Let us pray. (Use Proper 21, above, or a prayer of your own choosing.)

The chosen student lector reads from the class Bible (NRSV):

A *Reading from the Book of Isaiah, chapter 42, verses 5 through 9.*

Thus says God, the Lord,
who created the heavens and stretched them out,
who spread out the earth and what comes from it,
who gives breath to the people upon it
    and spirit to those who walk in it:
I am the Lord, I have called you in righteousness,
    I have taken you by the hand and kept you;
I have given you as a covenant to the people,
    a light to the nations,
    to open the eyes that are blind,
to bring out the prisoners from the dungeon,
    from the prison those who sit in darkness.
I am the Lord, that is my name;
    my glory I give to no other,
    nor my praise to idols.
See, the former things have come to pass,
    and new things I now declare;
before they spring forth, I tell you of them.

Reader: The Word of the Lord.
Response: Thanks be to God.

INTRODUCING THE STORY
(Time: 10–20 minutes)

Display Poster No. 5 in the Teacher's Packet entitled "Light" that shows a colorful sunset. Using information from the Getting Ready (above) and the article on page 1 of the *Community Times* (Unit I, Issue 7), tell the story of Second Isaiah.

Begin by reminding the class about the work of the prophet Isaiah whom we studied in Session 3 of this Unit. Explain why it is believed that chapters 40-55 in *Isaiah* were written by a second prophet nearly two centuries later.

Emphasize the dark mood among the Jewish exiles who were forced to live for such a long time in Babylon. Refer to the gloomy situation we learned about in Ezekiel in Session 6.

Call attention to Poster No. 5. Note that light is symbolic of the second part of the *Book of Isaiah*. This writer sees a bright future for God's people, who are destined to reflect the light of God to the whole world. You may want to read aloud *Isaiah 60:1-3* to illustrate this point.

Briefly introduce the Suffering Servant songs. Share the fact that Christians have believed that these poems point to the coming of Jesus Christ as "the light of the world." List the first verses of Isaiah's four servant songs: *Isaiah 42:1*; *42:5*; *49:1*; and *50:4*. Invite the students to find these lines in their Bibles and discover how each song begins.

EXPLORING
(Time: 15–20 minutes)

Option 1. Kings, Queens, and Servants

Divide the class into two groups. One group will be kings and queens; the other, servants. Bring enough props to "dress" the kings and queens, including long bathrobes or pageant costumes (the longer the better), big sticks or pieces of wood for "scepters," and construction paper to make tall (18 inches or more) crowns. Ask those in the servant group to help you dress the royalty.

Before the group arrives, lay out two identical obstacle courses with at least three barriers. For example, put a broomstick over two chairs just tall enough for a student to crawl under; set out a sturdy table to crawl over; and place a chair to be carrier from one point to another.

Divide the groups into two relay teams. Before you begin the race, tell the kings and queens that they can shed one of the symbols of royalty at each obstacle if they choose. The crown represents wealth, the robe is fame, and the scepter is power. If there is time let the groups switch roles and run the relay again.

Afterwards, talk about the race. How did the symbols of royalty make the race more difficult? Why did Jesus choose to come as a servant? Do "things" and activities sometimes get in our way of following Jesus?

Option 2. Dead Sea Scrolls

An article on page 3 of *Community Times* describes scrolls found near the Dead Sea that scholars have been studying for the last fifty years. One of the scrolls found was the *Book of Isaiah* recorded on sheets of leather bound with linen thread, 24 feet long by 10 inches high. The words in the scroll were very similar to the book we read in our Bibles now.

Divide into four groups. Ask each group to design a collage or manuscript about one of the four servant songs in *Isaiah 42:1-9* (justice); *49:1-13* (light); *50:4-9* (humble teacher); and *52:13-53:12* (man of sorrows). Give them a sheet of paper 10 inches high, and about 18 inches wide. When finished, roll paper like a scroll.

Consider using the scroll in telling the story of Second Isaiah to another group.

Option 3. Word Search

Turn in the student newspaper, *Community Times*, Unit I, Issue 7, to "Servant Search." Students may work alone or in teams to find the words associated with *Isaiah 40-55*.

MUSIC
(Time: 10 minutes)

Return to the hymn, "O praise ye the Lord! Praise him in the height" *(The Hymnal 1982*, 432). Read the first stanza or listen to it on the *Children Sing!* tape. Ask: How do these words remind us of the message of *Second Isaiah*?

CONNECTING/SPEAKING OUT
(Time: 15–20 minutes)

Option 1. Group Discussion

Present the fact that the early Christians reflected daily on the ministry of Jesus and the manner of his death. They said, "Aha! This is just what Isaiah was talking about. Jesus was the Servant who came to save the people."

Ask: Why do we call Jesus a "suffering" servant? What makes his coming "good news"? In what ways was the good news that Isaiah proclaimed like the good news we have in Jesus Christ? How does the risen Christ bring light into the world?

Option 2. Current Events

Ask the students to think about persons in our own time who have suffered (or now suffer) for other people. For example, Christians in Europe during World War II at places like Le Chambon in France risked their lives to help Jewish people escape to freedom. Terry Waite was imprisoned in Lebanon for years when he sought the release of other captives.

What causes people to suffer for others? How is it possible for people to have hope while they are actually suffering?

REFLECTING
(Time: 10 minutes)

Ask the students to think about the exiles who lived in Babylon 2,500 years ago when *Second Isaiah* was written. Think about how it would feel to be prevented, year after year, from returning to their home in Judah.

Picture yourself as an exile, taken far from your home to live in a foreign place where people do not share your language or your customs. What would you miss most about your home? How would you feel during holidays such as Thanksgiving and Christmas? What if someone like Isaiah came with good news about your future? What would you do?

The class members may write their reflections and compose their own prayers to be added to the private envelopes (as described in Session 1).

LEARNING SKILLS
(Time: 10–15 minutes)

Option 1. Class Memory Challenge

Note that the group has only one more verse to memorize from "The Song of Isaiah," Canticle 9 (BCP, p. 86). Introduce *Isaiah 12:7*, noting the key words, "Cry aloud," and "ring out." Work briefly in pairs, as in previous sessions.

Try saying the entire Canticle in unison without consulting the Prayer Book or the poster from the Teacher's Packet.

Point out that, in Christian worship, we add to the Canticle the words of the *Gloria Patri* (Latin for "Glory to the Father"), which praises the Holy Trinity.

Option 2. Learning Scripture

Add torches and flames as described in Session 1 for any verses students have learned, from suggestions offered in previous sessions.

Invite the students to learn one or both of the following verses before the next class session: *Isaiah 40:31* or *55:6-7*. See "Learning Scripture" in the student newspaper, *Community Times*.

ONGOING PROJECT
(Time: 5–10 minutes)

Make available a supply of materials for creating a collage on a sheet of posterboard. Second Isaiah is the subject for this piece to be added to the prophets' parade. Decide on a way to portray his image in the center, then add scenes suggesting that the prophet was a messenger of light and hope from God. Label the finished collage and place it next to Ezekiel.

SYMBOL CARD and TREASUREBOOK

Card 7 contains a picture of a Tau cross, a verse of Scripture, and an explanation on the back.

Ask the class members to read in *Chalice Year Treasurebook*, Part I, Section 7, about *Second Isaiah* and the relationship of these writings to the captivity of God's people in Babylon. Why do Bible scholars think more than one person wrote the *Book of Isaiah*?

GOING FORTH

Gather the group for the dismissal. The teacher or a student will say:
> I ask your prayers for all who seek God, or a deeper knowledge of him.
> Pray that they may find and be found by him.
> *Silence*

[Learners may add their petitions.]

> Praise God for those in every generation in whom Christ has been honored especially those whom we remember today.
> Pray that we may have grace to glorify Christ in our own day.
>
> From The Prayers of the People
> *The Book of Common Prayer*, p. 386

Teacher: Let us go forth in the name of Christ.
Students: Thanks be to God.

TEACHER'S ASSESSMENT

As you reflect on the work accomplished in this Unit, what evidence do you have that the students are able to understand the ministries of the Old Testament prophets? Are the class members able to associate words from *Isaiah* with the Christian faith and our worship in the Church?

LOOKING AHEAD

The next session, which is the last on the Hebrew prophets, highlights the work of so-called "minor prophets" from Hosea through Malachi. Look through this section of the Bible, focusing especially on *Hosea, Joel,* and *Jonah*. Are any familiar to you?

PROPHECY
SESSION 8
CENTURIES OF PROPHECY

FOCUS

In addition to the prophets studied in the earlier sessions of this Unit, others are included in the Hebrew Scriptures. They lived, spoke, and wrote over a period of 300 years. The students should be able to list these prophets' names and locate them in the Bible. They should also be able to link familiar verses with the lives of Hosea, Joel, and Jonah.

GETTING READY

The prophets from Hosea through Malachi (twelve in all) are frequently called the "Minor Prophets." This designation refers chiefly to the fact that they are shorter books.

In this Unit, we have devoted separate study sessions to Amos and Micah, both of whom play significant roles in the succession of literary prophets. The purpose of this session is to call the students' attention to the other ten shorter prophetic books. They were produced over a period of three centuries or more, from around 745-500 BCE or later.

(Note: The *Book of Daniel*, often labeled Major because of its length, is a very different kind of writing. It is believed to have been composed much later, perhaps not until 168 BCE. In Hebrew Bibles, *Daniel* is omitted from the Prophets and included with the section called Writings.)

In the teaching activities for this session, we focus on *Hosea, Joel,* and *Jonah* as key representatives of the shorter prophetic books.

• Hosea was a prophet of the northern kingdom of Israel prior to its fall in the eighth century BCE. He was a younger contemporary of Amos and their writings show a shift in the situation for God's people. In Amos' times, people enjoyed a superficial prosperity; he denounced their social life. Hosea, slightly later, focused on the people's idolatry, which he saw to be a cause of the crisis in their national life. We remember Hosea for his comparison of Israel's idol worship with the acts of an unfaithful spouse.

• Joel, writing around 500BCE, saw a coming day of the Lord which would include both judgment and grace. He calls for repentance and speaks of a time when the Spirit of God would take possession of the people. (His prophecy is recalled in the New Testament story of the Day of Pentecost. Peter's sermon, in *Acts 2:17-21*, includes a quotation from *Joel 2:28-32*.)

• The *Book of Jonah*, dating to 500 BCE or later, is not a prophecy. Instead, it is a book about a prophet to Nineveh. His message shows a deep insight into God's will for the non-Jewish peoples of the world. The Jewish people are called to bring others who are outside their faith community to worship God.

> You are God: we praise you;
> You are the Lord: we acclaim you; . . .
> The noble fellowship of prophets praise you. . . .
> *(Amen.)*
>
> You are God, Morning Prayer II
> *The Book of Common Prayer,* p. 95

TEACHING TIP

By this time, students should have a sense about the message of the prophets: their condemnation of the sins of the people, their predictions of a harsh judgment, and their good news about the future and the coming Messiah. It is important that students realize these messages are not just for people who lived 2,500 years ago. Help class members find relevance in their lives in these ancient words.

GATHERING

As the students arrive, ask volunteers to help place the ten names on the Prophets' TimeLine. Strips of names and dates (BCE) are included on Poster No. 2 in the Teacher's Packet as follows: Hosea, 745; Nahum, 650; Zephaniah, 640; Habakkuk, 625; Obadiah, 575; Haggai and Zechariah, 520; Joel, Jonah, and Malachi, 500. (All these dates are approximate; scholars differ in locating the times when these prophets lived.)

Encourage the class members to stand back and look at the prophetic period. How many years did the prophets cover? Compare this with our own country's history. How many years have passed since the colonists first arrived in the early 1600s? Think about all the changes that have occurred since that time. Do you think the people of Judah saw similar changes?

When everyone is present, say:

Let us pray. (Use the excerpt from "You are God," above, or a prayer of your own choosing.)

The chosen student lector reads from the class Bible (NRSV):

A Reading from the Book of Hosea, chapter 14, verses 4 through 7.

I will heal their disloyalty;
   I will love them freely,
 for my anger has turned from them.
I will be like the dew to Israel;
 he shall blossom like the lily,
 he shall strike root like the forests of Lebanon.
His shoots shall spread out;
 his beauty shall be like the olive tree,
 and his fragrance like that of Lebanon.
They shall again live beneath my shadow,
 they shall flourish as a garden;
 they shall blossom like the vine,
 their fragrance shall be like the wine of Lebanon.

Reader: The Word of the Lord.
Response: Thanks be to God.

INTRODUCING THE STORY
(Time: 10–20 minutes)

Ask the students to turn in their Bibles to find the books of the prophets from *Hosea* through *Malachi*. Point out that *Amos* and *Micah* were the subjects of earlier sessions and are represented on the timeline with pictures.

On a chalkboard or newsprint, write these words: repent, Spirit, mission, God's love.

From information in Getting Ready (above) and stories about Jonah, Hosea, and Joel in the student newspaper, *Community Times* (Unit I, Issue 8), weave a story about the ten prophets whose names have been added to the timeline. Focus especially on the following:

• Hosea, writing shortly after Amos, called on the people to repent and turn away from idol worship and become again faithful worshippers of the one true God. (Write Hosea's name under "repent.")

• Joel also spoke about repenting, but he also spoke of a day when God would pour out the Spirit upon the faithful in a new and powerful way. God desires graciously to restore the people. (Write Joel's name under "Spirit.")

• Jonah's story reminds the Jewish people that they are not to consider their faith as something to guard for themselves only. They are meant to share it with the Gentile (non-Jewish) world as well. That is the mission God has assigned to the chosen people. (Write Jonah's name under "mission.")

You may decide to briefly mention each prophet, and then focus on only one. The story of Jonah, for example, is full of adventure. While most students know about his sojourn in the belly of a great fish, they probably do not know how the people of Ninevah responded to his message and how he felt about God's forgiveness.

Underscore the words, "God's love," and remind the students that the prophets' writings—taken as a whole—teach us that God is always reaching out in love to bring us back into a faithful relationship.

EXPLORING
(Time: 15–20 minutes)

Option 1. Prophets Game

Create a playing board by cutting out and attaching the game squares from Poster No. 3 in the Teacher's Packet to a large piece of posterboard. Draw a thick line around each square to make a space big enough for a pebble or beanbag to land. The squares contain facts about prophets studied throughout this Unit, including especially Hosea, Joel, and Jonah.

Divide the class members into small teams. Each team takes a turn tossing the object onto the board. When it lands on a square, the challenge is to come up with the name of the prophet described.

(Material presented during Introducing the Story, the Bible, and the student newspaper, *Community Times*, may be consulted. Agree on a time limit for responding with each toss.)

Option 2. Prophets' Bookshelf

Supply sheets of construction paper, pencils, markers, glue, and rulers.

Invite the students to create their own versions of a shelf with the books of the prophets arranged in order. Individuals may choose to draw and label the books or to make small paper book spines that can be labeled and glued into place on the shelf.

Encourage them to be creative by color-coding the books, making them different sizes, and decorating the spines with appropriate symbols. Each person can make an individual bookcase or groups can work together in creating a single bookcase.

Option 3. Word Scramble

Turn in the student newspaper, *Community Times*, Unit I, Issue 8, to the word scramble titled "Prophets' Names." Students may work alone, in teams, or as a total group.

MUSIC
(Time: 10 minutes)

Sing or listen to the *Children Sing!* tape again "O praise ye the Lord! Praise him in the height" *(The Hymnal 1982*, 432). The central theme of this hymn embraces the messages of all the Hebrew prophets.

CONNECTING/SPEAKING OUT
(Time: 15–20 minutes)

Option 1. Group Discussion

Ahead of time, copy the following words onto a chalkboard or sheet of newsprint:

covenant   love   anger   return

Supply concordances to teams of students and invite them to take these steps:

1. Locate the word you were assigned.
2. Look to see whether the word appears in *Hosea, Joel,* or *Jonah*.
3. Find one or more of the cited verses in their Bibles.

Ask each team or individual to report their findings about the word assigned. Ask: Do any of the passages have anything to say to people today? What is the most important message? Why?

Option 2. Current Events

The prophets considered two types of human sin to be the worst: *idolatry* (the worship of false gods and following religious practices that leave out love for God); *social sins* (love of luxury, self-love, disregard for the needs of the poor, and the misuse of money).

Share these two categories with the students. Ask: What do you think prophets like Hosea, Joel, and Jonah would say to us about the way we live, worship, and treat others? Which of the sins mentioned by the prophets are still with us? What are we called to do about our situation?

REFLECTING
(Time: 10 minutes)

Encourage the class members to imagine they are with Jonah on the ship as he tried to run away. Jonah was angry at God about being asked to go on this mission. What kinds of situations make you angry? Have you ever been angry with God? How do you deal with your anger? Do you lash out or hold it in?

The students may write or draw their reflections, adding prayers that they have written. Store the sheets in the private envelopes, as described in Session 1.

LEARNING SKILLS
(Time: 10–15 minutes)

Option 1. Class Memory Challenge

Ask the students to locate "The First of Song of Isaiah" in *The Book of Common Prayer*, Morning Prayer II, Canticle 9, p. 86. Read the words aloud in unison, then close the books and repeat the canticle from memory. Add the *Gloria Patri*.

Display the poster from the Teacher's Packet at the conclusion of the recitation.

Option 2. Learning Scripture

Provide opportunity for students to add torches and flames as described in Session 1 for verses they have memorized.

Challenge the students to memorize *Jonah 2:2a* or *Zechariah 9:9*. (The passage from *Zechariah* is recalled each year on Palm Sunday.) See "Learning Scripture" in the student newspaper, *Community Times*.

ONGOING PROJECT
(Time: 5–10 minutes)

Use collage materials and posterboard to make a final entry into the parade of prophets. The students may design a way to incorporate all the remainder of the prophets added to the timeline at this session, or possibly focus on the familiar story of Jonah. Decide on an arrangement of scenes. When the project is finished, add the poster after Second Isaiah.

Discuss sharing the group's accomplishments with the wider congregation. Display the Ongoing Project during a presentation about the prophets' contributions to our faith. Include hymns learned, memory work, and creative projects in a program of celebration.

SYMBOL CARD and TREASUREBOOK

Card 8 contains a picture of a whale, a verse of Scripture, and an explanation on the back.

Ask the students to read in *Chalice Year Treasurebook*, Part I, Section 8, a survey of the parade of prophets whose ministry occurred over a 300-year period. Choose one to read in the Bible.

GOING FORTH

Gather the group for the dismissal. The teacher or a student will say:

> I ask your prayers for all who seek God, or a deeper knowledge of him.
> Pray that they may find and be found by him.
> *Silence*
> [Learners may add their petitions.]
> Praise God for those in every generation in whom Christ has been honored especially those whom we remember today.
> Pray that we may have grace to glorify Christ in our own day.
>
> From The Prayers of the People
> *The Book of Common Prayer*, p. 386

Teacher: Let us go forth in the name of Christ.
Students: Thanks be to God.

TEACHER'S ASSESSMENT

From your observations, have the students begun to sense the continuity among the "parade of prophets" in this Unit? In your estimation, would they be able to identify most with a few key images or phrases?

LOOKING AHEAD

The session that follows is designed for use around November 1 (All Saints' Day). Insert it in your teaching schedule at the most appropriate time.

PROPHECY
SESSION 9
HONORING THE SAINTS

FOCUS

When we celebrate All Saints' Day, we recall all the people who have spoken God's truth to the world, including our Hebrew spiritual ancestors. The students should be able to explain that this Principal Feast offers us an opportunity to honor the prophets among the host of God's saints.

GETTING READY

As one of the seven Principal Feasts of the Church, All Saints' Day was the latest celebration to be included in the calendar of the western Church. Not until the ninth century was the date of November 1 widely observed as a day to honor the memory of all devout Christians who had gone before. Hints of the concept can be found in earlier, fragmentary references to localized celebrations of a feast of All Martyrs.

Although unmistakably a Christian feast, All Saints' Day need not be seen as excluding the faithful people of the long centuries of Hebrew history. In the *Letter to the Ephesians*, the writer offers an image of the "household of God, built upon the foundation of the apostles and prophets, with Jesus Christ himself as the cornerstone." *(See Ephesians 2:19-20.)* As we have seen in this Unit, the prophets were laying the foundation for God's people to expect a coming Messiah who would redeem the nations.

In more recent times, another dimension of the festival has received increasing emphasis: the sainthood of all believers, including the present members of the Church. As a basis for this conclusion, we note that the apostle Paul frequently addressed Christians in local churches as "saints."

Intermediate-age students are in the intellectual stage that permits them to grasp the concept of history, to locate key figures on a timeline, and to appreciate the vast numbers of people who have lived in previous eras. It is appropriate for them to focus on their own place in history—especially as participants in a great procession of Christian believers, one generation after another.

Almighty God, you have knit together your elect in one communion and fellowship in the mystical body of your Son Christ our Lord: Give us grace so to follow your blessed saints in all virtuous and godly living, that we may come to those ineffable joys that you have prepared for those who truly love you; through Jesus Christ our Lord, who with you and the Holy Spirit lives and reigns, one God, in glory everlasting. *Amen.*
All Saints' Day
The Book of Common Prayer, p. 245

TEACHING TIP

Many intermediate-age students enjoy celebrating Halloween in their communities or at special activities at church. Share with them the relationship of Halloween and All Saints' Day using information from *Community Times* (Unit I, Issue 9), the student newspaper. All Saints' Day was established to honor those who had died. It came the day after a pagan rite from ancient Ireland was celebrated to chase away evil spirits of the dead. People would dress up in costumes and carry lanterns made from hollowed gourds. All Saints' Day is a time to remember all the saints who have led holy lives.

GATHERING

As the students arrive, invite them to examine the poster of the prophets' window on Poster No. 6 from the Teacher's Packet. What are the people carrying in the picture? Could you think of an explanation for each of the symbols?

At the end of the Prophets' Time-Line developed during the Unit, add the words "Christian church." Underneath, place the words "saints," "household," "foundation," and "cornerstone."

When everyone is present, say:

Let us pray. (Use the Collect "All Saints' Day," above, or a prayer of your own choosing.)

The chosen student lector reads from the class Bible (NRSV):

A Reading from the Letter of Paul to the Ephesians, chapter 1, verses 17 through 18, and chapter 2, verses 19 through 20.

I pray that the God of our Lord Jesus Christ, the Father of glory, may give you a spirit of wisdom and revelation as you come to know him, so that, with the eyes of your heart enlightened, you may know what is the hope to which he has called you, what are the riches of his glorious inheritance among the saints . . .

So then you are no longer strangers and aliens, but you are citizens with the saints and also members of the household of God, built upon the foundation of the apostles and prophets, with Christ Jesus himself as the cornerstone.

Reader: The Word of the Lord.
Response: Thanks be to God.

INTRODUCING THE STORY
(Time: 10–20 minutes)

Begin by inviting the class members to call out words and phrases that come to their minds when they hear the word "saint." Jot down the responses on a chalkboard or newsprint.

• In your own words, share briefly the outline about All Saints' Day found in Getting Ready (above). Emphasize the concept of the prophets as sharing with the apostles in forming the household of God. Discuss the importance of a foundation and speak of the image of Jesus Christ as "cornerstone."

• Include the story in the student newspaper, *Community Times*, about how the apostle Paul astounded religious authorities by addressing members of the Christian congregation as saints. Previously the term had been used only for specific people who were recognized as holy by the whole community. The authorities wondered how people who are sinful could be considered holy. Paul felt that anyone who belonged to Christ is beloved and a saint.

• Ask the students to work individually or in teams to locate the following: *Romans 1:7; I Corinthians 1:2; II Corinthians 1:1; Ephesians 1:1; Philippians 1:1; Colossians 1:2*. Point out that all these lines are from the apostle Paul's greetings to churches in which he speaks of the congregations as "saints."

• Note that saints include not only all the faithful Christians who have preceded us but also those in the present-day Church, including the students themselves.

In your presentation, use the students' list of words and phrases. In conclusion, ask the group whether they would now suggest adding other ideas.

EXPLORING
(Time: 15–20 minutes)

Option 1. Prophets Banner for the Feast of All Saints

Suggest that the students work together to prepare a large banner for All Saints' Day that includes names of Hebrew prophets along with well-known saints in Christian history. Encourage the group to include today's Christians as well. They may wish to add their own names to the finished banner.

For this project, stress simplicity. Use pieces of felt, burlap, or even heavy construction paper to fashion sections of the banner. Supply items such as yarn, colored markers, and all-purpose glue.

Option 2. Sun Catchers

To symbolize saints as persons who reflect the light of God (through their words and deeds), invite the students to make "sun catchers" for the classroom or to take home.

To make a sun catcher, use a black marker or pen to draw a selected shape on a piece of white paper. Clip a piece of waxed paper over the base sheet, followed by a piece of colored tissue paper. (The drawn shape should be clearly visible through the layers.) Cut a piece of yarn the same length as the shape's border and dip it into white glue that has been thinned with water. Holding one end of the wet yarn, pull it through your other hand's thumb and index finger so that excess glue is removed. (Work slowly so that the glue does not spatter on the work surface.)

Place the yarn on the tissue paper along the outline. (The wax paper underneath prevents the glue from seeping through to the white paper below.) When the yarn is completely dry, lift up the tissue paper and cut around the edges of the yarn, which forms a stiffened frame for the tissue sun catcher. Attach a string to the top and hang in a sunny window.

Option 3. Anagram

Turn in the student newspaper, *Community Times*, Unit I, Issue 9, to the anagram, "All Saints." Suggest that students work individually, in teams, or as a total group.

MUSIC
(Time: 10 minutes)

Listen on the *Children Sing!* tape or sing the short hymn, "For thy dear saints" *(The Hymnal 1982, 279)*. Explain that "strove" in the first stanza means "put forth great effort." Call attention especially to the third stanza, which is a prayer that God will "fit" (prepare) the people of today to join the saints of previous generations as one great community "knit" (woven together) into a loving fellowship.

CONNECTING/SPEAKING OUT
(Time: 15–20 minutes)

Option 1. Group Discussion

Point out that the saints of Christian history have included many different kinds of men and women. Some lived to an old age and died naturally; others' lives were cut short because they were martyred, often in hideous ways. Some were great scholars and teachers; others were poor folk who lived simple lives of devotion. Some left behind books and memorials; others are buried in unknown graves.

If possible, obtain a copy of the book, *Lesser Feasts and Fasts*, published by the Church Hymnal Corporation of the Episcopal Church. It contains brief sketches of the saints honored on the Church's calendar, from early centuries to the present. (You may want to photocopy several pages from the book to share with the students.)

Ask: What do the saints have in common, even though they are all different? Why do we call them a "communion of saints"?

Focus on the saints' common faith in God, their devotion to the truth that comes from God, and their wholehearted commitment to serve God at any cost.

Option 2. Current Events

Share a stack of recent issues of local newspapers and also newsletters from organizations in your community and church. Invite the class members to work in small groups to scan the publications for stories of individuals who seem to be "set apart" because they help others.

Prepare a display of items chosen by the students. Who are the people featured in the stories? How do they carry out their missions? What do others in the community say about them? Should they be considered "saints"? Why, or why not?

REFLECTING
(Time: 10 minutes)

Provide index cards (3 x 5 inches) and pencils for all the class members. Ask the group to reflect quietly on the great company of saints (from the Bible, from the history of the Church, or in present-day life). Encourage each student to write down the name of a favorite saint.

Ask: What do you like most about your favorite saint? In what ways would you want to be like her/him? Why?

Suggest that the students write their own prayers for All Saints' Day on the other side of their index cards.

If the students have prepared "Reflection Collection" envelopes (see Session 1), they may add the cards for this session.

LEARNING SKILLS
(Time: 10–15 minutes)

Option 1. Class Memory Challenge

Invite the class members to stand and say together, in unison, the words of "The First Song of Isaiah," Canticle 9 (BCP, p. 86), which has been memorized in previous sessions of the Unit.

Point out that the canticle could appropriately be called a "song of the saints of God."

Option 2. Learning Scripture

Invite class members to add torches and flames as described in Session 1 for verses they have committed to memory.

Suggest that the students memorize *Ephesians 1:17-18*. See "Learning Scripture" in the student newspaper, *Community Times*.

ONGOING PROJECT
(Time: 5–10 minutes)

Create a poster with these words in the center: "Prophets and Saints of Today." This poster can be moved to the end of the parade display at the conclusion of the Unit.

Ask the students to recall what it means to be a prophet (spokesperson for God), and also to think about persons they would identify as "saints" today (members of the community of faith). With crayons and markers, the class members can fill a sheet of posterboard with graffiti (words, phrases, drawings, symbols) that link their own lives to the communion of saints.

SYMBOL CARD and TREASUREBOOK

Card 9 contains a cross and crown, a verse of Scripture, and an explanation on the back.

Ask the students to read in *Chalice Year Treasurebook*, Part I, Section 9, about the foundation laid by Hebrew prophets for the coming of Jesus Christ, the Messiah. Why do Christians continue to read the prophets? Why are prophets considered to be saints?

GOING FORTH

Gather the group for the dismissal. The teacher or a student will say:

> I ask your prayers for all who seek God, or a deeper knowledge of him.
> Pray that they may find and be found by him.
> *Silence*

[Learners may add their petitions.]

> Praise God for those in every generation in whom Christ has been honored especially those whom we remember today.
> Pray that we may have grace to glorify Christ in our own day.
>
> From The Prayers of the People
> *The Book of Common Prayer*, p. 386

Teacher: Let us go forth in the name of Christ.
Students: Thanks be to God.

TEACHER'S ASSESSMENT

As you evaluate this session, what evidence did you glean that the students are gaining a broader knowledge and understanding of "saints"? Do the class members have a clearer vision of what it means for the Church to celebrate All Saints' Day?

Note: The following letter is for teachers and parents of children in the Intermediate level of church school. These pages can be reproduced or used as a model for a personalized letter.

Episcopal Children's Curriculum
Unit II: PARABLES OF PROMISE

Dear Parents and Guardians,

The theme of "promise" is the focus of the parables chosen for this Unit. Jesus teaches through his stories that life with God is filled with possibilities. God is at work to bring newness and saving health. Like a sower, a vineyard worker, a seeker of treasure, or a house builder, the Christian disciple thinks about the future and knows that God keeps the way open for new life, righteousness, and redemption.

We hope that this introduction to parables will encourage students to read more of Jesus' stories. His use of stories and metaphors helps us to grow in our relationship with God. The more we hear parables, the more meanings are revealed.

The parables invite questions: What is our relationship to God? What are we called to be and do? Where will we take our stand?

The first five sessions of the Unit are related to Advent, Christmas, and Epiphany. They are intended for use during those seasons as we prepare for and celebrate Jesus' birth as the incarnate Son of God. The last four sessions are devoted to Jesus' parables.

The transition between the two sets of sessions is natural: The long-expected Messiah who was born in Bethlehem of Judea becomes an incomparable teacher. He proclaims the reign of God and his parables are filled with hope and promise for all who respond in faith.

Plan to spend some time talking to your student about what he or she is learning. You can do this by reading the Scripture passages identified below, discussing the Symbol Cards and *Community Times* sent home each week, and by reading together Part II of the *Chalice Year Treasurebook*, which includes information about parables.

Following is a more detailed overview of the Unit:

Session 1: "A New Creation" introduces the season of Advent as a time of waiting and joyous expectancy. Activities center on words from the *Book of Isaiah* about a time when God would make "new heavens and a new earth"—what we believe to be the coming of Christ. The session stresses the Nativity as a new beginning for the people of God. (*Isaiah 65:17-18, 24-25*)

Session 2: "Preparing the Way" is about the ministry of John the Baptist. Quoting the prophet Isaiah, he announced that the reign of God was at hand: "In the wilderness prepare the way of the Lord, . . ." (*Isaiah 40:3b*). Many responded to his call for repentance and baptism. Students will contrast the Church's activities with those of the secular world during this season. (*Isaiah 40:1-5*)

Session 3: "The Genealogy of Jesus" looks at the introduction of Jesus' story in *Matthew*. Matthew was especially concerned about helping Jewish readers see that Jesus of Nazareth was the long-awaited Messiah. Listing Jesus' ancestors was a way of stressing that Christ's coming was a new "genesis," a new beginning for God's people. (*Matthew 1:1-2, 16-17*)

Session 4: "The Messiah Is Born" invites the students to explore the story of Jesus' birth. The birth in the Bethlehem manger during the Roman census is found only in *Luke*. The visit of the Wise Men comes from *Matthew*. The two accounts are often combined into one story. Students will be encouraged to reflect on the true meaning of Christmas. (*Luke 2:1-14*)

Session 5: "Flight into Egypt" tells of Herod the Great's threat to the life of the child Jesus. After a dream, the Holy Family fled to Egypt for protection. After Herod's death, Joseph returned with his family to Nazareth in Galilee. In this session, students will relate the plight of refugee children in the modern world to Jesus and his family's time in Egypt. (*Matthew 2:13-15*)

Session 6: "Parable of the Sower" focuses on a story of Jesus that is found in *Mark*, *Matthew*, and *Luke*. Students will be challenged to think about their own response to the good news of God. Will we be like the rocky soil where the Word cannot take root or like the good soil that brings a rich harvest? (*Mark 4:2-9*)

Session 7: "Parable of the Vineyard Workers" centers on the generosity of God. Everyone has equal access to divine blessing. As they think about this story, the students will have an opportunity to act out the scenes and to discover the parable's meaning. Class members will discuss fairness and God's love. (*Matthew 20:1-16*)

Session 8: "Parables of Treasure" is about two short stories Jesus used that are found only in *Matthew*. One is about a treasure found in a field, and the other about a pearl of great value. Both are about committing our whole lives to Christ. Activities will help students encounter the need to make important choices about priorities in their daily living. (*Matthew 13:44-46*)

Session 9: "The House upon a Rock" is about spiritual foundations. One builder constructed a house on rock and the other a house on sand. It was the house on a rock that withstood a severe rainstorm. Jesus declares that a person who hears and heeds his message is like the wise person who built on a solid foundation. To reject Jesus' teachings is to be like the foolish person who built on the sand. (*Matthew 7:24-27*)

Yours in Christ,

Church School Teachers

PARABLES OF PROMISE

SESSION 1
A NEW CREATION

FOCUS

For Christians, the season of Advent is marked by two dimensions: waiting and joyous expectancy. Both are related to the promises of God declared by the Hebrew prophets. The Church has understood the prophets' vision to be a foretelling of the kingdom of God in Jesus Christ. The students should be able to explain that the Messiah's birth is the beginning of a "new creation."

GETTING READY

The Christian Year begins with the Sunday nearest November 30 as the Church enters the Season of Advent. It is a four-week period with multiple themes. We prepare joyfully for celebrating Christ's birth, but we also engage in quiet reflection. Are we ready to receive the gift of the promised Messiah?

Throughout this season we recall the ancient prophecies in Hebrew Scriptures, with their announcement of a coming day of the Lord when life would be different. At Sunday Eucharists, we hear this message directly in readings from the prophets. In the three-year cycle of the Lectionary, most Old Testament selections for Advent are from the *Book of Isaiah*.

In *Isaiah 65:17-25* (NRSV), the voice of God declares, "For I am about to create new heavens and a new earth; the former things shall not be remembered or come to mind." Christians interpret this prophecy as a foretelling of the reign of God in Jesus Christ.

In the busyness of the days before Christmas, it is possible for us to lose sight of the Nativity's significance as a new beginning for the people of God. Sin and death were defeated by our Lord, who is our Savior.

Almighty and everlasting God, you made the universe with all its marvelous order, its atoms, worlds, and galaxies, and the infinite complexity of living creatures: Grant that, as we probe the mysteries of your creation, we may come to know you more truly, and surely fulfill our role in your eternal purpose; in the name of Jesus Christ our Lord. *Amen.*

For the Knowledge of God's Creation
The Book of Common Prayer, p. 827

TEACHING TIP

Although intermediate-age students no longer believe in the fantasies surrounding Christmas, they still get caught up in the excitement and expectancy of the season. Their waiting is often filled with impatience. Tap into these natural emotions as you talk about Advent. Use symbols such as the Advent wreath to focus on what it means to await the coming of Christ, the Savior.

GATHERING

Prepare a classroom Advent wreath. If a regular circular form is available, place the candles and surround them with greens. A good substitute holder can be made from a styrofoam ring or molding clay. Invite the students to replenish greens each week and tend the candles.

When everyone is present, gather around the wreath as the first candle is lighted. Invite the students to join in reading "Creator of the stars of night," found on Poster No. 7 in the Teacher's Packet (stanzas 1 and 3 of this hymn from *The Hymnal 1982,* 60; *We Sing of God,* 13).

The teacher then says:

Let us pray. (Use the prayer "For the Knowledge of God's Creation," above, or a prayer of your own choosing.)

The chosen student lector reads from the class Bible:

Unit II. Parables of Promise—Session 1
Chalice Year Intermediate—Copyright © 2000 Virginia Theological Sminary and Morehouse Publishing

A Reading from the Book of Isaiah, chapter 65, verses 17, 18, 24, and 25.

> For I am about to create new heavens
>   and a new earth;
> the former things shall not be remembered
>   or come to mind.
> But be glad and rejoice forever
>   in what I am creating;
> for I am about to create Jerusalem as a joy,
>   and its people as a delight. . . .
> Before they call I will answer,
>   while they are yet speaking I will hear.
> The wolf and the lamb shall feed together,
>   the lion shall eat straw like the ox;
>   but the serpent—its food shall be dust!
> They shall not hurt or destroy
>   on my holy mountain, says the Lord.

Reader: The Word of the Lord.
Response: Thanks be to God.

Since the candles of the Advent wreath will be lit during the Gathering for each week in Advent, extinguish them after the reading (above). They can be re-lit just before the Going Forth.

INTRODUCING THE STORY
(Time: 10 minutes)

Begin by wishing all the students "a joyful New Year." Repeat the greeting several times. Be alert to any expressions of puzzlement.

• Write the words, "Season of Advent," on a chalkboard or newsprint, and invite the class members to share their understanding of its meaning. Jot down key words and phrases suggested by individuals.

• Remind the group that Advent is the beginning of the Christian Year. It is a season for looking back, to recall the whole history of God's people, and a time for looking ahead to the newness of God's appearing in the birth of Jesus.

• Display the Nativity picture with prophets from the Teacher's Packet. Invite the students to examine the figures of Ezekiel and Isaiah in the side panels. Ask: Why would the artist include these two prophets beside the manger scene?

• Read aloud *Isaiah 65:17*. In your own words tell the story about Isaiah's vision from the Scripture passage and the article on page 1 of the student newspaper, *Community Times* (Unit II, Issue 1). Point out that this prophet had a vision of a time when God would act to make the world fresh and new again. All human troubles and evil would be replaced by a time of joy in which all God's creatures would live together in peace and unity. Christians believe that such newness in the world was begun by Jesus Christ. We remember this good news in Advent as we prepare to celebrate his birth.

• Invite the students to turn in their Bibles to *Isaiah 65:17-25*. Ask the class members to work as individuals or in teams to examine the passage and make a written list of ways in which life would be different in the "new creation" as told by the prophet. If time permits, allow the group to share what they wrote.

EXPLORING
(Time: 15–20 minutes)

Option 1. Pyramid Poem

The writing of pyramid poetry can be done individually or by the whole group. The poems form the shape of pyramids because each successive line contains one additional word.

Begin with the word "Advent" at the top center of a page, a sheet of newsprint, or a chalkboard. The next line will be two words; the third line, three words; and so on until the poem has seven lines.

Following are suggestions for a pyramid based on *Isaiah*, chapter 65:

(1. Title)
ADVENT
(2. Associated actions)
waiting   expecting
(3. When?)
time   before   Christmas
(4. Former things) . . . four words
(5. Words of rejoicing) . . . five words
(6. New conditions in new creation) . . . six words
(7. What Advent means to me) . . . seven words

Option 2. World Shape

Prepare a large sheet of posterboard with an outline of a sphere (the world). Provide magazines, newspapers, and/or plain paper. Ask the students to draw scenes, cut out illustrations, or compose phrases that depict the new kind of world described in *Isaiah 65*. Consider themes like health, rejoicing, joy, delight, gladness, and hope. The images and words are to be cut out and glued within the outlines of the world shape. Display the finished product in the classroom throughout this Unit.

Option 3. Advent Crossword

Turn in the student newspaper, *Community Times*, Unit II, Issue 1, to the crossword puzzle titled "Advent." Students may work individually, in pairs, or as a total group.

MUSIC
(Time: 10 minutes)

Introduce "Prepare the way, O Zion, your Christ is drawing near" *(The Hymnal 1982, 65; We Sing of God, 14)*. Read in unison or listen to all three stanzas on the *Children Sing!* tape. Practice the refrain, then sing the whole hymn with the tape.

CONNECTING/SPEAKING OUT
(Time: 15–20 minutes)

Option 1. Group Discussion

Talk with the students about the world situation during the time of the Hebrew prophets. Some of the problems of that period were dishonesty, lack of faithfulness, poverty, injustice, false prophets, bribery, idolatry, and disobedience. Encourage the class members to recall events in the Old Testament that illustrate these sins and failures. Do these problems exist today? Explain.

Work as a group to list characteristics of a "new creation" promised by God and announced by the Hebrew prophets, as in *Isaiah 65*. How would such a world be different? (The new creation would include faithfulness, redemption, hope, comfort, forgiveness, fruitfulness, deliverance, blessings, destruction of enemies, reconciliation, peace, and righteousness.)

Option 2. Current Events

Advent is a time of "waiting" and "expecting." Invite the students to think about these two dimensions of the season. What do Christians wait for as we worship in the weeks before celebrating Christ's birth? What are we expecting?

At this time in history, what do the world's people wait for? What might poor and neglected persons wait for? What are people who are lonely and without hope waiting for? What is waiting like for those who are ill? What can these people expect from their neighbors? from the Church? What would add "joy" to their expectations? What could you do for others who are in this time of waiting?

REFLECTING
(Time: 10 minutes)

For this Unit, set up a "Reflection Center" that encourages students to make personal responses to the session themes. Supply materials for colorful drawings, collages, and manuscripts. Students who prefer to write can respond with journal entries, poems, or essays. Plan to add new materials and replenish the supplies as needed for each session's work. (This activity may be done at each session or occasionally during the Unit.)

Provide an envelope approximately 9 x 12 inches in size for each student. Class members may add their names and decorate the envelopes, which will be used to keep items produced during the sessions. Store the envelopes safely between class meetings. Assure the students that the contents are private and may be taken home at the end of the Unit. Either orally or in writing, offer direction for student responses:

In Advent we remember the new beginnings promised by God. We can also think about new beginnings in our own lives. What are some things in your past that you would like to forget? What do you hope your own future will be like? What would be new and different?

Draw or write your reaction to these questions. When you are finished, you may compose a brief prayer.

LEARNING SKILLS
(Time: 10–15 minutes)

Option 1. Class Memory Challenge

For this Unit, the memory challenge is a listing of some of Jesus' parables. Knowing the Gospel(s) and chapter(s) for finding these stories can be helpful.

Share the fact that parables appear only in the *Gospels of Matthew, Mark,* and *Luke*. None is found in *John's Gospel*. The students' task will be to learn how to locate (by chapter number only) eighteen parables—six that appear in *Matthew* only, seven from *Luke* only, three found in both *Matthew* and *Luke*, and two appearing in all three of these *Gospels*.

For this session, concentrate on two parables from *Matthew 13*, known as "Hidden Treasure" and "Pearl of Great Price (Value)." Suggest that the class members turn to the chapter and find the stories (verses 44-46). Ask them to repeat the parable titles and chapter number several times. Suggest some form of association that would help them to recall the chapter whenever the parables are mentioned.

A block related to this Memory Challenge appears in each issue of the student newspaper, *Community Times*, for this Unit.

Option 2. Learning Scripture

For this Unit, prepare a very large outline of an Epiphany Star—with ten points—that can serve as the base for a mosaic. Cut gold and yellow paper into small triangular shapes and place in a basket or a bag. Display the outline at each session. As students memorize verses of Scripture, they can add small paper triangles (one for each verse) to fill in the star mosaic. Write the Scripture verses suggested for each session on large index cards and mount these near the Epiphany Star mosaic.

Offer students the opportunity to learn one of the following before the next class session: *Isaiah 7:14; Isaiah 35:1; Isaiah 65:17* (any version or translation). All the verses for the Unit are listed under "Learning Scripture" in the student newspaper, *Community Times*.

ONGOING PROJECT
(Time: 5–10 minutes)

As an ongoing project from Advent through the Feast of Epiphany, create a display of enlarged versions of seasonal symbols: 1. Advent wreath; 2. John the Baptist's symbol (staff, banner, and cross); 3. Jesse tree; 4. Nativity creche; 5. Epiphany star. These appear on Symbol Cards 10-14 and in the student newspaper, *Community Times*, Unit II, Issues 1-5.

Tear a white bedsheet into five long, thin panels that can be arranged in order on a clothesline or individual dowels. Use a permanent marker for outlining and assorted colors of poster or fabric paint. (Another option would be to glue colored fabric or paper to the panels.)

For this session, enlarge the picture of an Advent wreath. Use pencil to draw lightly on the cloth. When the students are satisfied with their design, go over the outline with permanent marker.

Spread the panel on a table or floor area to paint the symbol. When dry, place it on exhibit. The students may want to add decorative touches or a placard to explain the symbol.

SYMBOL CARD and TREASUREBOOK

Card 10 contains an advent wreath, a verse of Scripture, and an explanation on the back.

Suggest that the students read *Chalice Year Treasurebook*, Part II, Section 1. What were the people of God expecting the Messiah to do?

GOING FORTH

Gather the group for the dismissal. Re-light the Advent candle. The teacher or a student will say the following, pausing for the students' response of "Lord, have mercy":

> With all our heart and with all our mind, let us pray to the Lord, saying, "Lord, have mercy."
>
> For the peace from above, for the loving kindness of God, and for the salvation of our souls, let us pray to the Lord.
> *Lord, have mercy.*
>
> For the peace of the world, for the welfare of the holy Church of God, and for the unity of all people, let us pray to the Lord.
> *Lord, have mercy.*
>
> For _____ [learners may add their own petitions], let us pray to the Lord.
> *Lord, have mercy.*
>
> From The Prayers of the People
> *The Book of Common Prayer*, pp. 383-384

Teacher: Let us go forth in the name of Christ.
Students: Thanks be to God.

TEACHER'S ASSESSMENT

From your observations, were the students able to grasp the two concepts of waiting and expectancy during Advent? How did they react to the idea of God's "new creation"?

LOOKING AHEAD

In the next session, the students will be thinking about the ministry of John the Baptist as one who prepared the way for the coming of Jesus Christ. Think about your spiritual preparation during the season of Advent. How will you get ready for prayerful celebration of the Savior's birth?

PARABLES OF PROMISE

SESSION 2
PREPARING THE WAY

FOCUS

Advent is more than getting ready for Christ's birth. The season's theme of preparation is rooted in the work of John the Baptist, whose preaching prepared the way for Jesus' ministry. The students should be able to describe the role of John the Baptist and link the season of Advent with the theme of spiritual preparation.

GETTING READY

In Advent, we recall the ministry of John the Baptist who was a cousin of Jesus. The story of John's birth is found in *Luke*, chapter 1. His father, Zechariah, filled with the Holy Spirit, prophesied that John would become "the prophet of the Most High" who would "go before the Lord to prepare his ways" (verse 76).

John grew up to be a rugged outdoorsman who lived in the desert wilderness, wearing camel's hair clothing and eating locusts and wild honey. When the time was right, he began to preach an urgent message from God. He declared that the reign of God was at hand and he called on people to repent of their sins and be baptized. Many responded to his message.

All the Gospels identify John the Baptist as the one of whom the prophet Isaiah had written: "A voice cries out: 'In the wilderness prepare the way of the Lord, make straight in the desert a highway for our God.'" *(Isaiah 40:3)*. John's chief work was to serve as a forerunner, a herald, of Jesus' ministry. Indeed, Jesus later spoke of John as God's servant who had been foretold in *Malachi 3:1a*, "See, I am sending my messenger to prepare the way before me, . . ." (See *Luke 7:24-27*.)

John's ministry of preparation is a strong reminder to us in Advent. This is a season in which to prepare our own hearts and spirits, in prayer and worship, for the good news of Jesus' birth proclaimed at Christmas.

Stir up your power, O Lord, and with great might come among us; and, because we are sorely hindered by our sins, let your bountiful grace and mercy speedily help and deliver us; through Jesus Christ our Lord, to whom, with you and the Holy Spirit, be honor and glory, now and for ever. *Amen.*
Third Sunday of Advent
The Book of Common Prayer, p. 212

TEACHING TIP

Students of the intermediate-age level value their privacy. For this reason, they may begin to use personal diaries and journals. It follows naturally that this is a good age level for introducing the practice of private prayer. Encourage class members to pray each day for forgiveness and strength. Suggest they set aside the same time each day during this season of Advent.

GATHERING

As the students arrive, prepare the Advent wreath with fresh greens. When all are present, gather around the wreath. Light two candles and invite the students to join again in a choral reading, using the Teacher's Packet Poster No. 7, "Creator of the stars of night." (The poster includes stanzas 1 and 3 of this Advent hymn from *The Hymnal 1982,* 60; *We Sing of God,* 13.)

The teacher says:

Let us pray. (Use the Collect "Third Sunday of Advent," above, or a prayer of your own choosing.)

The chosen student lector reads from the class Bible (NRSV):

A Reading from the Book of Isaiah, chapter 40, verses 1 through 5.

Comfort, O comfort my people,
  says your God.
Speak tenderly to Jerusalem,
  and cry to her
that she has served her term,
  that her penalty is paid,
that she has received from the Lord's hand
  double for all her sins.
A voice cries out:
"In the wilderness prepare the way of the Lord,
  make straight in the desert a highway for our God.
Every valley shall be lifted up,
  and every mountain and hill be made low;
the uneven ground shall become level,
  and the rough places a plain.
Then the glory of the Lord shall be revealed,
  and all people shall see it together,
  for the mouth of the Lord has spoken."

Reader: The Word of the Lord.
Response: Thanks be to God.

Extinguish the candles after the reading. They can be re-lit just before the Going Forth.

INTRODUCING THE STORY
(Time: 10 minutes)

Begin by asking the students: How are you preparing for the coming celebration of Christmas? Encourage specific responses and jot down on a chalkboard or newsprint some of the main categories—such as plans for Church programs, gift-giving, parties, family meals, decorations, and baking.

• Point out that the season of Advent includes, of course, many activities related to the holiday season. It is important that we not lose sight of the chief reason for these weeks on the Church's calendar. Advent is a time of spiritual preparation as well. We take the time to pray quietly. We confess our sins and pray for forgiveness.

• Display Poster No. 9 in the Teacher's Packet that shows two pictures of John the Baptist. Retell his story, stressing his role as the one who prepared the way for Jesus' teaching. Use information from Getting Ready (above) and the front-page story in the student newspaper, *Community Times* (Unit II, Issue 2).

• Point out that Christians have interpreted the work of John as a fulfillment of Hebrew prophecy, especially that of *Isaiah 40:1-11*. This passage is one of the Advent readings in the Lectionary.

• Suggest that the group think about preparing themselves in heart and spirit for the true message of Christmas—that God has come into our midst in the person of Jesus Christ.

• Ask the students to work individually or in teams to locate *Isaiah 40:3* and the Gospels' use of this verse. See *Matthew 3:3; Mark 1:3; Luke 3:4; John 1:23*. Encourage the class members to notice the different ways in which the Gospel writers referred to the passage.

EXPLORING
(Time: 15–20 minutes)

Option 1. John's Message

Ask the class to look again at Poster No. 9 showing two artists' ideas of what John the Baptist looked like. Ask a volunteer to read a description of John in *Matthew 3:4*. Point out that John presented his message in a wilderness setting. Ask: How would you show John?

As a group or in teams, make your own drawings of John. Begin by making a general outline of a person by tracing the body of a class member lying on a large sheet of newsprint. (You may need to tape two or more sheets together.) Ask one or two artists to add details to the figure from students' suggestions. For example, one person might suggest a beard, while another recommends sandals or heavy boots.

When the drawings are complete hang them on a wall in front of the group. Spend a few minutes talking about ways we can prepare for Christ's birth. For ideas, read *Luke 3:10-14*. Note that prayer and forgiveness are important during this season of Advent. Ask: What do you think John would ask us to do as we get ready for Christmas?

Pass out post-it notes to the class members. Ask them to write down one thing they will do before Christmas to prepare for the celebration of Christmas. Encourage them to select something they would not ordinarily do. When they are finished, invite them to put their notes on the picture(s) of John the Baptist. Leave the picture(s) up as a reminder for the students through the season of Advent.

Option 2. Advent Prayer Cards

Distribute plain white index cards, either 4 x 6 or 3 x 5; pencils, pens, and markers; sheets of purple or blue construction paper; scissors and glue.

Ask the students to choose Advent Collects or other prayers from *The Book of Common Prayer* and copy them onto individual cards. Each card may be decorated or framed with construction paper and markers. Encourage class members to take their cards home and put them in places they are likely to see them each day.

Option 3. Word Scramble

Turn in the student newspaper, *Community Times*, Unit II, Issue 2, to the word scramble titled "Words of Isaiah." Students may work individually, in pairs, or as a total group.

MUSIC
(Time: 10 minutes)

Sing or listen on the *Children Sing!* tape the Advent hymn, "Prepare the way, O Zion" (*The Hymnal 1982*, 65; *We Sing of God*, 14). Point out that this hymn is a good example of Scripture rewritten as a rhythmic poem and set to music. The first two stanzas are based on *Isaiah 40:1-11*.

If time permits, lead the students in composing their own hymn from *Isaiah*—to the tune of "Twinkle, twinkle, little star." Each line of this nursery rhyme has eight beats (two for "star," "are," and other one-syllable words at the end of lines). Work on choosing thoughts and words from *Isaiah*, then setting them to the proper rhythm. Here is an example:

> Comfort, comfort, says our God.
> Christ the Savior comes to you.
> Hills and valleys will be straight,
> God's great glory shall be seen.
> Advent is the time to pray,
> Now for him prepare the way.

CONNECTING/SPEAKING OUT
(Time: 15–20 minutes)

Option 1. Group Discussion

Read a portion of the Scripture passage in *Isaiah 40:3-5*. Describe the wilderness that Isaiah wrote about and John lived in. That area of the Middle East is still considered a wilderness area. It is dry and incredibly rocky. While there are rocks the size of gravel, many are huge boulders. Roads in this area even today wind through rocks that are too big to remove. The land is very hilly; there are few places that are level.

Ask: What problems or issues do we face that seem like boulders in our lives? What problems would you like to be removed? What would a road crew have to do to make the roads straight and the ground level in the wilderness? How difficult would that be? How can Jesus help us remove some of the rocks in our lives?

Option 2. Current Events

In today's society, all the secular advertising and commercial activity in connection with the holiday season can easily distract us from the spiritual dimensions of the Nativity. Invite the students to compare the message of the marketplace with the message of the Church during Advent.

What are the themes of the pre-holiday advertising? How does the prophets' message of a Savior's birth contrast with these themes?

REFLECTING
(Time: 10 minutes)

Distribute the students' reflection envelopes and set up the Reflection Center, as described in Session 1—replenishing the art supplies as needed.

Either orally or in writing, offer direction for the student responses:

Advent can be a valuable time for thinking about our personal relationships with God. In what ways do you want to grow closer to God during this season? What are some of the "rough places" in your life? How could these places be made "smooth"?

Write or draw your reaction to these questions. Compose a prayer asking God to help you to use Advent for improving your relationship with God.

LEARNING SKILLS
(Time: 10–15 minutes)

Option 1. Class Memory Challenge

Review the memory challenge from Session 1 and introduce two more parables that appear in the *Gospel of Matthew* only: "Unforgiving Servant" (chapter 18) and "Laborers in the Vineyard" (chapter 20).

Ask the class members to find both stories in their Bibles and to link chapter numbers with these parables of Jesus. (A nonsense way might be to remember 18 servants and 20 laborers.) Refer to the related chart in the student newspaper, *Community Times*, Unit II, Issue 2.

Option 2. Learning Scripture

Ask whether class members have learned verses given in the previous session. Students can add paper triangles to the Epiphany Star mosaic outline as described in Session 1.

Encourage students to memorize *Isaiah 40:3*, *Mark 1:4*, or *Luke 7:27* before the next class session.

See "Learning Scripture" in the student newspaper, *Community Times*.

ONGOING PROJECT
(Time: 5–10 minutes)

Continue the seasonal project as described in Session 1. For the second cloth panel in the display, enlarge the picture of John the Baptist's symbol as it appears on Symbol Card 11 and in the student newspaper, *Community Times*, Unit II, Issue 2. This image combines a staff, banner, and cross.

When the task is finished, place the new panel to the right of the Advent wreath panel produced earlier.

SYMBOL CARD and TREASUREBOOK

Card 11 contains a staff, banner and cross, with a verse of Scripture, and an explanation on the back.

Ask the students to read in the *Chalice Year Treasurebook*, Part II, Section 2, the description of Jesus' ministry. His teaching and preaching are described in relation to "the kingdom of God," which was first announced by the prophet John the Baptist. How would you summarize what Jesus did during the three years?

GOING FORTH

Re-light the two candles on the Advent wreath. The teacher or a student will say the following, pausing for the students' response of "Lord, have mercy":

> With all our heart and with all our mind, let us pray to the Lord, saying, "Lord, have mercy."

> For the peace from above, for the loving kindness of God, and for the salvation of our souls, let us pray to the Lord.
> *Lord, have mercy.*

> For the peace of the world, for the welfare of the holy Church of God, and for the unity of all people, let us pray to the Lord.
> *Lord, have mercy.*

> For _____ [learners may add their own petitions], let us pray to the Lord.
> *Lord, have mercy.*
>   From The Prayers of the People
>   *The Book of Common Prayer*, pp. 383-384

Teacher: Let us go forth in the name of Christ.
Students: Thanks be to God.

TEACHER'S ASSESSMENT

How well did the students appear to grasp the concept of Advent as a season of spiritual preparation? In what ways did they demonstrate an understanding that the Church's message in this season is different from the typical holiday themes in our society?

LOOKING AHEAD

The next session is about the relationship of Jesus to the long story of God's people who had gone before. Think about your own spiritual ancestors. Where did they live? What did they believe? How have they influenced your life?

PARABLES OF PROMISE

SESSION 3
THE GENEALOGY OF JESUS

FOCUS

The Gospel writers make it clear that Jesus' birth is a climactic event in history. Jesus was born to Mary at a particular moment in God's time. Matthew begins his account with a genealogy divided into three periods of fourteen generations each. The students should be able to explain that Jesus the Messiah had a human family that spanned the whole biblical record and they should be able to identify key figures in the genealogy.

GETTING READY

The stories of Jesus' birth are found in *Matthew*, chapter 1, and *Luke*, chapter 2. At Christmas, we use both Gospel accounts in pageants and services.

The writer of *Matthew* was addressing Jewish readers whom he hoped to convince that Jesus, Son of Mary, was truly the long-awaited Messiah whose coming was foretold in Hebrew Scriptures. Consequently, he began his Gospel with a listing of Jesus' ancestors *(Matthew 1:1-17)*. For the chosen people of God, genealogies were extremely important. They helped Jewish people to recall their history and to be reassured of their continuing identity in the world.

Matthew's listing is inaccurate, when compared with Old Testament genealogies. But his purpose was to link Jesus Christ with all of Hebrew history. He named fourteen generations for each of three periods—from Abraham to David; from David to the exile in Babylon; and from the exiles' return until Jesus' birth. For the Jewish reader, the number fourteen would have been recognized as a symbol for completeness.

The ancestral list in *Matthew* includes three women—Rahab, Ruth, and "the wife of Uriah" (Bathsheba, mother of Solomon). Matthew implies that Christ's coming was a new "genesis," a new beginning, for humankind. Another genealogy of Jesus, extending all the way to Adam, appears in *Luke 3:23-38*.

Purify our conscience, Almighty God, by your daily visitation, that your Son Jesus Christ, at his coming, may find in us a mansion prepared for himself; who lives and reigns with you, in the unity of the Holy Spirit, one God, now and for ever. *Amen*.
Fourth Sunday of Advent
The Book of Common Prayer, p. 212

TEACHING TIP

Students may note that the genealogy in *Matthew 1* is for Joseph instead of Mary. In a patriarchal society, tracing lineage through males was common. Explain that this background was important to the Jewish people for whom the *Book of Matthew* was targeted. While we do not know exactly who Mary's ancestors were, we do know that her cousin Elizabeth was married to a priest from the tribe of Levi. The inclusion of Ruth, a non-Hebrew foreigner, in the genealogy in *Matthew* also makes clear that Jesus opened the reign of God to people other that Jews.

GATHERING

As the students arrive, place fresh greens around the Advent wreath. When everyone is present, light three candles and invite the students to join in reading "Creator of the stars of night." found on Poster No. 7 in the Teacher's Packet. (The poster includes stanzas 1 and 3 of this Advent hymn from *The Hymnal 1982*, 60; *We Sing of God*, 13.) If there are three purple and one pink candles in your wreath, light the pink candle along with two purple ones.

The teacher then says:

Let us pray. (Use the Collect "Fourth Sunday of Advent," above, or a prayer of your own choosing.)

The chosen student lector reads from the class Bible (NRSV):

A Reading from the Gospel of Matthew, chapter 1, verses 1 and 2, and verses 16 and 17.

Unit II. Parables of Promise—Session 3
Chalice Year Intermediate—Copyright © 2000 Virginia Theological Sminary and Morehouse Publishing

An account of the genealogy of Jesus the Messiah, the son of David, the son of Abraham. Abraham was the father of Isaac, and Isaac the father of Jacob, and Jacob the father of Judah and his brothers, . . . (The generations continued to) . . . Joseph the husband of Mary, of whom Jesus was born, who is called the Messiah.

So all the generations from Abraham to David are fourteen generations; and from David to the deportation to Babylon, fourteen generations; and from the deportation to Babylon to the Messiah, fourteen generations.

Reader: The Word of the Lord.
Response: Thanks be to God.

Extinguish the candles after the reading (above). Plan to re-light them just before the Going Forth.

INTRODUCING THE STORY
(Time: 10 minutes)

Begin by drawing a simple family tree on the chalkboard or a newsprint easel. Show spaces for several generations and encourage the students to think about how their own families' genealogies might look on such a chart. Many students have made family trees in school. Invite class members to share some of the information they discovered about their families.

Explain that the Hebrew ancestors of Jesus were careful in keeping family records. This was important to their identity, for they wanted always to remember all who had gone before them in the long story of their relationship to God as a chosen people.

Note aloud that the stories of Jesus' birth are found only in the *Gospels of Matthew* and *Luke*. The two stories are very different. We often piece them together at our Christmas celebrations. The writer of *Matthew* begins with Jesus' family tree (genealogy). This was to show that Jesus was truly the long-expected Messiah—a descendant of King David.

Ask the students to turn in their Bibles to *Matthew 1*, to examine the genealogy of Jesus. Draw on the material in Getting Ready (above) and the main story in the student newspaper, *Community Times* (Unit II, Issue 3) for additional details. The article begins with information about Mary and Joseph and then describes some of the people listed in the *Matthew* passage, such as Kings Solomon and David and David's great-grandmother Ruth. Include facts you know about these ancestors to make your story more interesting. Ask: What other names do you know?

Stress the fact that Matthew interprets the birth of Christ to be a new "genesis" (a new beginning) that God was undertaking for the benefit of humanity. Jesus, Son of Mary would be the Savior of the world.

EXPLORING
(Time: 15–20 minutes)

Option 1. *Matthew's* Genealogy

Many biblical names are unfamiliar to modern readers. Intermediate students often enjoy learning to pronounce strange, new words. Many Bibles include markings that show correct vowel sounds and accented symbols. Before beginning this activity, work with class members to practice saying the names of people and places in the Bible.

Then invite the class to work on a rap presentation of *Matthew 1*. The class can work as a whole or in three smaller groups, with each group taking one of *Matthew's* three divisions. Encourage students to include other information in their rap if they want to. For example, in introducing the third division, they may want to include a few mournful phrases that describe the deportation to Babylon.

After ten or fifteen minutes, ask the groups to perform their rap songs about the genealogy of Jesus. If the group is interested, they could perform the songs at an appropriate gathering of the congregation.

Option 2. Making Time Lines

For each class member, prepare a sheet of white 8 1/2 x 14 paper with a 10-inch straight line in the center. The sheets are to be used for creating a horizontal timeline. Invite the students to work alone or in teams to place biblical names and events on the line, beginning with Abraham at the left and moving to the present (at the right). Suggest that the finished lines should show David, the people's exile into Babylon and their return, and the birth of Jesus. Ask: What would you enter on the line between Jesus' birth and the present? Students may add illustrations on the page if they wish. Encourage the students to share with one another and to use Bible dictionaries if they need help.

Option 3. Matching Exercise

Turn in the student newspaper, *Community Times*, Unit II, Issue 3, to the matching exercise titled "Who

Am I?" Students may work individually, in pairs, or as a total group.

MUSIC
(Time: 10 minutes)

Reintroduce the Advent hymn, "Prepare the way, O Zion, your Christ is drawing near" *(The Hymnal 1982,* 65; *We Sing of God,* 14*).* Read or listen to it on the *Children Sing!* tape. Point out that "Zion" is a term for Israel, the chosen people of God. But it is also used for the Church as a faithful community devoted to the worship of God.

CONNECTING/SPEAKING OUT
(Time: 15–20 minutes)

Option 1. Group Discussion

Focus on the concept of a "new beginning." Ask the class members to think about times in their experience when they or people they know have made a new beginning. Ask if anyone remembers moving to a new house or a new city or town; entering a new school; going into a new classroom at school or church; or changing appearances by getting new a haircut or wearing different clothes.

Ask the group to share their feelings about new beginnings. Did they feel excited? Scared? Did they face new experiences with fear or anticipation? Did feelings change about places and people who had been familiar?

Describe the birth of Jesus, the long-expected Messiah, as a new beginning. God was breaking into human history in a new way. People had some of the same feelings class members described. Ask: How would the news of Jesus' coming cause people to feel about their past? Their future? How does Jesus help us make new beginnings in our own lives?

Option 2. Current Events

Matthew's genealogy of Jesus the Messiah includes pioneers and key figures in the history of God's people. At Jesus' birth, the people around him could recall with gladness all that the prophets had said about the Savior whom God would send.

The sharing of genealogies in Scripture did not begin with *Matthew.* Tracing the history of God's people through the generations was common in the Hebrew tradition. Ask the students to find and scan one or more of the following: *Genesis 5* (Adam through the sons of Noah); *Genesis 10* (descendants of Noah's sons); *I Chronicles,* chapters 1-8 (all the generations up to the time of the exile in Babylon). Read together the summary in *I Chronicles 9:1-2.* Ask: Do you find any names that are also in *Matthew?*

REFLECTING
(Time: 10 minutes)

Hand out the students' reflection envelopes and set up the Reflection Center as described in Session 1. Make certain that a good supply of varied art materials is on hand.

Offer directions for the students' responses. For this session, use the following:

Imagine a year in the far distant future, a hundred or more years from now. Think about young persons living in that future time. What will they remember about Christians from the past? Would you be one of their spiritual ancestors? If so, what would you like them to know about you? What kind of ancestor do you hope to be for a coming generation?

Write or draw your thoughts about being a spiritual ancestor. When you have finished, add a brief written prayer.

LEARNING SKILLS
(Time: 10–15 minutes)

Option 1. Class Memory Challenge

Invite the students to call out the chapter numbers for the parables from *Matthew* that have been memorized in Sessions 1 and 2. For this session, the task is to learn the chapter locations for two more parables that appear only in the first Gospel: "Two Sons" (chapter 21) and "Talents" (chapter 25).

Ask class members to find the stories in their Bibles. One way to remember the Parable of the Two Sons would be to think of two sons and one father (2-1, to suggest "chapter 21").

See the chart that appears in the student newspaper, *Community Times,* Unit II, Issue 3.

Option 2. Learning Scripture

Ask whether class members have learned verses given in the previous sessions. Add paper triangles to the Epiphany Star mosaic as described in Session 1.

Encourage students to memorize *Matthew 1:17* or *Mark 1:7-8* before the next class session.

See "Learning Scripture" in the student newspaper, *Community Times.*

ONGOING PROJECT
(Time: 5–10 minutes)

See Session 1 for a description of this project. For the third cloth panel, design an enlarged version of a Jesse tree as pictured on Symbol Card 12 and in the student newspaper, *Community Times*, Unit II, Issue 3. Add the new panel to the display alongside the two that were completed in previous sessions.

SYMBOL CARD and TREASUREBOOK

Card 12 contains a Jesse tree, a verse of Scripture, and an explanation on the back.

Ask the students to read in *Chalice Year Treasurebook*, Part II, Section 2, a brief discussion on the mission of Jesus as teacher, preacher, and healer. Which mission interests you the most?

GOING FORTH

Re-light the candles on the Advent wreath. The teacher or a student will say the following, pausing for the students' response of "Lord, have mercy":

> With all our heart and with all our mind, let us pray to the Lord, saying, "Lord, have mercy." For the peace from above, for the loving kindness of God, and for the salvation of our souls, let us pray to the Lord.
> *Lord, have mercy.*
> For the peace of the world, for the welfare of the holy Church of God, and for the unity of all people, let us pray to the Lord.
> *Lord, have mercy.*
> For _____ [learners may add their own petitions], let us pray to the Lord.
> *Lord, have mercy.*
> From The Prayers of the People
> *The Book of Common Prayer*, pp. 383-384

Teacher: Let us go forth in the name of Christ.
Students: Thanks be to God.

TEACHER'S ASSESSMENT

Reflect on the students' response to this session's emphasis on Jesus' birth in relation to the history of Israel. Was it clear to the class members that Jesus the Messiah belonged to a centuries-long family tradition? How well are the class members able to handle concepts involving past, present, and future time?

LOOKING AHEAD

In preparation for the next session, read the story of Jesus' birth *(Luke 2:1-20)*. Try to recall what interested you most when you heard this story as a young person of the intermediate-age level. What kinds of knowledge have you gained through the years that have added to your understanding of the story?

PARABLES OF PROMISE

SESSION 4
THE MESSIAH IS BORN

FOCUS

Centuries of waiting and preparing had ended for the people of God—and months of waiting had ended for Mary and Joseph. In Bethlehem, city of David, the child Jesus was born. The students should be able to retell the Nativity story. They should also be able to explain the significance of Jesus' being born in Bethlehem of Judea.

GETTING READY

Scholars have not been able to reconcile a puzzling difference of ten years or more between the implied dates of the Nativity in *Matthew* and in *Luke*.

According to *Luke 2:1-20*, Jesus' birth occurred in the time of the Emperor Augustus and a local governor named Quirinius. Joseph and Mary had traveled to Bethlehem because of a general enrollment (census) required by the Roman government that occupied their land.

This account does not square with data available outside the New Testament. There is no record of a worldwide census under Caesar Augustus. And Quirinius did not serve as local governor until 6-7 CE.

The story in *Matthew* places Jesus' birth in the time of Herod, king in Jerusalem *(Matthew 2:1)*. Thus Jesus' birth could have been no later than 4 BCE, which was the year Herod died.

Most researchers have concluded that Luke did not have access to accurate dates. But far more important than the historical details is the main thrust of the accounts in both *Matthew* and *Luke*: Jesus' Nativity heralded the coming of the long-awaited Messiah. His birth in Bethlehem fulfilled the words of the prophet Micah:

"But you, O Bethlehem . . . , who are one of the little clans of Judah, from you shall come forth for me one who is to rule in Israel, whose origin is from old, from ancient days" *(Micah 5:2)*. See *Matthew 2:6*.

Bethlehem was the ancestral home of King David and Jesus' birth in that place was a sign that he was to be the long-expected "Son of David" (Messiah). See *Luke 2:11*. The Child born to the Virgin Mary would be the Savior of the whole world.

> O God, who wonderfully created, and yet more wonderfully restored, the dignity of human nature: Grant that we may share the divine life of him who humbled himself to share our humanity, your Son Jesus Christ; who lives and reigns with you, in the unity of the Holy Spirit, one God, for ever and ever. *Amen.*
>
> Second Sunday after Christmas Day
> *The Book of Common Prayer*, p. 214

TEACHING TIP

During the weeks before Christmas, the shopping malls and the commercials on radio and television portray a sentimental season of gift-sharing and eager celebration. It is easy for all of us to be caught up in these seasonal activities. The message of Christ's birth and infancy, preserved in Scripture and proclaimed in the Church, is very different from the secular version of Christmas. Point out the distinction between popular culture and the Christian faith. Stress the presence of God, who loved us enough to send Jesus as our Savior.

GATHERING

As the students arrive, replenish the greens on the Advent wreath and prepare to gather around it. When everyone is present, light four candles. Invite the students to join in a choral reading of "Creator of the stars of night," found on Poster No. 7 in the Teacher's

Packet. (The poster includes stanzas 1 and 3 of this Advent hymn from *The Hymnal 1982*, 60; *We Sing of God*, 13.)

The teacher then says:

Let us pray. (Use the Collect "Second Sunday after Christmas Day," above, or a prayer of your own choosing.)

The chosen student lector reads from the class Bible (NRSV):

A Reading from the Gospel of Luke, chapter 2, verses 1 through 14.

In those days a decree went out from Emperor Augustus that all the world should be registered. This was the first registration and was taken while Quirinius was governor of Syria. All went to their own towns to be registered. Joseph also went from the town of Nazareth in Galilee to Judea, to the city of David called Bethlehem, because he was descended from the house and family of David. He went to be registered with Mary, to whom he was engaged and who was expecting a child. While they were there, the time came for her to deliver her child. And she gave birth to her firstborn son and wrapped him in bands of cloth, and laid him in a manger, because there was no place for them in the inn.

In that region there were shepherds living in the fields, keeping watch over their flock by night. Then an angel of the Lord stood before them, and the glory of the Lord shone around them, and they were terrified. But the angel said to them, "Do not be afraid; for see—I am bringing you good news of great joy for all the people: to you is born this day in the city of David a Savior, who is the Messiah, the Lord. This will be a sign for you: you will find a child wrapped in bands of cloth and lying in a manger." And suddenly there was with the angel a multitude of the heavenly host, praising God and saying,

"Glory to God in the highest heaven, and on earth peace among those whom he favors!"

Reader: The Word of the Lord.
Response: Thanks be to God.

Extinguish the candles on the wreath, and plan to re-light them at the Going Forth. If your wreath has a fifth, white Christ Candle, talk about how it is to be lit on Christmas Day and through the twelve days of the season.

INTRODUCING THE STORY
(Time: 10 minutes)

Begin by speaking briefly about the period in Jewish history that surrounds Jesus' birth. The Roman government was in control and local kings and governors were subordinate to authorities in Rome. The people continued to hope for a day when they would be free under the reign of a Messiah sent from God.

Suggest that the students divide into two groups or teams. Ask each team to prepare a way of telling the story of Jesus' birth up through the visit of the Magi. Encourage them to reconstruct the events from memory and to avoid looking in the Bible for this exercise.

Call on each group to present their version of Jesus' infancy. Compare the stories. In what ways did they differ? Are they both accurate? Was anything left out?

Be alert to the students' use of details from the Gospels of *Matthew* and *Luke*. List these on a chalkboard or newsprint. You may want to read or tell the story of Jesus' birth from the student newspaper, *Community Times*, Unit II, Issue 4. It describes the crowded scene in Bethlehem and townspeople who shared the event with Mary and Joseph. Compare the facts you listed with those on page 2 in the story that compares the infancy narratives in the *Gospels of Matthew* and *Luke*.

Ask the students to turn in their Bibles to both *Matthew 1* and *Luke 2*, to find the accounts of Jesus' birth. Ask them to look for details they may have missed in their accounts. Do you need to add anything to the lists?

Point out that both Gospel writers agree on the central truth that Jesus was the expected Messiah, Son of David. His birth in Bethlehem, the city of David, was understood to be a sign that he was the very One for whom the people of God had waited such a long time.

EXPLORING
(Time: 15–20 minutes)

Option 1. St. Francis and the Creche

Tell the story about the legend of the first Christmas creche (see the student newspaper, *Community Times*). St. Francis of Assisi had struggled to find a way for people to understand the real meaning of Christmas. First he found the perfect place at the nearby hillside. When everything was ready, he led the villagers to the clearing.

In a cave stood a manger filled with straw surrounded by an ox and a small gray donkey. As St. Francis read the Christmas story, it came alive in a brand new way. Since that time, the creche (Nativity scene) has been a part of the Christmas celebration.

On a table, spread out pieces of junk or other materials you have collected, along with adhesive tape and glue. Ask the students to construct a creche using only the items on the table to remind others about the real meaning of Christmas. See how creative students can be in constructing their creche. Afterward, display it in the classroom or another place in the church.

Option 2. Making Ornaments

Obtain a supply of round wooden clothespins, pens and markers, bits of cloth, yarn, colored paper, and glue. Invite the students to choose figures from the Nativity story (the Holy Family, angels, shepherds, Magi) and create their versions of each one in the form of a Christmas tree ornament. A clothespin forms the head and body. Features and costumes can be made from the materials at hand.

Option 3. Word Puzzle

Turn in the student newspaper, *Community Times*, Unit II, Issue 4, to the word puzzle titled "Jesus' Birth." Students may work individually, in pairs, or as a total group.

MUSIC
(Time: 10 minutes)

Sing or listen on the *Children Sing!* tape "O little town of Bethlehem" *(The Hymnal 1982, 78, 79)*. This carol was written by a well-known Episcopal preacher and teacher, Phillips Brooks (1835-1893). Note especially the phrase, "the hopes and fears of all the years." How has Jesus' birth affected both our hopes and our fears? If time permits, try both tunes from the hymnal. Which of these do the students prefer?

CONNECTING/SPEAKING OUT
(Time: 15–20 minutes)

Option 1. Group Discussion

Ask: When do we have a census in our country? Why? What do we learn from asking all the questions on a census form? Point out that census-taking is an ancient custom.

Under the Roman government, periodic registrations (enrollments, censuses) were common, probably for the purpose of collecting taxes or conscripting people for military service. For example, a census occurred in Egypt every fourteen years. In *Luke's* story of Jesus' birth, Mary and Joseph went to Bethlehem, the city of his ancestors, for a registration.

Option 2. Current Events

It is common for nations and local groups to preserve the places where famous people in history were born. Invite the students to recall any birthplaces they may have seen or heard about (Presidents, writers, and others). Ask: Why do we like to make visits to these sites?

If possible, bring in picture books that have pictures of the countryside in modern Israel. Note that annual celebrations are held during the Christmas season in Bethlehem where Jesus was born. How would it feel to be in the place where Mary gave birth to the Christ Child? How is the area similar to or different from the place where you live?

REFLECTING
(Time: 10 minutes)

Give out the reflection envelopes, and arrange the Reflection Center as described in Session 1. Replenish art supplies.

Offer direction for the students' responses, using the following:

Pretend that you are living in the time of Jesus' birth. You have heard about the babe lying in a manger, and you rush to see him with your very own eyes.

After you arrive home, you want to save your memories of this visit. What would you write down or draw as a reminder? Who else would be at the manger?

When you have completed either writing or drawing your reflections, write a brief prayer.

LEARNING SKILLS
(Time: 10–15 minutes)

Option 1. Class Memory Challenge

Review the parable locations memorized in earlier sessions of the Unit, all of which are found only in *Matthew*. This session's challenge focuses on two parables from a group that appear only in the *Gospel of Luke*. The selected stories are "Good Samaritan" (chapter 10) and "Friend at Midnight" (chapter 11).

Ask the students to locate the parables in their Bibles. The Parable of the Good Samaritan is one of the best-known teachings of Jesus. Note that the Parable of the Friend at Midnight *(Luke 11:5-13)* comes immediately after *Luke's* version of the Lord's Prayer, as Jesus teaches the importance of praying persistently.

Refer to the Memory Challenge block in the student newspaper, *Community Times*, Unit II, Issue 4.

Option 2. Learning Scripture

For each student who has learned a verse, add a paper triangle to the Epiphany Star mosaic described in Session 1.

Encourage students to memorize *Luke 2:7* or *Luke 2:14* before the next class session.

See "Learning Scripture" in the student newspaper, *Community Times*.

ONGOING PROJECT
(Time: 5–10 minutes)

For this session, make a fourth cloth panel as described in Session 1. Prepare an enlarged version of a Nativity creche similar to the one pictured on Symbol Card 13 and in the student newspaper, *Community Times*, Unit II, Issue 4. Display the panel alongside the Advent wreath, symbol for John the Baptist, and the Jesse tree.

If this project was not started in earlier sessions, the class members may want to form teams to complete four panels at one time. The fifth and final panel will be an Epiphany star, to be added at the next session.

SYMBOL CARD and TREASUREBOOK

Card 13 contains a creche, a verse of Scripture, and an explanation on the back.

Encourage the students to look again at *Chalice Year Treasurebook*, Part II, Section 3. How does the story of Jesus' infancy fit into the picture of Jesus as Messiah?

GOING FORTH

Re-light all the candles on the Advent wreath. The teacher or a student will say the following, pausing for the students' response of "Lord, have mercy":

> With all our heart and with all our mind, let us pray to the Lord, saying, "Lord, have mercy."

For the peace from above, for the loving kindness of God, and for the salvation of our souls, let us pray to the Lord.
Lord, have mercy.

For the peace of the world, for the welfare of the holy Church of God, and for the unity of all people, let us pray to the Lord.
Lord, have mercy.

For _____ [learners may add their own petitions], let us pray to the Lord.
Lord, have mercy.

> From The Prayers of the People
> *The Book of Common Prayer*, pp. 383–384

Teacher: Let us go forth in the name of Christ.
Students: Thanks be to God.

TEACHER'S ASSESSMENT

As a result of this session's activities, have the students gained an understanding of the historical context for Jesus' birth? How do they express their understanding of the Nativity's significance?

LOOKING AHEAD

The next session, on the theme of Epiphany, focuses on *Matthew's* account of the Holy Family's flight into Egypt to escape Herod. In preparation, think and pray about reasons people have had to leave their homes in recent history.

PARABLES OF PROMISE

SESSION 5
FLIGHT INTO EGYPT

FOCUS

The visit of the Magi resulted in two warning dreams: The Wise Men were warned not to go back to see Herod, so they returned home by a different route. And Joseph was warned that Herod would seek to destroy Jesus. The students should be able to retell the story of the Holy Family's flight into Egypt.

GETTING READY

In *Matthew 2:13-23*, the infancy of Jesus is placed in the time of King Herod the Great. He had gained favor with Julius Caesar and was rewarded by the Romans who made him procurator of Judea in 47 BCE. Ten years later he became king and exercised power with great cruelty.

As Matthew tells it, Herod became alarmed at the news of Jesus' birth. He assumed, along with the Jews of his time, that the long-awaited Messiah would become an earthly king who could replace him. When the Magi arrived and were sent to Bethlehem to find the infant Jesus, Herod asked them to return and let him know where they found the Child so that he could "also go and pay him homage" *(Matthew 2:8)*.

When Herod discovered he had been tricked by the Wise Men, who had been warned in a dream not to return to Jerusalem, he was furious. Fearing that he might lose his kingship, Herod ordered the killing of all infant boys in Bethlehem who were two years old and under. He assumed this would include Jesus. Herod died a short time after this. He never knew that Joseph had heeded a dream of his own, taking Mary and the Child to Egypt.

Egypt played a significant role in Hebrew history, frequently as a place of refuge. Patriarchs from Abraham to Jacob and his sons had gone to that country to survive in times of crisis. Joseph, son of Jacob, ended up in the household of Pharaoh, where he was able to help his family in a period of famine.

It does not surprise us that Joseph, husband of Mary, acted on a dream message and took Mary and Jesus to Egypt. After the death of Herod, Joseph feared his successor, Archelaus. Again, he was led through a dream to return to Nazareth of Galilee rather than to Bethlehem of Judea.

> Assist us mercifully, O Lord, in these our supplications and prayers, and dispose the way of your servants towards the attainment of everlasting salvation; that, among all the changes and chances of this mortal life, they may ever be defended by your gracious and ready help; through Jesus Christ our Lord. *Amen.*
> For Protection
> *The Book of Common Prayer*, p. 832

TEACHING TIP

Intermediate-age students are often very concerned about fairness—at school, in sports, in their families, and among their friends. The story of the killing of the innocents is the height of unfairness. Use this story to describe the harsh world that Jesus entered. His message of God's love and the coming reign of God was counter to the prevailing culture and the people's hopes for an earthly messiah who would overthrow foreign oppression.

GATHERING

As the students arrive, invite them to reflect on the Advent wreath. Its candles may be burned low by now. The seasons of Advent and Christmas have been observed. When everyone is present, gather around a Christ Candle and light it. (This may be the fifth candle of the wreath, or you may need to provide a large white candle for this session.)

Unit II. Parables of Promise—Session 5
Chalice Year Intermediate—Copyright © 2000 Virginia Theological Sminary and Morehouse Publishing

Encourage the group to share special events or traditions they celebrated with family and friends during the holidays. Invite the class members to say or sing together the words of the familiar first stanza of "We three kings of Orient are" *(The Hymnal 1982, 128; We Sing of God, 27).*

When everyone is present, the teacher says:

Let us pray. (Use the prayer "For Protection," above, or a prayer of your own choosing.)

The chosen student lector reads from the class Bible (NRSV):

A Reading from the Gospel of Matthew, chapter 2, verses 13 through 15.

Now after the (wise men) had left, an angel of the Lord appeared to Joseph in a dream and said, "Get up, take the child and his mother, and flee to Egypt, and remain there until I tell you; for Herod is about to search for the child, to destroy him." Then Joseph got up, took the child and his mother by night, and went to Egypt, and remained there until the death of Herod. This was to fulfill what had been spoken by the Lord through the prophet, "Out of Egypt I have called my son."

Reader: The Word of the Lord.
Response: Thanks be to God.

Extinguish the Christ Candle and plan to re-light it for the Going Forth.

INTRODUCING THE STORY
(Time: 10 minutes)

Display Poster No. 10 from the Teacher's Packet showing carvings of the Magi who visited the Christ Child in Bethlehem, the Holy Family, and the shepherds. Invite the students to comment on the artist's impressions.

Tell, in your own words, the story found in *Matthew 2.* Stress the danger posed by Herod the Great and emphasize the significance of the dreams by which God offered guidance to the Wise Men and assisted Joseph in protecting the Christ Child.

Using the student newspaper, *Community Times* (Unit II, Issue 5), for ideas, describe Joseph's dream and how he abruptly left Bethlehem for Egypt. Ask the students to turn in their Bibles to *Matthew 2:12-23.* In which verses does the word "dream" appear? Who had the dreams? What was the message of each dream? How seriously were the dreams taken?

Briefly describe Epiphany as a time to proclaim that Jesus Christ came for the sake of the whole world. The Wise Men symbolize the people of the non-Jewish world to whom God reached out in the sending of God's son.

Remind the students that the Church remembers the infants who were slaughtered in Jerusalem in its observance of Holy Innocents' Day, December 28. See page 3 of the student newspaper for more information. (You may want to suggest that the class members observe a moment of silence in remembrance of the innocent children and their families who suffered their loss.)

Point out the importance of Egypt as a place of refuge for figures in Hebrew history. (See Getting Ready, above.)

EXPLORING
(Time: 15–20 minutes)

Option 1. Events in Order

Prepare a scrambled list of events from *Matthew 2,* and give a copy with each student. Ask the class members to work in groups to unscramble the list, putting the events in proper sequence. When they are finished, the groups can compare their work with one another. Following is a suggested scrambling:

Herod summons Wise Men secretly; Wise Men warned in a dream; Joseph takes his family to Egypt; Bethlehem children killed; Wise Men return home by a different way; an angel appears to Joseph in a dream; Wise Men bow down and pay homage to Jesus; Archelaus succeeds Herod; Herod is infuriated; Joseph and his family settle in Nazareth; Wise Men follow a star to Jerusalem; Joseph is visited by an angel in a dream; Wise Men present gifts to Jesus; Jesus is born in Bethlehem during Herod's reign.

(Place the list vertically on the sheet, with a short blank line before each item, so that students may number them to indicate the correct order.)

Option 2. Epiphany Gift

Epiphany is a season of light. Invite the students to prepare miniature lights to be shared with residents of a nearby nursing home or with selected shut-ins or hospital patients. For this project, assemble small white candles, molding clay, paper placemats, construction paper, pens, and markers.

Make appropriate candle holders from the clay. Write or draw messages on Epiphany cards made from construction paper. The finished items can be assembled by placing the candles in their holders on individual place mats, with a card attached just below each candle.

Option 3. Secret Code

Turn in the student newspaper, *Community Times*, Unit II, Issue 5, to the secret code titled "Fulfillment." Students may work individually, in pairs, or as a total group.

MUSIC
(Time: 10 minutes)

Sing with the *Children Sing!* tape "What star is this, with beams so bright" *(The Hymnal 1982*, 124; *We Sing of God*, 26). Notice that the Wise Men are called "Gentiles" in stanza 1, and "eastern sages" in stanza 2. Stanza 4 is a prayer addressed to Jesus. What does the prayer ask?

CONNECTING/SPEAKING OUT
(Time: 15–20 minutes)

Option 1. Group Discussion

Focus on the Wise Men's visit. Ask: Where could they have come from? What was the significance of their gifts to the Christ Child? Why did King Herod ask the Wise Men to return to Jerusalem?

Tell the group the following scenario: You are the director of a Christmas pageant set in the present. You must decide where Jesus will be born and who will visit. What countries will your Magi come from? What will they bring to the Christ child?

In discussion, underscore the sense of mystery surrounding this story in *Matthew*. Jesus came into the world as a hidden king. He was not recognized and honored by his own people. But visitors appeared from the non-Jewish world and paid him homage. The Magi's gifts were symbols of royalty and honor.

Option 2. Current Events

Herod's order that children in Jerusalem be slaughtered is a grim reminder that human history, including our own time, is filled with cases of cruel abuse and outright persecution of innocent people. Ask the students to recall any such incidents they know about.

Share examples of refugee people in recent times, such as families leaving Cuba or Haiti by boat or seeking safety from armed conflict in various parts of the world. In every instance, many young children are among the victims.

Ask: Where can refugees turn for help? What are some of the organizations who offer gifts and support? (Describe the role of the Presiding Bishop's Fund for World Relief.)

REFLECTING
(Time: 10 minutes)

Distribute the reflection envelopes and set up the Reflection Center as described in Session 1.

Direct the students to think about the following:

Close your eyes and imagine that you are one of the Wise Men—or that you are Joseph around the time of the Wise Men's visit. Which one do you choose to be?

Now you lie down to sleep and you have a very vivid dream. If you are a Wise Man, your dream includes a serious warning. What will you do about it? If you are Joseph, an angel appears in your dream. What does the angel say? What will you do?

Write or draw your reflections. When you have finished, write a brief prayer.

LEARNING SKILLS
(Time: 10–15 minutes)

Option 1. Class Memory Challenge

Review parables of Jesus memorized in earlier sessions, along with their locations by chapter number. For this session, focus on two more parables that are found only in the *Gospel of Luke*: "Rich Fool" (chapter 12) and "Great Banquet (Dinner)" (chapter 14).

Ask the class members to find the stories in their Bibles. Invite the group to link the chapter numbers with the titles.

Refer to the Memory Challenge chart provided in the student newspaper, *Community Times*, Unit II, Issue 5.

Option 2. Learning Scripture

Find out if class members have learned verses given in the previous sessions. Add paper triangles to the Epiphany Star mosaic described in Session 1.

Encourage students to memorize *Matthew 2:6* or *Matthew 2:15b* before the next class session.

See "Learning Scripture" in the student newspaper, *Community Times*.

ONGOING PROJECT
(Time: 5–10 minutes)

This ongoing project is to be completed at this session. For the final cloth panel in the series of five, create an Epiphany star like the one pictured on Symbol Card 14 and in the student newspaper, *Community Times*, Unit II, Issue 5.

The total display can be shared with the entire congregation, either in an assembly room or as a traveling exhibit to be shown to other classes. The project's completion offers a chance for the students to reflect on the symbols' meanings and the significance of the seasons, Advent through Epiphany.

SYMBOL CARD and TREASUREBOOK

Card 14 contains an Epiphany star, a verse of Scripture, and an explanation on the back.

Suggest that the students read in the *Chalice Year Treasurebook*, Part II, Section 3, to review the role of Jesus as Messiah.

GOING FORTH

Re-light the Christ Candle. The teacher or a student will say the following, pausing for the students' response of "Lord, have mercy":

> With all our heart and with all our mind, let us pray to the Lord, saying, "Lord, have mercy."
>
> For the peace from above, for the loving kindness of God, and for the salvation of our souls, let us pray to the Lord.
> *Lord, have mercy.*
> For the peace of the world, for the welfare of the holy Church of God, and for the unity of all people, let us pray to the Lord.
> *Lord, have mercy.*
> For _____ [learners may add their own petitions], let us pray to the Lord.
> *Lord, have mercy.*
>
> From The Prayers of the People
> *The Book of Common Prayer*, pp. 383-384

Teacher: Let us go forth in the name of Christ.
Students: Thanks be to God.

TEACHER'S ASSESSMENT

More than likely, the students were well acquainted with the story of the Wise Men's visit to Bethlehem. How did they react to this session, with its emphasis on the flight into Egypt? Did they appear to gain new information about Herod's period in history? How do they relate the slaughter of the Innocents to contemporary events?

LOOKING AHEAD

The next four sessions in this Unit focus on Jesus' parables of promise about the Kingdom of God. The first of these will be the parable of the sower (or the parable of the soils). Think about the parable prayerfully. How do Jesus' words speak to you?

PARABLES OF PROMISE
SESSION 6
PARABLE OF THE SOWER

FOCUS

Jesus' story of the sower who scatters seed freely assures us that hearers of the word of God who accept it will bear fruit—that is, they will have productive lives in the kingdom of God. The students should be able to retell the parable with an emphasis on the promise that God acts in the lives of people who are attentive to God's good news in Christ.

GETTING READY

The traditional name for Jesus' teaching in *Mark 4:2-20* is "the parable of the sower." All Christians are called by God to "sow" the good news of the Gospel. We cannot always control the way people respond to that message: We must trust that God will use the gift of our words and actions.

In the story, the seed scattered by a sower fell on four kinds of soil, and each of these had characteristics that either prevented or promoted growth. This parable also appears in *Matthew 13* and *Luke 8*.

In the Near East of Jesus' day, the typical method of planting was to rake and hoe the area to work the seed into the soil. It was expected that some seeds would go to waste in the process. The parable describes what happens as the seeds fall on the varied surfaces.

Jesus' parable—interpreted in the same way in the three Gospels—takes the form of a challenge. As hearers of the Lord's word, we have a choice before us: We can be like the poor soils or we can be the good ground that brings growth and a good harvest.

The parable also reminds us that seeds must first be planted before anything can grow.

Almighty God, Lord of heaven and earth: We humbly pray that your gracious providence may give and preserve to our use the harvests of the land and of the seas, and may prosper all who labor to gather them, that we, who are constantly receiving good things from your hand, may always give you thanks; through Jesus Christ our Lord, who lives and reigns with you and the Holy Spirit, one God, for ever and ever. *Amen.*

For fruitful seasons
The Book of Common Prayer, p. 258-259

TEACHING TIP

Students of the intermediate-age level have varying abilities to use analogies and metaphors. While some find it easy to think abstractly, most still think very concretely. Offer frequent opportunities for students to explore and discuss Jesus' parables and teachings. Encourage them to make concrete connections of the stories to their own experiences.

GATHERING

As the students arrive, direct their attention to the enlarged photograph from Poster No. 11 in the Teacher's Packet, showing soil that is severely cracked with a few green plants growing from it. Stimulate discussion of the picture by asking: What may have caused the soil to develop such fissures? What do you think will happen to the plants? If you were trying to grow plants or grass in this kind of soil, what would you do about it? Why?

When everyone is present, say:

Let us pray. (Use the Collect "For fruitful seasons," above, or a prayer of your own choosing.)

The chosen student lector reads from the class Bible (NRSV):

A Reading from the Gospel of Mark, chapter 4, verses 2 through 9.

(Jesus) began to teach them many things in parables, and in his teaching he said to them: "Listen! A sower went out to sow. And as he sowed, some seed fell on the path, and the birds came and ate it up. Other seed fell on rocky ground, where it did not have much soil, and it sprang up quickly, since it had no depth of soil. And when the sun rose, it was scorched; and since it had no root, it withered away. Other seed fell among thorns, and the thorns grew up and choked it, and it yielded no grain. Other seed fell into good soil and brought forth grain, growing up and yielding thirty and sixty and a hundredfold." And he said, "Let anyone with ears to hear listen!"

Reader: The Word of the Lord.
Response: Thanks be to God.

INTRODUCING THE STORY
(Time: 10 minutes)

Begin by announcing that this is the first of four study sessions on Jesus' teaching through the use of parables. Write the word "parable" on a chalkboard or newsprint. See if anyone knows the meaning of the word. Explain that Jesus used stories to help people better understand his message.

Try to give examples the students may be familiar with, such as the story of the tortoise and the hare. Briefly tell the story of the race between the animals and how the hare's carelessness allowed the plodding tortoise to win the race. This familiar fable has a "moral" just as Jesus' parables have deeper meanings.

We hear Jesus' parables over and over, but each time they seem to speak to us in different ways. We can learn new things from these teachings all our lives.

Explain that the first parable the group will examine appears in *Mark, Matthew,* and *Luke*. Mark's version was probably written down first.

Tell the story in your own words from *Mark 4:1-9*. Use the story in the student newspaper, *Community Times* (Unit II, Issue 6), to describe where Jesus was teaching and who was in the crowd.

Encourage the students to explain what they think the parable is about. Ask: Why would Jesus talk about farming? What did Jesus want his disciples to learn? Which part of the story did you identify with?

Ask the students to turn in their Bibles to *Mark 4:1-9* to find Jesus' parable of the sower. Then suggest that they locate the same parable in *Matthew 13:1-9* and *Luke 8:4-8*. What are the similarities and differences among the three versions?

EXPLORING
(Time: 15–20 minutes)

Option 1. Parable Drama

Good teachers often use stories to help students understand lessons that may be difficult to understand. Drama and storytelling are closely related; understanding sometimes comes when words are put into action.

Act out the parable of the sower. Assign one person to be the sower and others to be birds and seeds. Assign at least four students to be seeds to fall on 1.) a pathway, 2.) rocky ground, 3.) thorns, and 4.) good soil. Another student can be the sun. The teacher or a volunteer can read the story from the Bible or tell it in their own words.

Replay the drama to give everyone in the class a chance to be an actor. Encourage the "seeds" to be as creative as possible as they dry up or thrive in the soil. Afterward, talk about the meaning of the parable.

Option 2. Depicting the Sower

Spend a few minutes talking about things the students like to do that they do well. Pass out paper and markers and ask each person to draw a stick figure that represents him or her.

Based on the earlier discussion, ask the class members to add features that represent things they like to do and things they do well. Label each feature that is added. For example, a soccer player might draw a foot in his or her stick figure, while an artist might draw a hand with a paintbrush. Someone who is known for kindness could add a big heart.

Ask the students to share their drawings when everyone is finished. Put each drawing on a bulletin board or hang them from a string in the room. Inform the students that they all have gifts that enable them to be sowers. Ask: How can your gifts be used to help others hear Jesus' good news? Brainstorm ways that the group's gifts could be used to help others and to spread the good news of the Gospel.

Option 3. Word Puzzle

Turn in the student newspaper, *Community Times*, Unit II, Issue 6, to the word puzzle titled "Soils." Students may work individually, in pairs, or as a total group.

MUSIC
(Time: 10 minutes)

Listen on the *Children Sing!* tape to "Almighty God, your word is cast" *(The Hymnal 1982,* 588, 589*)*. Read the words in unison, pausing after each stanza. Then sing the tune. Ask: How has the hymn writer interpreted Jesus' parable?

CONNECTING/SPEAKING OUT
(Time: 15–20 minutes)

Option 1. Group Discussion

Jesus' disciples asked him privately to interpret his parables. Jesus gave a detailed explanation of the parable of the sower in *Mark 4:13-20*. Assist the students in listing the analogies that are used. On a chalkboard or newsprint, print the headings: "Parable" and "Meaning." Under the first heading, list words and phrases from the parable, including sower, birds, seed, on the path, rocky ground, thorns, good soil, grain.

Ask the class members to help you find meanings for each word. Ask questions to guide the discussion. For example, What happened to the seed sown along the pathway? Who is compared to seed along the path? (See *Mark 4:15*) In your life, who are the birds?

What happened to seed planted on rocky ground? Whose lives are like that? (*Mark 4:16-17*).

What happened to seed that grew up among thorns? Whose life turns out to be like that? (*Mark 4:18-19*)

What resulted when seed was sown on good soil? Who are the people who bear good fruit in their lives? (*Mark 4:20*)

In the parable, the good soil resulted in a big harvest of grain. Ask the students to name things that could represent the grain in the parable. For example, helping a younger sibling with homework without being asked or comforting a friend who is lonely.

Option 2. Current Events

In our present-day world, we observe many different ways people show their faith and obedience to God. While some persons and groups are indifferent to the Church's teaching, many other people take the word of God seriously and devote themselves to living productive and healthy lives.

Talk about the different opportunities people have been offered to serve God at your church and in the community. Ask: What activities do you find most interesting?

Explore groups or events in which the students could participate. As a group, select one activity that class members would like to be involved in. Contact the appropriate person to find out how the class can be like the seed that fell on good soil.

REFLECTING
(Time: 10 minutes)

Distribute the students' reflection envelopes and arrange the Reflection Center as described in Session 1. Replenish the art supplies if necessary.

For this session offer the following directions:

Think about your own life, now and in the future. How would you like God to help you to bear good fruit? What attitudes or characteristics would you like to develop?

Name to yourself the gifts that God gave you to serve others and how you can best use these gifts.

Write down a promise to God or yourself or write some of your personal hopes and resolutions. If you wish, illustrate your writing with simple drawings. When you have finished, compose a short prayer.

LEARNING SKILLS
(Time: 10–15 minutes)

Option 1. Class Memory Challenge

Invite the class members to form small groups for reviewing the parable titles and chapters memorized in preceding sessions, from both *Matthew* and *Luke*.

For this session, turn to two more parables found only in the *Gospel of Luke*: "Lost Coin" and "Prodigal" (both found in chapter 15). A way to remember these stories is to associate "lost" with *Luke 15* (a lost coin and a lost son).

Call attention to the Memory Challenge chart in *Community Times*, Unit II, Issue 6.

Option 2. Learning Scripture

Find out whether class members have learned verses given in previous sessions. Add mosaic triangles to the Epiphany Star outline described in Session 1.

Encourage the students to memorize *Mark 4:2a* and *Mark 4:8* before the next class session.

See "Learning Scripture" in the student newspaper, *Community Times*.

ONGOING PROJECT
(Time: 5–10 minutes)

For Sessions 6-9, on parables of Jesus, produce a series of tape-recorded interviews exploring people's reactions to the stories. The interviews will be conducted by students and the interviewees may be members of the congregation who represent all age groups. Decide whether to make the tapes with guests invited to the class sessions or with people interviewed by teams of roving reporters.

For each tape, the students will need to take these steps:

a. Choose a method of presenting the content of the parable. The Scripture could be printed on a card for easy reading, presented orally, or acted out.

b. As a group, compose suitable interview questions. Generally avoid yes/no-type questions.

c. Select a team to make the recording.

d. Decide whom to interview.

e. Complete the interview and arrange a time to play it for the whole group.

Examples of questions for this session: Some call this the Parable of the Sower and others call it the Parable of the Soils. Which name do you prefer? Why? When did you first hear this story? What does it mean to you?

SYMBOL CARD and TREASUREBOOK

Card 15 contains a seed bag and seeds, a verse of Scripture, and an explanation on the back.

Ask the students to read, in *Chalice Year Treasurebook*, Part II, Section 4, on the parable of the sower, also known as the parable of the soils. What do you think Jesus was teaching in this story?

GOING FORTH

Gather the group for the dismissal. The teacher or a student will say the following, pausing for the students' response of "Lord, have mercy":

With all our heart and with all our mind, let us pray to the Lord, saying, "Lord, have mercy."

For the peace from above, for the loving kindness of God, and for the salvation of our souls, let us pray to the Lord.
Lord, have mercy.

For the peace of the world, for the welfare of the holy Church of God, and for the unity of all people, let us pray to the Lord.
Lord, have mercy.

For _____ [learners may add their own petitions], let us pray to the Lord.
Lord, have mercy.

From The Prayers of the People
The Book of Common Prayer, pp. 383-384

Teacher: Let us go forth in the name of Christ.
Students: Thanks be to God.

TEACHER'S ASSESSMENT

This session on the parable of the sower invited the students to think about their own lives. From your observations, were they able to respond to the story? What kinds of help do the students need as they struggle to find personal meaning from Jesus' parables?

LOOKING AHEAD

The next session is on Jesus' parable of workers in a vineyard. The story requires interpretation of employee relations in Jesus' day. What questions does the parable raise for a modern reader?

PARABLES OF PROMISE

SESSION 7
PARABLE OF THE VINEYARD WORKERS

FOCUS

Jesus' parable of the workers in a vineyard describes a landowner who hired people at different times of the day but paid them all the same at sundown. It is understandable that those who worked longest thought this was unfair. The students should be able to explain that the parable focuses on the generosity of God. The promise of God's reign is that everyone can receive God's blessing.

GETTING READY

The parable of the workers in the vineyard *(Matthew 20:1-16)* frequently distracts modern readers who question whether the landowner acted justly. Such discussion misses the parable's urgent theme: All the workers received generous treatment. The parable is about God's generosity in welcoming all people into the kingdom of heaven.

In Jesus' time, a working day was from sunrise to the appearance of the stars. The landowner went out to recruit workers at four intervals during the day. Finally, he hired the last workers just an hour before quitting time.

According to Hebrew law *(Leviticus 19:13; Deuteronomy 24:15)*, laborers were to be paid no later than the end of each day. The usual daily wage was a denarius, and some scholars believe this to have been a generous amount.

Verbal agreement to work for this pay was binding in law. A worker who agreed to accept an employer's offered wage was bound by a solid contract. What other workers contracted to do, and the wage offered them, could not alter the binding agreement. This custom was so well understood in the Jewish tradition that any complaints about differences in pay were simply out of place.

In the parable, the owner paid everyone the same without regard to the number of hours they worked. The workers who toiled all or most of the day complained about their contracted wage. They had no legal grounds for complaint, but they felt they deserved a greater reward in appreciation for their steady work. The owner asked them, ". . . are you envious because I am generous?"

The workers were like the elder son in the parable of the Prodigal, who envied the attention lavished on his brother. He had no legal reason to complain but he, too, felt unappreciated.

We are not in a position to assess the fairness of God, because God's fairness and generosity operate on a different level we cannot fully understand. However, we can be reassured by this parable that shows us that God extends the same generosity to all.

Almighty God, whose Son Jesus Christ in his earthly life shared our toil and hallowed our labor: Be present with your people where they work; make those who carry on the industries and commerce of this land responsive to your will; and give to us all a pride in what we do, and a just return for our labor; through Jesus Christ our Lord, who lives and reigns with you, in the unity of the Holy Spirit, one God, now and for ever. *Amen.*

For commerce and industry
The Book of Common Prayer, p. 259

TEACHING TIP

Intermediate-age students are beginning to test their skills for debate about meanings. For teachers, this stage in young persons' development can be both an opportunity and a challenge. It is important to allow class members freedom to express their points of view and to encourage honest sharing. On the other hand, it may be necessary at times to guide discussions to prevent inaccuracies and misimpressions. In examining the parable of the vineyard workers, the students may be sidetracked into the "fairness" issue and miss the parable's message about God's generosity.

GATHERING

Display the photograph of a vineyard from Poster No. 12 in the Teacher's Packet. As the students arrive, invite them to speculate about the kinds of labor required for establishing and maintaining such a large planting of grapevines. How are the grapes protected? How is the harvesting done? Have class members ever visited or worked in a vineyard?

When everyone is present, say:

Let us pray. (Use the Collect "For commerce and industry," above, or a prayer of your own choosing.)

The chosen student lector reads from the class Bible (NRSV):

A Reading from the Gospel of Matthew, chapter 20, verses 1 through 16.

"For the kingdom of heaven is like a landowner who went out early in the morning to hire laborers for his vineyard. After agreeing with the laborers for the usual daily wage, he sent them into his vineyard. When he went out about nine o'clock, he saw others standing idle in the marketplace; and he said to them, 'You also go into the vineyard, and I will pay you whatever is right.' So they went. When he went out again about noon and about three o'clock, he did the same. And about five o'clock he went out and found others standing around; and he said to them, 'Why are you standing here idle all day?' They said to him, 'Because no one has hired us.' He said to them, 'You also go into the vineyard.' When evening came, the owner of the vineyard said to his manager, 'Call the laborers and give them their pay, beginning with the last and then going to the first.' When those hired about five o'clock came, each of them received the usual daily wage. Now when the first came, they thought they would receive more; but each of them also received the usual daily wage. And when they received it, they grumbled against the landowner, saying, 'These last worked only one hour, and you have made them equal to us who have borne the burden of the day and the scorching heat.' But he replied to one of them, 'Friend, I am doing you no wrong; did you not agree with me for the usual daily wage? Take what belongs to you and go; I choose to give to this last the same as I give to you. Am I not allowed to do what I choose with what belongs to me? Or are you envious because I am generous?' So the last will be first, and the first will be last."

Reader: The Word of the Lord.
Response: Thanks be to God.

INTRODUCING THE STORY
(Time: 10 minutes)

The parable of the workers in the vineyard lends itself to role play in both smaller and larger classes. Choose a student to be the landowner and select small groups or individuals to be hired at the different times of day. Act out each scene in the story, concluding with the payment to the workers (the same amount for each one). Allow time for the workers to react to their equal pay.

It will be helpful to write out a few notes for each actor and group to help define roles clearly. For ideas, read the story about the parable on page 1 of the student newspaper, *Community Times* (Unit II, Issue 7). Lay out an imaginary marketplace and vineyard in the classroom.

Draw on the material in Getting Ready (above) to provide background information about the parable.

After the role play, talk about the story. Emphasize the parable's message about God's generosity. Ask: Did the workers appreciate the landowner's generosity? Why or why not?

Ask the students to locate and read *Matthew 20:1-16* in their Bibles. What preceded this parable, in chapter 19? What comes afterward, beginning with *Matthew 20:17*?

EXPLORING
(Time: 15–20 minutes)

Option 1. Parable Strip

Assign the following seven scenes from *Matthew 20:1-16* to teams or individuals: verses 1-2; verses 3-4; verse 5; verses 6-7; verse 8; verses 10-12; verses 13-16.

Provide sheets of 12 x 18-inch drawing paper and ask the class members to prepare illustrations of all the passages. Supply pens, pencils, markers, and crayons. When the drawings are completed, tape them together into a continuous strip. The ends may be fastened to dowels or wrapping paper rolls. If time permits, choose a narrator and reread the parable, unfurling the strip one scene at a time.

Option 2. Portraying the Landowner

Supply paper, pens, and markers. Ask the students to prepare a cartoon-like panel showing the figure of the landowner in the parable of the vineyard workers. Add a balloon in which to enter words the owner might say. Encourage the class members to think of the owner as a very generous employer. What will he say? How will he explain how he pays people? Suggest a caption for the panel, such as "A Generous Landowner."

Option 3. Word Puzzle

Turn in the student newspaper, *Community Times*, Unit II, Issue 7, to the crossword puzzle titled "Workers in the Vineyard." Students may work individually, in pairs, or as a total group.

MUSIC
(Time: 10 minutes)

Listen on the *Children Sing!* tape to "Rise up, ye saints of God!" *(The Hymnal 1982, 551)*. Call the students' attention to "King of kings" and "kingdom" in stanzas 1 and 2. The hymn is a call to Christian obedience.

CONNECTING/SPEAKING OUT
(Time: 15–20 minutes)

Option 1. Group Discussion

You may want to tackle the fairness issue head-on. Many students will be unable to hear the primary message of this parable (God's generosity) because they are caught up in the situation that on the surface seems so unfair.

This would be a good time to talk about the reign or kingdom of God. For background, see the article about the reign of God on page 2 of the student newspaper.

Invite students to think of all the unfairness that now exists in the world. Encourage them to talk about fairness in their families, at school, and in the community. Then invite them to think about the way they live and the way people in poverty live. Suggest they compare their lifestyles with young people from nations facing war, starvation, or natural disasters.

Emphasize that the kingdom of God sets new standards of fairness and justice. God's fairness and generosity operate on a level we do not fully understand. In the parable we read today, we learn that God is a generous God who welcomes everyone to the kingdom at any time.

Option 2. Current Events

In our time, people enter into contracts almost daily. When agreeing to do things, we make informal but binding agreements about what is expected and how we will be rewarded. Invite the students to name examples of such agreements (such as doing household chores, accepting school assignments, or taking jobs like babysitting).

Ask: When you make an agreement (contract), what do you expect to do? What do you expect of others? Have you ever been paid more than you thought you deserved? Share your experience.

Pose a situation in which a student agrees to do something for a given reward. Then someone else does the same task, perhaps in shorter time, and is paid the same. How would it feel to know that this had happened?

Encourage class members to cite any examples they know about in which people complain about the conditions of a contract. Ask: How are such occurrences connected to the parable Jesus told? What is different or the same?

REFLECTING
(Time: 10 minutes)

Hand out the students' reflection envelopes and prepare the Reflection Center, as described in Session 1. Check to be sure the art supplies are adequate.

Share directions for the students, such as the following:

Think about the goodness of God. Think about some of the gracious gifts God has given to you and people you know. How does it feel to be loved and accepted by God at all times in our lives?

Has there ever been a time when you received more from God than you thought you deserved?

Write or draw your thoughts or feelings. Add a brief prayer.

LEARNING SKILLS
(Time: 10–15 minutes)

Option 1. Class Memory Challenge

The memory task for this session is to link the parable of "The Pharisee and the Tax Collector (Publican)" with the *Gospel of Luke*, chapter 18, the only place it is found in the New Testament.

Review all the titles and chapter numbers previously memorized. Begin by asking the students to call out parables that are only in *Matthew*, then the ones that are only in *Luke*.

Refer to the Memory Challenge block in the student newspaper, *Community Times*, Unit II, Issue 7.

Option 2. Learning Scripture

Ask whether class members have learned verses given in the previous sessions. Add paper triangles to the mosaic outline of the Epiphany Star described in Session 1.

Encourage students to memorize *Matthew 20:1* and *Matthew 20:16* before the next class session.

See "Learning Scripture" in the student newspaper, *Community Times*.

ONGOING PROJECT
(Time: 5–10 minutes)

Introduce or continue the series of tape-recorded interviews described in Session 6. Review the steps to be taken and plan questions about the Parable of the Laborers in the Vineyard. Examples: How do you feel about the laborers who complained at the end of the day? Why? What do you think Jesus wants us to think about when we hear this story?

SYMBOL CARD and TREASUREBOOK

Card 16 contains a grapevine, a verse of Scripture, and an explanation on the back.

Encourage the students to look at *Chalice Year Treasurebook*, Part II, Section 5, on Jesus' parable of the vineyard workers. How would you explain this parable in your own words?

GOING FORTH

Gather the group for the dismissal. The teacher or a student will say the following, pausing for the students' response of "Lord, have mercy":

With all our heart and with all our mind, let us pray to the Lord, saying, "Lord, have mercy."

For the peace from above, for the loving kindness of God, and for the salvation of our souls, let us pray to the Lord.
Lord, have mercy.

For the peace of the world, for the welfare of the holy Church of God, and for the unity of all people, let us pray to the Lord.
Lord, have mercy.

For _____ [learners may add their own petitions], let us pray to the Lord.
Lord, have mercy.

From The Prayers of the People
The Book of Common Prayer, pp. 383-384

Teacher: Let us go forth in the name of Christ.
Students: Thanks be to God.

TEACHER'S ASSESSMENT

As you reflect on the students' participation, what seemed to interest them most in this session? How well were they able to focus on the generosity of the landowner as a sign of God's graciousness? What evidence did you gather of the class members' varying abilities to interpret parables?

LOOKING AHEAD

The next session is on two short parables: treasure in a field and a pearl of great value. In preparation, think about priorities in your own life. What is most important of all?

PARABLES OF PROMISE
SESSION 8
PARABLES OF TREASURE

FOCUS

Matthew's Gospel includes the parables of a treasure in a field, and of a pearl of great value. They focus on the unbelievable worth of God's good news in Christ; we can trust the promise that this news is worth the commitment of our lives. The students should be able to dramatize these short parables imaginatively and explain the meaning they get from them.

GETTING READY

Jesus' very short parables of the buried treasure and the costly pearl are found only in *Matthew 13:44-46*. Both make the same point—that the kingdom of heaven (the reign of God) is so desirable and valuable that a person would joyfully give up everything in order to have it. To do so would not even be considered a sacrifice.

In Jesus' time, people of the Near East were known to bury money for safekeeping. Even in recent decades, hoarded coins have occasionally been uncovered during excavations in Israel. Pearls were bought and sold by Palestinian traders who would sometimes search as far as the Persian Gulf or India for especially fine ones.

Jesus compared God's reign (kingdom) to a sought-after treasure or fine jewel. He said that the most important priority in the life of a committed disciple is the pursuit of God's reign (kingdom).

Intermediate-age students, caught up in a complex society like our own, may find it a difficult task to think about turning aside from all the "things" that surround us in order to place a high value on a lasting relationship with God. But it is important that they have an opportunity to weigh personal priorities and make choices about their life commitments.

O merciful Creator, your hand is open wide to satisfy the needs of every living creature: Make us always thankful for your loving providence; and grant that we, remembering the account that we must one day give, may be faithful stewards of your good gifts; through Jesus Christ our Lord, who with you and the Holy Spirit lives and reigns, one God, for ever and ever. *Amen.*
For stewardship of creation
The Book of Common Prayer, p. 259

TEACHING TIP

The intermediate years are usually filled with many options for students: extracurricular activities, hobbies, music lessons, and sports. Young people are faced with the need to set priorities and make choices. This session on parables of treasure offers an opportunity for class members to think about what they treasure. Teachers can discuss personal priorities, sharing examples from their own experience.

GATHERING

As the students arrive, invite them to look at the photograph of an oyster and pearl on Poster No. 12 in the Teacher's Packet. Who has seen a raw pearl? What causes one to form in an oyster? What is the value of a large, perfect pearl? Why are pearls valuable?

When everyone is present, say:

Let us pray. (Use the Collect "For stewardship of creation," above, or a prayer of your own choosing.)

The chosen student lector reads from the class Bible (NRSV):

Unit II. Parables of Promise—Session 8
Chalice Year Intermediate—Copyright © 2000 Virginia Theological Sminary and Morehouse Publishing

A *Reading from the Gospel of Matthew, chapter 13, verses 44 through 46.*

> (Jesus said) "The kingdom of heaven is like treasure hidden in a field, which someone found and hid; then in his joy he goes and sells all that he has and buys that field.
>
> Again, the kingdom of heaven is like a merchant in search of fine pearls; on finding one pearl of great value, he went and sold all that he had and bought it."

Reader: The Word of the Lord.
Response: Thanks be to God.

INTRODUCING THE STORY
(Time: 10 minutes)

Invite the students to find, in their own Bibles, the parables of the buried treasure and the costly pearl, in *Matthew 13:44-46*.

Suggest that the class members form teams to prepare two short dramatic scenes—"Seeking Buried Treasure" and "Finding the Best Pearl." Encourage them to use their imaginations freely. Supply simple directions:

Team 1: Reread the parable of the buried treasure *(Matthew 13:44)*. For ideas, read the articles about the parable and buried treasure on page 2 of the student newspaper, *Community Times* (Unit II, Issue 8). Decide on an area to be the "field" where a treasure is buried. Where is the treasure located? Choose a person who will find it. How will the treasure be kept a secret? What will he sell? How will he purchase the field? from whom? (Time limit for presenting the scene: 6 minutes.)

Team 2: Reread the parable of the costly pearl *(Matthew 13:45-46)*. An article about the merchant and the pearl is on page 1 of *Community Times*. Another story on page 3 explains why natural pearls are rare and valuable. Set up a trader's area. Who will take the part of the merchant? Where will this person search for fine pearls? Where will the one costly pearl be located? What will be sold? to whom? What will the merchant do with the money? (Time limit for presenting the scene: 6 minutes.)

After the teams have made their presentations, talk about the two stories. Ask class members to think about things that they value. To help them identify objects of value, ask: If your house caught on fire and you had time to grab one or two items, what would you take?

Encourage students to describe the things they named. Why are they valuable? Would they have value for someone else? What does Jesus say we should value the most?

EXPLORING
(Time: 15–20 minutes)

Option 1. Treasure Chest

Obtain a medium-size cardboard box with a lid, construction paper or colored tissue, scissors, glue, and glitter (optional). Ask the students to cover and decorate the box so that it looks like a treasure chest.

Distribute 3 x 5 file cards, pens, and markers. Encourage each class member to decide what might be a treasure of great value, then use a card to describe it in writing and/or draw a picture of it. They may want to describe the item of value they thought of earlier. Ensure the group that no one will look at the cards if they want to include something personal. Place the treasure cards in the chest and put it away for safekeeping.

Option 2. Pearl Mementos

Purchase, from an art supply store, enough imitation pearl beads to provide one for each class member. (As an alternative, other beads may be spray-painted to look like pearls.) Give the students 4 x 6 cards or pieces of posterboard, along with pens and markers. Suggest that they decorate the borders of the cards, then copy *Matthew 13:45-46* on the lower half. Use glue to attach a pearl just above the parable. The mementoes may be displayed at home as a reminder of Jesus' teaching about the kingdom of heaven.

Option 3. Code Puzzle

Turn in the student newspaper, *Community Times*, Unit II, Issue 8, to the code puzzle titled "Secret Message." Students may work individually, in pairs, or as a total group.

MUSIC
(Time: 10 minutes)

Sing with the *Children Sing!* tape "Rise up, ye saints of God!" *(The Hymnal 1982, 551)*. Notice the words, "Have done with lesser things," in Stanza 1. What does the hymn ask us to do? What connection could we make between the hymn and the parables of the treasure and the pearl?

CONNECTING/SPEAKING OUT
(Time: 15–20 minutes)

Option 1. Group Discussion

Suggest that the students describe, in their own words, the man who wanted the hidden treasure more than anything else. What was he like? Why did he want the money so much? What could he have done with it after he owned it?

In the same manner, invite imaginative descriptions of the merchant who wanted the valuable pearl. What kind of person was he? Why would he sell everything in order to get one pearl? What might he do with this valuable gem after it was his?

Encourage the group to consider "the kingdom of heaven (God)" as a treasure that is worth more than anything else. Ask: What do you think Jesus meant? How do people show their desire for God's reign today?

Option 2. Current Events

Pass out old magazines and catalogues that can be cut up. Ask students to look for items that they believe people value and tear or cut them out. Ask them to focus on the kinds of "treasure" that attract people's attention and commitment in our society.

After about five to ten minutes, ask class members to share the items they found, such as cars, electronic equipment, the latest styles of clothing, jewelry, travel. Ask: Why do people develop such strong desires for such possessions? To what lengths will we go in order to obtain such treasures?

Ask: What is of greatest value to you personally? What would you give up in order to have it? In what way does our faith in Jesus Christ affect what we treasure most? What might cause our values to change?

REFLECTING
(Time: 10 minutes)

Set up the Reflection Center, as described in Session 1. Distribute the reflection envelopes, check the art supplies, and offer these directions:

Think about all that you possess. Which of your possessions would you call treasures? How long have you had them? Where did they come from? If you had to give up one or more of these, which would be hardest to part with? Why are the things you value most so precious to you?

Now think about the reign of God in our lives. Jesus said that God's kingdom is the greatest treasure of all. Is that true for you? Why, or why not?

Write or draw your responses. As you complete a page for your envelope, write a brief prayer to be added.

LEARNING SKILLS
(Time: 10–15 minutes)

Option 1. Class Memory Challenge

The memory task for this session focuses on three parables of Jesus that are all found in both the *Gospel of Matthew* and the *Gospel of Luke*: "House on the Rock" *(Matthew 7* and *Luke 6)*; "Yeast (Leaven)" (found in *Matthew 13* and *Luke 13)*; "Lost Sheep" *(Matthew 18* and *Luke 15)*.

Ask the students to find all three stories in their Bibles, locating them in both Gospels. Work out together a way to link the chapter numbers with the parables. Note that the Parable of the Yeast can be associated with the same chapter number (13).

Call attention to the Memory Challenge block in the student newspaper, *Community Times*, Unit II, Issue 8.

Option 2. Learning Scripture

Ask class members who have learned verses given in the previous sessions to add mosaic triangles to the Epiphany Star outline described in Session 1.

Encourage the students to memorize either or both of two parables before the next class session: *Matthew 7:28* (Jesus' teaching authority); *Matthew 13:44* (hidden treasure); *Matthew 13:45-46* (costly pearl).

See "Learning Scripture" in the student newspaper, *Community Times*.

ONGOING PROJECT
(Time: 5–10 minutes)

Consult Session 6 for steps to be taken in producing another in the series of tape-recorded interviews on the parables. For this session on the Parables of the Hidden Treasure and the Pearl of Great Price (Value), consider using these questions: How important are these parables for you? Why? If Jesus were telling these parables today, what examples might he use instead of buried treasure or pearls?

SYMBOL CARD and TREASUREBOOK

Card 17 contains an oyster with a pearl, a verse of Scripture, and an explanation on the back.

Suggest the students look in the *Chalice Year Treasurebook*, Part II, Section 6, about Jesus' parables of the kingdom of God. If Jesus were telling this story to a group of young people today, what treasures would he use?

GOING FORTH

Gather the group for the dismissal. The teacher or a student will say the following, pausing for the students' response of "Lord, have mercy":

> With all our heart and with all our mind, let us pray to the Lord, saying, "Lord, have mercy."
>
> For the peace from above, for the loving kindness of God, and for the salvation of our souls, let us pray to the Lord.
> *Lord, have mercy.*
>
> For the peace of the world, for the welfare of the holy Church of God, and for the unity of all people, let us pray to the Lord.
> *Lord, have mercy.*
>
> For _____ [learners may add their own petitions], let us pray to the Lord.
> *Lord, have mercy.*
>
> From The Prayers of the People
> *The Book of Common Prayer,* pp. 383-384

Teacher: Let us go forth in the name of Christ.
Students: Thanks be to God.

TEACHER'S ASSESSMENT

As the students explored the parables of treasure, what clues to their own priorities and values did you pick up? Were they receptive to the concept that the kingdom (reign) of God is the highest value humanity can seek?

LOOKING AHEAD

The next session is devoted to Jesus' teaching about a house built on a rock, in contrast to a house built on shifting sand. In preparation, consider the foundations of your own spiritual journey. How firm are they? Why?

PARABLES OF PROMISE

SESSION 9
THE HOUSE UPON A ROCK

FOCUS

Jesus compares a person who listens to and acts upon Jesus' teachings to one who built a house on a firm rock foundation. The house survived destructive rains and winds. This story focuses on the necessity for a strong spiritual base for one's life. The students should be able to locate and explain this passage in their own words.

GETTING READY

Biblical scholars do not agree on whether Jesus' teaching about "the house upon the rock" *(Matthew 7:24-27)* is a genuine parable. If a parable is defined as a story that can have more than one meaning, then the test of a real one is whether it causes us to wonder and reflect—especially about the nature of God and what God does.

The four verses (see also *Luke 6:47-49*) form the conclusion of the Sermon on the Mount. Jesus contrasts a wise person who builds a house on a solid-rock foundation to another person who foolishly builds on sand. Wisdom consists in hearing and doing what Jesus teaches. Folly is the rejection of Jesus' teaching.

These words of judgment are crystal clear, and there is little that would puzzle a hearer. One either accepts or rejects Jesus' message. So, for some students of Scripture, the passage is a strong and important admonition but not a true parable (story) that invites imagination and varied interpretations.

Other scholars have no problem with classifying the scene as a parable. Jesus' words are similar to a very old rabbinical parable contrasting two reactions to the study of Torah. According to this teaching, a person of good works who learns Torah is like one who builds a house with stone at the bottom with adobe (clay bricks) at the top. When heavy rain comes, such a house stands firm. But a person who has no good works while learning Torah is like one who builds a house first of adobe with stone at the top. When the water comes, the house topples over.

O God, the strength of all who put their trust in you: Mercifully accept our prayers; and because in our weakness we can do nothing good without you, give us the help of your grace, that in keeping your commandments we may please you both in will and deed; through Jesus Christ our Lord, who lives and reigns with you and the Holy Spirit, one God, for ever and ever. *Amen.*
Sixth Sunday after the Epiphany
The Book of Common Prayer, p. 216

TEACHING TIP

Intermediate-age students are making decisions about how seriously to take their faith and where to place their loyalties. This session on Jesus' words about the house on the rock underscores the necessity for each person to have a strong spiritual foundation. The words and messages that come from television, movies, music, and the media are powerful influences in your students' lives. It is appropriate to challenge class members to examine their priorities and loyalties.

GATHERING

Display the photograph on Poster No. 12 from the Teacher's Packet showing a rocky shore alongside a sandy beach. As the students arrive, point out the picture and encourage individuals to react to what they see. Ask: What are the contrasts in the picture? If you were in the scene, where would you want to stand? Why? If a rainstorm and high winds came, where would you prefer to be?

Unit II. Parables of Promise—Session 9
Chalice Year Intermediate—Copyright © 2000 Virginia Theological Sminary and Morehouse Publishing

When everyone is present, say:

Let us pray. (Use the Collect "Sixth Sunday after the Epiphany," above, or a prayer of your own choosing.)

The chosen student lector reads from the class Bible (NRSV):

A Reading from the Gospel of Matthew, chapter 7, verses 24 through 27.

(Jesus said) "Everyone then who hears these words of mine and acts on them will be like a wise man who built his house on rock. The rain fell, the floods came, and the winds blew and beat on that house, but it did not fall, because it had been founded on rock. And everyone who hears these words of mine and does not act on them will be like a foolish man who built his house on sand. The rain fell, and the floods came, and the winds blew and beat against that house, and it fell—and great was its fall!"

Reader: The Word of the Lord.
Response: Thanks be to God.

INTRODUCING THE STORY
(Time: 10 minutes)

Begin by asking, What is the first thing a builder must consider when starting to build a house or other structure? Encourage class members to talk about the importance of solid footing for buildings, and the need for good foundations.

Explain that Jesus was familiar with house-building of his day. For information about houses in Palestine of New Testament times, see the article on page 2 of *Community Times* (Unit II, Issue 9). Housing materials and weather both had impacts on buildings. Jesus could count on his hearers to understand when he talked of a house built on a rock in contrast to a house built on unstable sandy soil. Perhaps Jesus had experience as a carpenter, like his father Joseph.

At the end of his Sermon on the Mount, Jesus wanted to draw a sharp contrast between people who built their lives on the solid foundation of his teaching and others who refused to do so. He used the figure of two builders—one who built a house on a rock and the other who built on sand instead. The first withstood the fury of a rainstorm. The second fell with a mighty thud.

The difference between the two builders is clear. One was wise, the other foolish. Wise listeners to Jesus will actually do what he teaches, for theirs is a good spiritual foundation. Foolish listeners who fail to act as Jesus teaches are building their lives on a very shaky and easily undermined foundation.

Invite the students to turn in their Bibles to *Matthew*, chapters 5-7. Note that these three chapters form Jesus' Sermon on the Mount. Examine the sermon's conclusion in *Matthew 7:24-27*.

The story on page 1 of *Community Times* describes this famous sermon, where it occurred, and who gathered to hear it. Ask: Why did Jesus end his sermon with this story? What is he trying to tell us today?

EXPLORING
(Time: 15–20 minutes)

Option 1. Diorama

Obtain a shoe box or another box of similar size, a small flat rock, some sand, brown and sky-blue construction paper, markers, scissors, and clear plastic tape. Invite the students to construct a diorama showing two houses, one built on a rock and the other on sand. Use construction paper and tape to create the structures, and line the box in blue to represent the sky in the background. Ask the students to name the diorama with a phrase that reminds the viewer of Jesus' teaching in *Matthew 7:24-27*.

Option 2. Building Foundations

Divide the class into two groups. Give each a set of wooden blocks of various sizes. Make sure both groups have a number of very small blocks and larger blocks. Tell each that the goal is to make a structure as high as possible. There is only one hitch. Group one can use any blocks in any sequence. Group two must use the smallest blocks first, and then move up to the largest. Set a time limit of five to ten minutes.

Afterward, examine the two structures. Is one structure taller than the other? Why? How sturdy are both structures? Would both withstand a strong wind?

Take a few minutes to brainstorm ways that class members could build strong spiritual foundations for their lives, such as prayer, Bible study, attending worship, and helping others. Tear down both structures the students built. Attach the words or phrases from the brainstorm to the largest blocks. Give the students about five minutes to construct a new structure using the largest blocks as the foundation.

Option 3. Word Search

Turn in the student newspaper, *Community Times*, Unit II, Issue 9, to the word search titled "Key Names and Words." Students may work individually, in pairs, or as a group.

MUSIC
(Time: 10 minutes)

Listen on the *Children Sing!* tape to "If thou but trust in God to guide thee" *(The Hymnal 1982, 635)*. Change stanza 1 into a class prayer, changing the pronouns to the vernacular first person: "thou" to "I"; "thee" to "me"; "thy" to "my." Note the reference to a rock in the final phrase. Students may copy this altered version onto 3 x 5 cards that can be taken home and used as their personal morning or evening prayer. Sing the first verse with the tape or say it together.

CONNECTING/SPEAKING OUT
(Time: 15–20 minutes)

Option 1. Group Discussion

Jesus' teaching at the end of the Sermon on the Mount contrasts "wise" and "foolish" persons who built houses. Ask: What made their construction either wise or foolish?

Remind the students that the contrasting structures and their fate (either standing or falling during a storm) are intended to make us think about the spiritual foundations for our own lives. We cannot stand up to unwholesome influences and temptations unless we take care to form a solid base for our lives as children of God.

Ask: How would you describe a good foundation for a Christian's life? To whom does a Christian listen with care? What kinds of background and teaching will help to strengthen one's base for living?

Option 2. Current Events

If possible, bring in clips of television advertisements aimed at young people or find similar examples in teen magazines. Look at the ads and talk about the values that are suggested in the messages. Ask: What are they trying to sell? What do the messages imply about what is important?

Ask class members to take a mental check to see how successful advertisers are. For example, suggest that they look at their clothing. Where did it come from? Does it have some kind of label that identifies it? What kind of tennis shoes do you wear? Why did you select them? What else is essential in your life? A television? CD player? Computer? Game system? Why are these important?

Talk about the things Jesus said are important in life. If you built your life on the items in the advertisements, would you be very stable? Why or why not?

REFLECTING
(Time: 10 minutes)

Distribute the reflection envelopes and prepare the Reflection Center as described in Session 1. Check the art supplies.

Offer these directions for the students' response:

Close your eyes and think about people you have known who had a strong spiritual influence in your life. How did they help you to become a stronger, more faithful Christian person? What did they do? What did they say?

Now think about your present life. What are some of your greatest temptations right now? How does the teaching of Jesus Christ help you to stand on a solid foundation? How could God help you now?

When you have completed writing or drawing your reflections, write a brief prayer.

LEARNING SKILLS
(Time: 10–15 minutes)

Option 1. Class Memory Challenge

Direct the class members' attention to the final memory challenge, shown in chart form in the student newspaper, *Community Times*, Unit II, Issue 9. The block to be memorized contains two parables that are found in *Matthew, Mark,* and *Luke* (all three): "Sower" *(Matthew 13; Mark 4,* and *Luke 8);* "Mustard Seed" *(Matthew 13; Mark 4,* and *Luke 13).*

After the students have accomplished the task, encourage them to reconstruct the complete list of Jesus' parables they have memorized, with corresponding locations by Gospel and chapter. Use a chalkboard or newsprint easel. Check the list against the newspaper chart.

Option 2. Learning Scripture

Add mosaic pieces to the Epiphany Star outline described in Session 1 for verses class members have learned from previous sessions.

See "Learning Scripture" in the student newspaper, *Community Times.*

For this final session of the Unit, memorize *Matthew 7:24* and review all the other Scripture verses that have been learned. In Unit III, another group of verses will be introduced, together with a way to record what has been memorized.

ONGOING PROJECT
(Time: 5–10 minutes)

The tape-recording project, as described in Session 6, may be continued, or a single tape may be produced for this session. Examples of questions related to the Parable of the House on the Rock: What pictures do you see in your mind's eye as you hear this parable? Why is this a story we remember?

If the class members have completed a series of tapes, they may want to plan a way to share the interviews with others. Depending on their length, the tapes may need to be edited and spliced for easier listening.

SYMBOL CARD and TREASUREBOOK

Card 18 contains a house on a rock, a verse of Scripture, and an explanation on the back.

Encourage students to review all of *Chalice Year Treasurebook*, Part II. Look especially at Section 7, which summarizes Jesus' parables and other teachings, including the story of two house builders. Why do some people wonder whether this is a parable?

GOING FORTH

Gather the group for the dismissal. The teacher or a student will say the following, pausing for the students' response of "Lord, have mercy":

> With all our heart and with all our mind, let us pray to the Lord, saying, "Lord, have mercy."

For the peace from above, for the loving kindness of God, and for the salvation of our souls, let us pray to the Lord.
Lord, have mercy.

For the peace of the world, for the welfare of the holy Church of God, and for the unity of all people, let us pray to the Lord.
Lord, have mercy.

For _____ [learners may add their own petitions], let us pray to the Lord.
Lord, have mercy.

> From The Prayers of the People
> *The Book of Common Prayer,* pp. 383-384

Teacher: Let us go forth in the name of Christ.
Students: Thanks be to God.

TEACHER'S ASSESSMENT

This session invited students to think about the spiritual foundations for their lives. What evidence did you hear that the class members were reflecting on personal priorities and choices? In what ways can future sessions build on this Unit's study of Jesus' parables and teachings?

Note: The following letter is for teachers and parents of children in the Intermediate level of church school. These pages can be reproduced or used as a model for a personalized letter.

Episcopal Children's Curriculum
Unit III: EUCHARIST—SHARED LIFE

Dear Parents and Guardians,

Students will be studying the sacrament of Eucharist during this Unit. Each time we renew the Baptismal Covenant, we promise to "continue in the apostles' teaching and fellowship, in the breaking of bread, and in the prayers." With these words, we renew our intention to be faithful participants in worship around the Lord's Table.

In the Episcopal Church, our architecture and art, music and prayers reflect the importance of Holy Communion in our worship. Young persons should come to understand and appreciate the celebration of the Lord's Supper.

Activities are designed to help intermediate-age students understand the structure of the Church's worship. Although many class members at this age level are currently involved in congregations as acolytes or choir members, they may not be aware of the meanings and symbolism of the liturgy.

Spend some time talking to your student about what he or she is learning. Do this by reading the Scripture identified below, discussing the Symbol Cards and *Community Times* sent home each week, and by reading together Part III of the *Chalice Year Treasurebook*, which includes information about the different sections of Holy Eucharist.

In the first five sessions of this Unit, students are invited to look at the form of worship, from the time of gathering until the dismissal. The final four sessions are centered on themes of Lent, Holy Week, and Easter. These sessions give us an opportunity to examine the meaning of Christ's suffering, death, resurrection, and ascension.

Following is a more detailed overview of the Unit:

Session 1: "Gathering for Liturgy" is devoted to the opening part of the Service of Holy Eucharist. The students will explore the meaning of liturgy as "the work of the people" and learn about the traditional ways of gathering for worship. The session emphases the significance of gathering for worship using prayer and song as key elements. (*Colossians 3:14-17*)

Session 2: "The Word of God" explains where Scriptures are read in the Service of Holy Eucharist. The Sermon, the Nicene Creed, the Prayers of the People, Confession of Sin and Absolution, and the Peace follow. Students will concentrate on the central place of Scripture in worship. Activities will help them become more familiar with the lectionary. The Bible passage for this session is about Jesus' reading of Scripture during worship. (*Luke 4:14-21*)

Session 3: "Offering the Gifts" has a two-fold purpose: to emphasize our own giving as a response to God's gift of Jesus, and to supply information about the way the bread and wine are prepared for the service. The work of clergy and servers will be recognized, and students will learn more about rubrics or instructions in *The Book of Common Prayer.* (*Ephesians 5:1-2*)

Session 4: "The Great Thanksgiving" shows that prayer is at the heart of the Sacrament of Holy Eucharist. The word "eucharist" can be translated as "giving thanks." Students will look at the six forms of The Great Thanksgiving in the Prayer Book to discover similarities in the following: praise, words of institution of the Lord's Supper, words of remembering, and invocations of the Holy Spirit. (*I Corinthians 11:23-26*)

Session 5: "Going Forth into the World" focuses on the mission of Christians as God's people in the world. The prayers after communion stress our going forth "to love and serve." Students will prepare to take their places in the Christian community as active participants. (*Philippians 4:4-7*)

Session 6: "Holy Week Begins" surveys the events of Jesus' last week, from Palm Sunday through the trial before Pilate and Peter's denial. Students will discuss the context for the Last Supper and how the celebration of the Eucharist dramatizes the life and mission of Jesus. They will also discover the relationship of the Supper to Passover.
(*Mark 14:16, 22-25, 28-31*)

Session 7: "The Passion of Christ" describes the three sections of Mark's account of Jesus' last hours: the mocking, the crucifixion, and the death. Intermediate-age students are ready to hear and discuss the events of Good Friday. They will learn why the crucifixion is a central focus for the Church's liturgy in Holy Week. (*Mark 15:25-39*)

Session 8: "The Resurrection of Christ" is about the glad news of Easter. Students will compare and contrast this account with the resurrection stories in the other three Gospels. They will discover that the Eucharist is a proclamation of the joyous announcement, "Christ has died. Christ is risen. Christ will come again." (*Mark 16:1-8*)

Session 9: "Breakfast by the Sea of Galilee" shifts to the *Gospel of John*. The breakfast scene, in which the disciples knew Jesus as Lord, is understood by the Church to be a Eucharist story. Just as the living Jesus was with his followers that morning, he is present at the table as we gather to receive the bread and wine of Holy Communion. For Christians, every Sunday is a "little Easter." (*John 21:1-14*)

Yours in Christ,

Church School Teachers

EUCHARIST: SHARED LIFE

SESSION 1
GATHERING FOR LITURGY

FOCUS

Christ's people come together around the Holy Table to celebrate Eucharist. The time of gathering, marked by prayer and song, is the beginning of the Church's most important liturgical assembly. The students should be able to define liturgy as "the work of the people," and to explain the significance of the moment of gathering.

GETTING READY

The first five sessions of this Unit follow the structure of the service of The Holy Eucharist. In the Church's worship, Word and Sacrament are linked together. The Rites for Holy Eucharist in *The Book of Common Prayer* have two main headings. The word of God and the Holy Communion. This session begins with the gathering, sometimes called The Entrance Rite.

The New Testament includes few details about the planning of Christian worship. The apostle Paul urged the Church to gather for teaching, singing, and giving thanks *(Colossians 3:16-17)*. He also provided the words of institution for the Lord's Supper and gave instructions about its observance *(I Corinthians 11:17-34)*.

In times of persecution, Christians were forced to meet in secret. When they gathered, the priest would visit with the people as they arrived, and the worship probably began with the first reading from Scripture.

As congregations and buildings grew larger, the need arose for more formal ways of gathering people for worship. Through the centuries, entrance rites tended to become more and more elaborate.

In Anglican tradition, the early practice was to sing a psalm at the beginning. This gave way to other customs as new versions of *The Book of Common Prayer* evolved.

O Almighty God, who pours out on all who desire it the spirit of grace and of supplication: Deliver us, when we draw near to you, from coldness of heart and wanderings of mind, that with steadfast thoughts and kindled affections we may worship you in spirit and in truth; through Jesus Christ our Lord. *Amen.*
Before Worship
The Book of Common Prayer, p. 833

TEACHING TIP

Intermediate-age students may have very different experiences of Holy Eucharist as participants or observers. Stress a sense of reverence as the people of God enter the church building and prepare themselves in heart and mind to worship. During activities and discussions, be sensitive to class members' different backgrounds and help students acknowledge their feelings.

GATHERING

For use during the Gathering at Sessions 1-5 of this Unit, the Teacher's Packet contains a sheet of word placards that can be cut apart or displayed as printed on Poster No. 13. Place the poster near a chalkboard, newsprint easel, or large sheet of posterboard. Supply chalk or markers.

As the students arrive, encourage them to think about the words on the poster and write or draw any responses that occur to them. If possible, display the poster and the students' observations during Sessions 1-5.

When everyone is present, say:

Let us pray. (Use the prayer "Before Worship," above, or a prayer of your own choosing.)

The chosen student lector reads from the class Bible (NRSV):

A Reading from the Epistle to the Colossians, chapter 3, verses 14 through 17.

Above all, clothe yourselves with love, which binds everything together in perfect harmony. And let the peace of Christ rule in your hearts, to which indeed you were called in the one body. And be thankful. Let the word of Christ dwell in you richly; teach and admonish one another in all wisdom; and with gratitude in your hearts sing psalms, hymns, and spiritual songs to God. And whatever you do, in word or deed, do everything in the name of the Lord Jesus, giving thanks to God the Father through him.

Reader: The Word of the Lord.
Response: Thanks be to God.

INTRODUCING THE STORY
(Time: 10 minutes)

Begin by asking the class members: Why do Christians come together on Sundays in a special place? In your own words, tell the story about Christians in other parts of the world from the article on page 1 of *Community Times* (Unit III, Issue 1). The countries highlighted are Hong Kong (a part of China), Peru, and Tanzania. Each describes the words they say when they gather for worship.

Call attention to the words LITURGY (LAOS+ERGON) on the poster used at the Gathering. The word "liturgy" comes from two Greek words: *laos* (people) and *ergon* (work). Put them together and we see that when Christians gather for Word and Sacrament, they are about "the work of the people." Everyone is an active participant. Share the literal meaning of liturgy as "the work of the people," and point out that the Episcopal Church has a liturgical tradition. Using *The Book of Common Prayer*, the people follow established ways of worshiping that come from old traditions. Point out the "rubrics" in the Prayer Book—the italicized type that offers instructions for each part of the services.

Explain that this is session is on the gathering part of the liturgy of the Holy Eucharist, which is the principal form of Sunday worship.

Ask the students to turn, in their Bibles, to *Colossians 3:14-17.* What does this passage urge people to do? After examining the following list, ask: How many items are mentioned in the scripture passage?

On a chalkboard or newsprint, list the following elements:
    Hymn, psalm, or anthem
    Opening acclamation *(three forms)*
    Collect for Purity
    Ten Commandments or Summary of the Law
    The Kyrie/The Trisagion, *before or in place of:*
    Song of praise
    Salutation and Collect

Describe your own congregation's customs as the people gather for Eucharist. Which Rite is used (I or II)? Which of the elements (above) are included? Obtain several copies of a service bulletin. Identify and name the parts of the entrance rite (See the list that appears in the student newspaper, *Community Times*, Unit III, Issue 1.)

EXPLORING
(Time: 15–20 minutes)

Option 1. Gathering Together—Silent Skits

Ahead of time, prepare several index cards that describe actions, encounters, or events that might occur as a congregation gathers and the liturgy begins. Arrange for individuals, pairs, or small teams to select a card, and prepare a brief silent skit dramatizing the event. As the silent skit is presented, other class members can provide commentary about the actions being portrayed. Simple props will prove helpful, such as Prayer Books, hymnals, kneelers, candles, and service bulletins.

Some suggestions for the skits: person taking off coat and kneeling in prayer; acolyte lighting candles; person using bulletin to locate where to look in the hymnal, and then singing; Celebrant and choir in procession; people rising to begin the entrance hymn.

Option 2. Telling Our Story

Share information from the article on page one of *Community Times* (Unit III, Issue 1) that describes worship experiences in three countries. What is similar to or different from services at your church?

Ask students to remember everything the congregation does before, during, and after the services. Encourage students to picture the church as services begin. What is already in place? Who puts it there? What happens first? When are candles lit? Do young people participate in the services? How? Find one or two volunteers to record the group's ideas on a piece of newsprint.

After the students have written down everything they can think of, put the list in order by putting numbers by each item. When all the items are numbered, ask another volunteer to rewrite the list in the correct order.

Option 3. Matching Puzzle

Turn in the student newspaper, *Community Times*, Unit III, Issue 1, to the matching puzzle titled "Matching Word Scramble." Students may work alone, in pairs, or as a total group.

MUSIC
(Time: 10 minutes)

Introduce and sing "We gather together to ask the Lord's blessing" *(The Hymnal 1982, 433)*, and then listen to it on the *Children Sing!* tape. Note that the words of this hymn were written more than 350 years ago by an anonymous poet. Ask: What do the stanzas ask of God?

CONNECTING/SPEAKING OUT
(Time: 15–20 minutes)

Option 1. Group Discussion

Following is a series of "search questions" related to the directions for celebrating the Eucharist, found in *The Book of Common Prayer*, pp. 322 or 354, and pp. 406-409.

What color is the linen on the Holy Table? Under what circumstances can the Gospel be read in a language other than English? What can deacons do in the liturgy? Who can be the celebrant? Add more questions if you wish.

Divide the class members into small groups, or students may work in pairs. You may want to conduct the quiz as a game with time limits.

Option 2. Current Events

Suggest that the class members list the people who take part in the liturgy in their own congregation. Diagram a procession, putting names and titles on stick figures representing various persons. Be sure to include acolytes and servers. Acolytes who carry candles are usually called torchbearers, while those who carry crosses are called crucifers. If two crosses are carried in a processional, the smaller one is often called the clergy cross.

This is a good opportunity to emphasize names and function of the participants in the services. Lay readers also take part in the liturgy but are not always in the procession. Are any others included?

REFLECTING
(Time: 10 minutes)

Suggestions are provided in this Unit for times of "guided meditation." The teacher leads, and students are encouraged to provide details. The intent is to encourage private, personal reflection.

Ask the students to think about that morning. When did they get up? What did they do? Did everyone in their families get ready for church? Were you calm?

Allow time for the students to think about these questions and share their thoughts. Then ask them to close their eyes and relax in silence as you lead them in meditating. Speak slowly, with pauses between sentences to allow the class members to absorb the images. Incorporate the students' contributions from the earlier sharing.

Describe a calm beginning to the day as the students prepare for church. No one is hurried; there is time for breakfast and getting dressed. You arrive a few minutes early. After greeting several people, you enter the worship area. It is quiet. You enjoy watching people enter and find their seats.

After a minute or so of silence, invite the class members to open their eyes. Ask them to describe how they felt. Do you need to change your Sunday routine to make the worship experience better? Is there something you could do differently next Sunday to start the day better?

LEARNING SKILLS
(Time: 10–15 minutes)

Option 1. Class Memory Challenge

The memory challenge for this Unit is the Nicene Creed, in the version found in *The Book of Common Prayer*, p. 358. Some class members may already know it by heart; for those who do, suggest that this is an opportunity to reflect on the meaning of the words.

For this session, ask the students to turn to the Creed in their Prayer Books and read aloud together the first sentence: "We believe in one God, the Father, the Almighty, maker of heaven and earth, of all that is, seen and unseen." Point out the key words: one God; maker . . . of all that is.

Close the Prayer Books and say the sentence again at least twice.

Option 2. Learning Scripture

Suggest that the students memorize *Psalm 146:1-2* or *Colossians 3:17* before the next class session. See

"Learning Scripture" in the student newspaper, *Community Times*.

To record the class members' progress in learning Scripture during this Unit, make a large cardboard chalice (symbol for the Eucharist) in the same shape as the one on the front of this Teacher's Guide. Attach a series of long, colored ribbons to the chalice—one for each Bible verse memorized. Explain that each verse that has been learned will be written on a card and added to the end of a ribbon.

Add a sticker for each person who has accomplished the task.

ONGOING PROJECT
(Time: 5–10 minutes)

As an ongoing project for Sessions 1-5, invite the class members to become a liturgy planning group. It will be their task to prepare in detail a service bulletin for a Sunday Eucharist. The students will need copies of *The Book of Common Prayer*, the Bible, and *The Hymnal 1982*.

Choose a particular Sunday in the current Church Calendar from the weeks between Easter Day and Pentecost. Planning for a Sunday in the future may allow the students to submit their plan to the rector or worship planning committee. At this first session, the group will do the following:

1. Who will be at the altar (Celebrant, assistants, acolytes, and others)? Who will be the lector(s)? Will there be a choir? What other decisions need to be made?

2. How will the Celebrant begin the service

3. On a Sunday of Easter, it is likely the congregation will sing or say, "Glory to God in the highest . . ." (BCP, p. 356). What other hymn or song of praise might be used?

4. What will be the Collect of the Day? (See *The Book of Common Prayer*, pp. 159-261.)

Encourage the students to write down their decisions so that they can be saved for use in the following session.

SYMBOL CARD and TREASUREBOOK

Card 19 contains a bell in a steeple, a verse of Scripture, and an explanation on the back.

Ask the students to read, in the *Chalice Year Treasurebook*, Part III, Section 1 about the parts of the entrance rite.

GOING FORTH

Gather the group for the dismissal. The leader will say the following, pausing for the response of "Lord, have mercy":

> For our Bishop, and for all the clergy and people, let us pray to the Lord.
> *Lord, have mercy.*
>
> For this city (town, village, ____), for every city and community, and for those who live in them, let us pray to the Lord.
> *Lord, have mercy.*
>
> That we may end our lives in faith and hope, without suffering and without reproach, let us pray to the Lord.
> *Lord, have mercy.*
>
> For _____ [learners may add their own petitions], let us pray to the Lord.
> *Lord, have mercy.*
>
> From The Prayers of the People
> *The Book of Common Prayer*, pp. 384-385

Teacher: Let us go forth in the name of Christ.
Students: Thanks be to God.

TEACHER'S ASSESSMENT

What impressions concerning liturgy emerged from the students' discussions? How familiar were they with the Episcopal liturgy? In what ways could students appreciate the different parts of the entrance rite?

LOOKING AHEAD

The next session focuses on the remainder of The Word of God section in the service of Holy Eucharist. Included are the readings, the sermon, the Creed, the prayers, and the peace. Reflect on the ways in which this part of the liturgy provides a foundation for what follows—the Great Thanksgiving of Holy Eucharist.

EUCHARIST: SHARED LIFE

SESSION 2
THE WORD OF GOD

FOCUS

Following the entrance rite in the Eucharistic celebration, the section of The Word of God continues with Scripture, the sermon, the Nicene Creed, the Prayers of the People, Confession of Sin and Absolution, and the Peace. The students should be able to describe and explain the various parts of the liturgy of the Word.

GETTING READY

The portion of the service called The Word of God begins with the entrance rite (examined in Session 1). It continues with the reading of Holy Scripture, the sermon, the Nicene Creed, the Prayers of the People, Confession of Sin and Absolution, and the Peace.

Regular reading and interpreting of Scripture in the community of faith is rooted in Hebrew tradition. Jesus followed the custom of the Jewish people when he went to the synagogue each sabbath day. In *Luke 4:14-21*, we read the story of his visit to his home town of Nazareth, where he was invited to read from the *Book of Isaiah*. He stunned the people by declaring that he had come to fulfill the prophet's words.

The liturgy of the Word focuses on the Scripture selections listed in the Lectionary (BCP, pp. 889-931). This listing of Old Testament, Epistle, and Gospel lessons follows a three-year cycle. Generally speaking, Year A features the *Gospel of Matthew*; Year B, *Mark*; and Year C, *Luke*. Passages from John's Gospel are also used with frequency. Readings from the Old Testament (Hebrew Scriptures) were chosen for their compatibility with the themes of the Gospel readings. Except in the period of Advent through Easter, the Epistle readings are *seriatim* (one section at a time, in order).

The present Lectionary, an outgrowth of the Roman Catholic Vatican Council II, of the 1960s, is used in the liturgies by many Christian churches in the Western world.

Almighty God, the fountain of all wisdom: Enlighten by your Holy Spirit those who teach and those who learn, that, rejoicing in the knowledge of your truth, they may worship you and serve you from generation to generation; through Jesus Christ our Lord, who lives and reigns with you and the Holy Spirit, one God, for ever and ever. *Amen.*
For Education
The Book of Common Prayer, p. 261

TEACHING TIP

The use of class lectors for sharing selected passages of Scripture in the Intermediate Units is an opportunity to offer students early training in the tradition of the Episcopal liturgy of the Word. Encourage students who are appointed for this task to practice their reading ahead of time, to announce the readings in the correct way, and to read with understanding and an appropriate sense of reverence.

GATHERING

Gather as many different translations of the Bible as possible. Open each to one of the lessons, the Gospel reading for this Sunday, or a passage of your choosing. As students arrive, ask them to read the same passage in two or more of the Bibles.

Ask: What comes to mind when you see the word "Bible"? Why are translations of the same passages different? Is it helpful or confusing to read more than one translation?

When everyone is present, say:

Let us pray. (Use the Collect "For Education," above, or a prayer of your own choosing.)

The chosen student lector reads from the class Bible (NRSV):

A Reading from the Gospel of Luke, chapter 4, verses 14 through 21.

Then Jesus, filled with the power of the Spirit, returned to Galilee, and a report about him spread through all the surrounding country. He began to teach in their synagogues and was praised by everyone.

When he came to Nazareth, where he had been brought up, he went to the synagogue on the sabbath day, as was his custom. He stood up to read, and the scroll of the prophet Isaiah was given to him. He unrolled the scroll and found the place where it was written:

"The Spirit of the Lord is upon me,
  because he has anointed me
    to bring good news to the poor.
He has sent me to proclaim release to the captives
    and recovery of sight to the blind,
  to let the oppressed go free,
to proclaim the year of the Lord's favor."

And he rolled up the scroll, gave it back to the attendant, and sat down. The eyes of all in the synagogue were fixed on him. Then he began to say to them, "Today this scripture has been fulfilled in your hearing."

Reader: The Word of the Lord.
Response: Thanks be to God.

INTRODUCING THE STORY
(Time: 10 minutes)

Ask the students to name, in order and from memory, everything that happens at a service of the Holy Eucharist from the time the people gather until the Peace. To check their memories, look up the order in *The Book of Common Prayer* for Rite I, beginning on page 323, or Rite II on page 355.

Explain that the first part of the liturgy of Holy Eucharist is called The Word of God. It is a time for hearing the Bible read aloud, and a sermon on the readings. The sermon is followed by the Nicene Creed and the Prayers of the People. Then comes the Confession of Sin, and the passing of the Peace.

Call attention to the second word placard on Poster No. 13. The word "Bible" comes from the Greek *biblos* which means "papyrus" (book). Demonstrate the use of the Prayer Book's Lectionary to find the prescribed Scripture readings for Sunday Eucharists. Describe the cycle of Years A, B, and C, and locate the readings for the week the class is meeting.

Ask the students to turn in their Bibles to *Luke 4:14-21*. What happened when Jesus went to his home town? How did the people react? What clues does this story offer concerning synagogue worship?

Explain that the use of lectionaries is an ancient tradition, established to assure that the whole spectrum of Holy Scripture is included in public worship. Lectionaries were used in Hebrew worship before the beginning of the Christian faith.

EXPLORING
(Time: 15–20 minutes)

Option 1. Paper Making

Share with students information from the article about writing materials in ancient times found on page 2 of the student newspaper, *Community Times*. It describes the use of papyrus by biblical writers, such as the apostle Paul.

Let the group make its own paper to help students understand better how time-consuming the preparation of writing materials was in ancient times. Bring in a bucket partially filled with water, several sheets of a newspaper, a tiny amount of bleach, a colander, paper towels, and a piece of plastic. You will need a flat surface, such as a table, for the drying process.

Tear the newspaper in strips and put it in the water. Stir until the paper is the consistency of thick paste. Add a few drops of bleach to remove the ink coloring. Press the material into the colander to remove as much water as possible. Arrange the paper towels over the plastic on a flat surface. Carefully press the paper mixture on the towels. Decide beforehand if you want to make a small piece for each person in the group or one larger piece of paper.

As the materials dry, talk about the relation of words and paper. Ask students to name different ways that words are spread—through books, magazines, papers, over airwaves, and from person to person.

Option 2. The Lectionary

Bring in enough large, un-iced sugar cookies for each person in the class. Also have on hand several tubes of icing gel in different colors, enough Prayer Books for each person in the class, and several calendars that include church feasts and seasons.

Invite class members to look up the Daily Office Lectionary, beginning on page 936 of the Prayer Book. Using the calendars and the lectionary, help students find the Scripture passages for their birthdays and invite them to write them down on an index card.

When each person has found the appropriate references, pass out the cookies. Ask students to write down one or more of the passages on their cookies with the icing gel. Then eat the cookies as a snack.

Option 3. Word Puzzle

Turn in the student newspaper, *Community Times*, Unit III, Issue 2, to the word puzzle titled "The Word of God." Students may work individually, in pairs, or as a total group.

MUSIC
(Time: 10 minutes)

Sing or listen on the *Children Sing!* Tape to "I come with joy to meet my Lord" *(The Hymnal 1982, 304)*. This modern hymn for Holy Eucharist is set to an American folk melody that has been adapted for use in the hymnal.

CONNECTING/SPEAKING OUT
(Time: 15–20 minutes)

Option 1. Group Discussion

Begin by sharing the story of how one minister prepares a sermon from the article on page 1 of the student newspaper, *Community Times*. Write on a chalkboard the Scripture references used in worship this Sunday and *Luke 4:14-21* (the passage for this session).

Announce to the group that they are going to prepare a sermon for intermediate-age youth. First one or more students will need to look up each Scripture passage to find out what it is about. Then the group needs to select one that they believe has something to say to young people their age.

After selecting a passage, talk about different ways to present the ideas or story in the Scripture. Can anyone think of an appropriate story? How can they grab someone's attention?

Option 2. Current Events

Bring in several daily newspapers with sections of local and national news, your church newsletter, and diocesan publications. On the board write down the different sections of the prayers for the people, including the Church, its members, and its mission; the nation and those in authority; the welfare of the world; the concerns of the local community, those who suffer and those in any trouble; and those who have died (including the commemoration saints).

Ask students to look through the different publications for stories that fall in each category. For example, the diocese may be planning the next convention, a community may be considering zoning issue, and a fire or other tragedy may have injured people in a neighboring state. Find at least one story or picture for each of the categories above.

As a group, write a "prayers of the people" using the stories the group found. You may wish to use this prayer in your dismissal.

REFLECTING
(Time: 10 minutes)

Review the approach to "guided meditation" described in Session 1. For this session, pose these questions: Who are the readers or lectors in your congregation? How do they prepare? Where do they stand? How do they introduce the passage?

Invite the students to be quiet, with their eyes closed, for a period of meditating. Incorporate the students' contributions into an outline like the following:

"You have been asked to read one of the Scripture passages at a family worship service. Think about how you would prepare. Where would you go for help?

On the day of the service, where would you sit? At what point in the service would you go to the front of the congregation? Would you use a microphone? How would you introduce the passage and end it?

After a moment of silence, ask: Did you enjoy being a part of the service? Did you feel nervous? Would you like to find out if you could be a lector at your church?

LEARNING SKILLS
(Time: 10–15 minutes)

Option 1. Class Memory Challenge

Continue the study and memorizing of the Nicene Creed, as found in *The Book of Common Prayer*, p. 358.

Begin by reviewing the first sentence. Introduce the second sentence that begins "We believe in one Lord, Jesus Christ, . . ." and ending "of one being with the Father."

Ask the students to read and then recite the sentence aloud in unison. The key words are "one Lord, Jesus Christ." Note that Jesus Christ is described in seven ways. Challenge the students to make a chalkboard list from memory: 1. God's only Son; 2. eternal (everlasting); 3. God from God; 4. Light from Light; 5. true God from true God; 6. begotten, not made; 7. one Being with the Father.

Remind the students that the Nicene Creed is always said by the Celebrant and people at Holy Eucharists on Sundays and Major Feasts.

Option 2. Learning Scripture

If students have learned verses given in the previous session, add ribbons, cards, and student symbols to the Chalice described in Session 1.

Invite the class members to memorize *Luke 4:21* or *II Timothy 3:16* before the next session. See "Learning Scripture" in the student newspaper, *Community Times*.

ONGOING PROJECT
(Time: 5–10 minutes)

Continue planning a Sunday service of Holy Eucharist, as described in Session 1. Remind the students that the finished project will be a service bulletin suitable for a congregation's use.

At this session, make the following decisions:

1. Which lessons from Scripture will be read in the service—Old Testament, Epistle, or both? What is the Gospel reading? Look at the Lectionary (BCP, pp. 889-921). What are the themes of the Scriptures? Each lesson may be followed by a Psalm, hymn, or anthem. (See the italicized rubric, *The Book of Common Prayer*, p. 357.) In your church, what would be the usual custom?

2. Choose a processional hymn appropriate for the service. See Easter hymns in *The Hymnal 1982*, 174-213. Which hymn goes with the Scripture readings?

3. Who will preach the sermon? Note that the Nicene Creed follows immediately.

4. Which form will be used for the Prayers of the People? (See *The Book of Common Prayer*, pp. 328-330 and 383-393.) Will the Confession of Sin be included in the service? What follows?

SYMBOL CARD and TREASUREBOOK

Card 20 contains a Gospel book, a verse of Scripture, and an explanation on the back.

Ask the students to look in the *Chalice Year Treasurebook*, Part III, Section 2, about the part of the liturgy called The Word of God. Which section do you like best in this part?

GOING FORTH

Gather the group for the dismissal. The leader will say the following, pausing for the response of "Lord, have mercy":

> For our Bishop, and for all the clergy and people, let us pray to the Lord.
> *Lord, have mercy.*
> For this city (town, village, ____), for every city and community, and for those who live in them, let us pray to the Lord.
> *Lord, have mercy.*
>
> That we may end our lives in faith and hope, without suffering and without reproach, let us pray to the Lord.
> *Lord, have mercy.*
> For _____ [learners may add their own petitions], let us pray to the Lord.
> *Lord, have mercy.*
> From The Prayers of the People
> *The Book of Common Prayer*, pp. 384-385

Teacher: Let us go forth in the name of Christ.
Students: Thanks be to God.

TEACHER'S ASSESSMENT

As students explored the liturgy of the Word, did they have new insights? What would help them appreciate this part of the Holy Eucharist?

LOOKING AHEAD

The next session focuses on preparing the gifts of bread and wine and placing them on the altar for the celebration of Holy Communion. The lessons tell us that our lives and all we possess are gifts from God, calling for generous giving on our part. Reflect on what this has meant in your life.

EUCHARIST: SHARED LIFE

SESSION 3
OFFERING THE GIFTS

FOCUS

Following the Peace, the offerings of the people are brought to the Table (altar). The gifts of bread and wine for the Eucharist are received and prepared by the clergy and servers. Gifts of money are also brought to the Altar. The students should be able to explain the significance of the Offertory.

GETTING READY

In the early centuries of the Church's history, people came to the Sunday liturgy bringing gifts of bread and wine. A sufficient amount was placed on the Altar for the Eucharist, and the remainder was set aside for the clergy and for distribution to the poor.

The tradition of a deacon, an ordained member of the church, preparing the table began in the second century. A white cloth was spread on the table to receive the gifts, and offerings were collected by deacons.

Water was added to the wine to dilute it—a custom that continues to this day. In time, various prayers and ritual acts were added to the act of preparing the gifts.

The use of Scripture sentences to invite the people's offering is a very old practice. See suggestions in *The Book of Common Prayer*, pp. 343-344 or 376-377. A much-used Offertory sentence is adapted from *Ephesians 5:2*. Other appropriate sentences from the Bible or singing a hymn, psalm, or anthem can be used.

In today's Episcopal congregations, representatives bring the bread, wine, and money to the deacon or celebrant. The rubrics direct that the people are to stand as the offerings are presented and placed on the altar.

This preparatory period preceding Holy Communion is done with care and grace, in anticipation of the Great Thanksgiving that follows.

Almighty and everlasting God, increase in us the gifts of faith, hope, and charity; and, that we may obtain what you promise, make us love what you command; through Jesus Christ our Lord, who lives and reigns with you and the Holy Spirit, one God, for ever and ever. *Amen.*

Proper 25
The Book of Common Prayer, p. 235

TEACHING TIP

Ushers perform a significant service as the congregation gathers for worship. Later they receive the people's offerings of money and deliver them to the altar. Volunteers from the congregation carry the oblations (bread and wine) for the Eucharist. Intermediate-age students may enjoy serving as ushers or carrying the bread and wine. Are there such opportunities for youth in your congregation?

GATHERING

At the top of a piece of newsprint write the heading "Offerings—Time and Talent." Draw a line down the middle of the sheet. As students arrive, ask them to list in the right column offerings of talents they make to God at church. For example, serving as an acolyte or choir member.

In the left column, ask them to list offerings they make to God outside of church, such as visiting someone in a nursing home. Encourage class members to think of other ways they could serve God in the church, such as ushers or helping to take care of toddlers during coffee hour or other times.

When everyone is present, say:

Let us pray. (Use Proper 25 above, or a prayer of your own choosing.)

Unit III. Eucharist: Shared Life—Session 3
Chalice Year Intermediate—Copyright © 2000 Virginia Theological Sminary and Morehouse Publishing

The chosen student lector reads from the class Bible (NRSV):

A Reading from the Epistle to the Ephesians, chapter 5, verses 1 and 2.

Therefore be imitators of God, as beloved children, and live in love, as Christ loved us and gave himself up for us, a fragrant offering and sacrifice to God.

Reader: The Word of the Lord.
Response: Thanks be to God.

INTRODUCING THE STORY
(Time: 10 minutes)

In your own words, tell the story about a young person's experience taking gifts to the Altar from the article on page 1 of the student newspaper, *Community Times* (Unit III, Issue 3). Or, describe your own experience in presenting the gifts of bread and wine at the Altar.

Point out the word placard on Poster No. 13 in the Teacher's Packet that says: SACRAMENT (SACRAMENTUM, SACER). Point out that the word "sacrament" comes from the Latin "sacramentum." Its root is "sacer" which means sacred. A related word is "sacrifice." At the Eucharist, the offerings of bread and wine are blessed by prayer. In the mystery of this act, Jesus Christ is truly present. The Holy Eucharist is a sacred moment for the people of God.

Explain the significance of the Offertory or the presenting of gifts by sharing information provide in Getting Ready (above) and the *Chalice Year Treasurebook*.

Describe briefly how the gifts are presented and prepared in your congregation. Find out if anyone in the class has had similar experiences. Ask them to describe what they did and how they felt.

Name people who assist as servers and in other roles. In some churches there is only a simple passing of the bread and wine to the Celebrant, who places them on the altar. In other churches, the custom is more elaborate.

Ask the students to turn in their Bibles to *Luke 21:1-4*. Jesus spoke about the spirit in which we offer gifts to God. What would be some examples of sacrificial giving in today's Church? Look at the lists made during the Gathering exercise for ideas.

Find out if students are interested in serving as ushers or in taking the wine and bread to the altar at the Offertory. Talk to the clergy or someone who is responsible for these functions to see if class members could participate.

EXPLORING
(Time: 15–20 minutes)

Option 1. Baking Bread

With advance planning, it may be possible to arrange for the class members to make bread for a celebration of Holy Communion at your church. Use the recipe provided in the student newspaper, *Community Times*, or one provided by the church.

The class could meet in a kitchen, or they could mix the ingredients in the classroom and take the dough home to bake. Designate a worship service in which the bread could be used. If necessary, freeze the bread until that time.

Option 2. Altar Frontal

Prepare a length of plain fabric for an Altar frontal. Invite the students to discuss designs and symbols to include on the cloth. Look at the Chalice Year symbol cards for ideas. Use fabric markers and crayons (available at craft stores) in making the designs.

Each student may be assigned to work in a marked-off square of the cloth or on separate 12-inch squares of fabric to be attached to a larger cloth background. The finished frontal could present a scattered mosaic effect, or it could have an orderly border of squares along the edge.

Arrange for the completed Altar frontal to be used in a service, or displayed for the congregation to see. If separate squares are made, they could be returned to the individuals who created them.

Option 3. Word Puzzle

Turn in the student newspaper, *Community Times*, Unit III, Issue 3, to the word puzzle titled "Offering the Gifts." Students may work alone, in pairs, or as a total group.

MUSIC
(Time: 10 minutes)

Introduce the hymn, "For the bread which you have broken" (*The Hymnal 1982*, 340; *We Sing of God*, 55). How many different notes are used in this hymn? (Only g, a, c, f, and d—five in all). Explain that much music in Asia is written in a "Pentatonic" scale using just five notes to produce a distinctive sound. Listen to the hymn on the *Children Sing!* tape.

CONNECTING/SPEAKING OUT
(Time: 15–20 minutes)

Option 1. Group Discussion

The Offertory in the Church's liturgy is a special moment in which the people respond to The Word of God by presenting gifts. Call the students' attention to the rubrics in *The Book of Common Prayer*, at the top of page 333 or page 361.

Ask: What are the gifts to be presented? In addition to bread, wine, and money, what "other gifts" could be offered? Food to be shared with the hungry is especially appropriate.

Some churches collect food, coats, or other items through the church school. If your church does not do this, class members might explore a gathering for a community group or other church. Participants in the church school could present gifts at the Altar at a designated service.

What do the gifts represent? Why are they collected and carried by people from the congregation? Point out that our gifts are an expression of praise to God. They are to be used for God's purposes in the world. We give ourselves prayerfully as we present offerings that come from our daily work.

Option 2. Current Events

If possible, arrange to show how the Altar in your church is prepared for Holy Communion: the spreading of the linens and the arranging of the vessels. Consider inviting Altar Guild members or servers to assist in a demonstration and discussion.

REFLECTING
(Time: 10 minutes)

A process for guided meditation is described under Reflecting in Session 1 of this Unit. For this session, lead the students in meditating about the preparation of gifts for the Service of Holy Eucharist.

To get ready, ask the students: What happens at the Eucharist just after the Peace? What are the gifts that are brought to the Altar? Who carries them? How is the altar prepared during the Offertory? Who assists?

Ask the group to close their eyes and be silent. Remind them about the gifts of time and talent they listed during the Gathering exercise by reading both lists slowly.

Then say: "Think of one new way you could bring an offering to God. Mentally think about services and activities at your church. Are there opportunities for you to serve God and others?

"Now think about your activities outside of church. Is there something you could do at school to help a teacher or a classmate? Is there something you could do at home to help a parent or sibling?"

After a brief silence, encourage class members to identify one new offering. Pass out slips of paper and ask them to write it down. Tell students the slips will be collected at the dismissal. Before you say the final prayers at the end of the session, say one of the offertory sentences in *The Book of Common Prayer*, pp. 376-377, and then collect the slips by passing a basket or other container.

LEARNING SKILLS
(Time: 10–15 minutes)

Option 1. Class Memory Challenge

Continue the process of reflecting on the Nicene Creed as it is memorized by the group. Begin by reviewing the portions learned at previous sessions.

Introduce the two sentences about Jesus Christ that begin "Through him . . . ." and "For us . . . ." Explain the importance of both claims about the Son of God: He was present at the creation of "all things." He was fully human. You may want to point out that, in some churches, the people bow or kneel as they say the words "by the power of the Holy Spirit he became incarnate from the Virgin Mary, and was made man."

Say the sentences in unison, pausing after each one to reflect on its meaning.

Option 2. Learning Scripture

Ask class members to add ribbons, cards, and student symbols to the chalice for any Scripture verses learned since the last session as described in Session 1. Remind the students that any verse cited during this Unit may be memorized at any time; the complete list of passages for the Unit appears in the student newspaper, *Community Times*.

Suggest that the group memorize *Psalm 96:8* or *Ephesians 5:1-2* before the next session.

ONGOING PROJECT
(Time: 5–10 minutes)

Continue with the project of planning a liturgy for a given Sunday, as begun in Sessions 1-2.

Review the details worked out in previous meetings, then consider the following:

1. After the Peace, the Celebrant may begin the Offertory with a sentence of Scripture—probably cho-

sen from *The Book of Common Prayer*, p. 376. Which of these would the group prefer?

2. As the Celebrant and others move to the Altar, the preparation at the Holy Table begins. What will be needed? In your church, who will be responsible for preparing the linens, vessels, bread, wine, and water on the chosen Sunday? When will they carry out the various tasks?

3. Will a hymn, psalm, or anthem be used during the Offertory? If so, what would be appropriate for the chosen Sunday?

4. Who will bring the bread and wine and the money to the Altar?

Be sure the group keeps a written record of the discussion and decisions at this meeting.

SYMBOL CARD and TREASUREBOOK

Card 21 shows bread, cruet, and wine, with a verse of Scripture and an explanation on the back.

Encourage the students to read in *Chalice Year Treasurebook*, Part III, Section 3, to reexamine how gifts are offered at the Eucharist. The section also describes how the gifts are prepared at the Holy Table. What do our gifts represent?

GOING FORTH

Gather the group for the dismissal. The leader will say the following, pausing for the response of "Lord, have mercy":

> For our Bishop, and for all the clergy and people, let us pray to the Lord.
> *Lord, have mercy.*

For this city (town, village, ____), for every city and community, and for those who live in them, let us pray to the Lord.
Lord, have mercy.

That we may end our lives in faith and hope, without suffering and without reproach, let us pray to the Lord.
Lord, have mercy.

For _____ [learners may add their own petitions], let us pray to the Lord.
Lord, have mercy.

> From The Prayers of the People
> *The Book of Common Prayer*, pp. 384-385

Teacher: Let us go forth in the name of Christ.
Students: Thanks be to God.

TEACHER'S ASSESSMENT

From your observations, do the students appreciate the significance of the Offertory? How familiar are they with the steps in preparing the gifts of bread and wine for Holy Communion? What would help the class members adopt a stronger sense of stewardship and sacrificial giving?

LOOKING AHEAD

The next session is devoted to the Great Thanksgiving in the liturgy of the Eucharist. This prayer reviews what God has done for us in the life, death, and resurrection of Jesus Christ. The prayer also calls us into the living presence of the risen Lord. What are some of the "great thanksgivings" you can offer in your own life?

EUCHARIST: SHARED LIFE

SESSION 4
THE GREAT THANKSGIVING

FOCUS

The Eucharistic Prayer of The Holy Communion follows forms dating to the earliest Christian celebrations of the liturgy. This great prayer of the Eucharist, followed by the breaking of the bread and the distribution of the Sacrament, is the central act of the sacred meal. The students should be able to locate one version of the Great Thanksgiving in *The Book of Common Prayer*, and to describe their own understanding of the Eucharist.

GETTING READY

When we gather for a family meal and someone says "grace," the prayer is an expression of our thanks for the food and other good gifts that God has provided. We then eat together and enjoy one another's company.

In the same way, when we gather for the sacred meal of Holy Communion, the Celebrant says "grace" in the form of a prayer called the Great Thanksgiving. Then the bread is broken and we all receive the gifts of God.

The word "Eucharist" is formed from a combination of the Greek "eu" (well, or good) and "charis" (favor, or grace). The act of celebrating Eucharist is a "good grace"—an expression of profound thanksgiving.

Through the centuries, Christian churches have prepared many forms of the prayer at the heart of the Sacrament. Essential elements are:

—praise to God for the sacrifice of Jesus Christ;

—the words of the "institution" of the Lord's Supper (based on *I Corinthians 11:23-26*);

—words of "memorial," or remembering;

—invoking the Holy Spirit's presence in the Sacrament and in the people's lives as they serve the Lord.

The Book of Common Prayer offers a choice of six forms for the Great Thanksgiving—two in Rite I and four in Rite II. Each form has grown out of the experiences of Christian people over the many generations of Church history.

The Great Thanksgiving is followed by the Lord's Prayer and the Fraction (the breaking of the consecrated bread). Then the elements are distributed to the people with the words given in the Prayer Book, pp. 338 and 365.

God our Father, whose Son our Lord Jesus Christ in a wonderful Sacrament has left us a memorial of his passion: Grant us so to venerate the sacred mysteries of his Body and Blood, that we may ever perceive within ourselves the fruit of his redemption; who lives and reigns with you and the Holy Spirit, one God, for ever and ever. *Amen.*
Of the Holy Eucharist
The Book of Common Prayer, p. 252

TEACHING TIP

Students at the intermediate-age level can have a deeper understanding of the significance of receiving the bread and wine. Some class members may have been receiving the gifts all their lives. Others may only now be preparing to receive for the first time. Be aware of questions or concerns that may arise as a result of these sessions on the Eucharist. Help the students to reflect on their journey into the holy mysteries of this Sacrament.

GATHERING

At the top of a piece of posterboard, write "Great Thanksgivings." As students arrive, invite them to think of events, people, or items that they are thankful for. Encourage them to write descriptions of these things or draw them on the posterboard underneath the title. Let them know that their ideas will be used later in the session.

When everyone is present, say:

Let us pray. (Use the Collect "Of the Holy Eucharist," above, or a prayer of your own choosing.)

The chosen student lector reads from the class Bible (NRSV):

A Reading from the First Epistle to the Corinthians, chapter 11, verses 23 through 26.

For I received from the Lord what I also handed on to you, that the Lord Jesus on the night when he was betrayed took a loaf of bread, and when he had given thanks, he broke it and said, "This is my body that is for you. Do this in remembrance of me." In the same way he took the cup also, after supper, saying, "This cup is the new covenant in my blood. Do this, as often as you drink it, in remembrance of me." For as often as you eat this bread and drink the cup, you proclaim the Lord's death until he comes.

Reader: The Word of the Lord.
Response: Thanks be to God.

INTRODUCING THE STORY
(Time: 10 minutes)

Describe in your own words the different parts of The Holy Communion and how you experience each part. Use the article on page 1 of the student newspaper, *Community Times* (Unit III, Issue 4) as a guide. You may wish to relate a Communion experience that has special meaning for you that occurred during a wedding, a retreat, funeral, or other time.

Refer to the fourth set of words on Poster No. 13 in the Teacher's Packet: EUCHARIST (EU+CHARIS). Use the information in Getting Ready (above) and the *Chalice Year Treasurebook* to expand on the meaning of Holy Eucharist.

The most important moment of Holy Communion is the Great Thanksgiving. In *The Book of Common Prayer*, there are six forms of this prayer.

Rite I includes two forms: Eucharistic Prayer I (beginning on page 333) and Prayer II (p. 340). Both are based on the prayers composed by Bishop Thomas Cranmer, who wrote the first prayer book for the Church of England.

Rite II offers four forms: Prayer A (pp. 361-363); Prayer B (pp. 367-369); Prayer C (pp. 369-372); and Prayer D (pp. 372-375).

Mention each of the essential elements of the Great Thanksgiving (praise, words of institution, remembrance, offering, and the breaking of the bread. At this time the Holy Spirit is asked to make the bread and wine the spiritual food of Christ's Body and Blood and to help the people become faithful servants of the risen Lord). A more detailed description of the parts of The Great Thanksgiving are on page 2 of the student newspaper, *Community Times*.

Discuss your own congregation's way of distributing the bread and wine to the people. Ask class members if they have participated in services at other churches, including those of a different denomination, during communion. Invite them to share their experiences.

Ask the students to turn in their Bibles to *I Corinthians 11:23-26*, and compare the words of the apostle Paul with the "words of institution" found in the Great Thanksgiving, Rite I, Prayer I (BCP, pp. 334-335). What is the same? different?

EXPLORING
(Time: 15–20 minutes)

Option 1. Thanksgiving

Look at the events, people, and items that students listed under "Great Thanksgivings" on the posterboard used during the Gathering. Ask them to explain some of the things on the list.

Provide paper, markers, pens, and envelopes. Encourage students to describe a way to offer thanksgivings for one or more of the things they put on the list. For example, they may choose to write someone a thank you note for being a good friend or to a teacher for spending extra time with them. Students may want to write and illustrate a prayer thanking God for creating a place that has special meaning or beauty. Encourage them to be creative.

When everyone has finished, ask students to put their letters or prayers in separate envelopes. If it is a letter to a specific person, ask them to write that person's name on the envelope. At the dismissal, gather the letters in a basket as an offering of thanksgiving. Encourage students who wrote letters to individuals to take their envelopes home to be addressed and mailed.

Option 2. Chalice Cutwork

Display the picture from Poster No. 14 in the

Teacher's Packet of the cutwork chalice. Invite close observation and discussion. This is a particularly fine example of paper folding and cutwork. The chalice or cup is one of the great symbols of the Eucharist.

For each student, provide a sheet of paper that can hold a crisp fold and a pair of sharp-tipped scissors, not blunt-ended. Invite the students to create their own versions of a cutwork chalice. The general technique is much like cutting snowflakes. Mount the finished chalices on sheets of paper in contrasting colors.

Option 3. Word Puzzle

Turn in the student newspaper, *Community Times*, Unit III, Issue 4, to the crossword titled "Eucharist." Students may work alone, in pairs, or as a total group.

MUSIC
(Time: 10 minutes)

Sing again or listen on the *Children Sing!* tape to "For the bread which you have broken" *(The Hymnal 1982, 340; We Sing of God, 55)*. Call attention in stanza 3 to "our Father's board." This means the table. How does the hymn writer feel about coming to Communion?

CONNECTING/SPEAKING OUT
(Time: 15–20 minutes)

Option 1. Group Discussion

In Rite II of the Holy Eucharist, the Great Thanksgivings include varying forms of the "the Memorial Acclamation," said by the Celebrant and people together. These lines come immediately after the consecration of the bread and wine, as a summary of the good news of Jesus Christ. He lived, died, and rose again. (See Prayer A, p. 363; Prayer B, p. 368; Prayer C, p. 371.)

In Prayer D, p. 374, the recalling of Christ's death, proclaiming of his resurrection and ascension, and awaiting his "coming in glory" are included in the words of the priest. Similarly, in Rite I, the priest's words include "having in remembrance his (Christ's) blessed passion and precious death, his mighty resurrection and glorious ascension; . . . " (See Prayer I, p. 335, and Prayer II, p. 342.)

Invite the class members to compile a chart of the six forms. What do they have in common? How are they different? Ask: Which of the forms appeals most to you?

Option 2. Current Events

At the Last Supper, Jesus instituted the Eucharist with "common" elements of bread and wine, parts of any ordinary meal at that time. Invite the students to discuss the similarities between regular meals and the sacred meal of the Holy Eucharist (gathering, saying grace, eating and drinking together, and expressing care for one another).

Explore with the students the concept of the Great Thanksgiving as a prayer of "grace." (See Getting Ready above.) Ask: In what ways do we offer prayers of thanks at family meals? You may want to turn to page 835 of *The Book of Common Prayer* to examine four examples of "Grace at Meals."

Note words, phrases, and meanings from the Eucharist that we sometimes use in speaking about our everyday (common) meals, such as: "Let us give thanks," "Let us share the feast," or "Let us break bread together."

REFLECTING
(Time: 10 minutes)

Ask the group to sit quietly and think about the last time they went to the communion rail to receive the bread and the wine. (Note: If students in your class do not receive at Communion, say "blessing" instead of "bread and wine.")

Ask: What were you thinking about? Did you hear the words preceding Communion? Did you think about Jesus having the Last Supper with his disciples? Did you think about people and things you were thankful for?

Encourage them to be prepared to fully participate the next time they are in a Communion service. Ask them to think about ways they can get more out of the service by listening or praying.

Allow a few moments of silent prayer. Then lead the class members in reflecting on their feelings about receiving Holy Communion.

LEARNING SKILLS
(Time: 10–15 minutes)

Option 1. Class Memory Challenge

Continue working reflectively on the task of memorizing the Nicene Creed. Begin by reciting the portions learned in previous sessions.

Introduce the section that includes the death and resurrection of Jesus Christ, beginning "For our sake he was crucified . . . ." and ending "in accordance with the Scriptures; . . . " Point out that the earliest Christians were eager to show that Jesus' mission was the fulfillment of Hebrew prophecy.

Say this portion of the Creed in unison more than once.

Option 2. Learning Scripture

Add ribbons, cards, and symbols to the cardboard chalice prepared for this Unit for verses learned by students since the last session.

Remind the class members that any verse cited during the Unit may be memorized at any time. The complete list for the Unit is under the heading, "Learning Scripture," in the student newspaper, *Community Times*.

Invite the students to learn either or both of the following before the next session: *Mark 14:22-24* or *I Corinthians 11:26*.

ONGOING PROJECT
(Time: 5–10 minutes)

Continue the group's liturgy planning, as outlined in previous sessions. Ask the students to use their Prayer Books as they consider the following:

1. Which of the Great Thanksgiving prayers will be used? If the liturgy is Rite I, the two options begin on pages 333 and 340 of *The Book of Common Prayer*. In Rite II, Prayers are designated A, B, C, and D (pp. 361-376).

2. Where will the Celebrant find the Proper Preface for the chosen Sunday? (For the Sundays of Easter, see *The Book of Common Prayer*, pp. 346 and 379.)

3. Will a musical setting be used for the Sanctus ("Holy, holy, holy, . . . ")? If so, which one? Consult *The Hymnal 1982*, S-113 through S-117.

4. If Rite II is chosen for this service, which form of the Lord's Prayer will be used? (See *The Book of Common Prayer*, p. 364.)

5. If Rite I is used, will the Celebrant lead in the Agnus Dei ("O Lamb of God, . . . ")? Will the prayer of humble access be used? ("We do not presume . . . .")? See *The Book of Common Prayer*, p. 337.

6. Will words at the Fraction—when the Celebrant breaks the consecrated Bread—be sung or said? If sung, what anthem will be used? (See *The Hymnal 1982*, S-151 through S-172. For Sundays of Easter, S-151 and S-152 are preferred.)

7. On the chosen Sunday, who will assist the Celebrant in serving the consecrated Bread and Wine to the people?

Keep a written record of its decisions for use at the final planning meeting.

SYMBOL CARD and TREASUREBOOK

Card 22 contains a chalice and wafer, a verse of Scripture, and an explanation on the back.

Suggest that the students read Part III, Section 4, in the *Chalice Year Treasurebook* that describes the Great Thanksgiving, including the serving of the consecrated bread and wine. It is a helpful introduction to its structure as it has been developed from the New Testaments accounts of the Last Supper. Ask: How does the Holy Eucharist echo what happened at Jesus' Last Supper?

GOING FORTH

Gather the group for the dismissal. The leader will say the following, pausing for the response of "Lord, have mercy":

> For our Bishop, and for all the clergy and people, let us pray to the Lord.
> *Lord, have mercy.*
>
> For this city (town, village, ____), for every city and community, and for those who live in them, let us pray to the Lord.
> *Lord, have mercy.*
>
> That we may end our lives in faith and hope, without suffering and without reproach, let us pray to the Lord.
> *Lord, have mercy.*
>
> For _____ [learners may add their own petitions], let us pray to the Lord.
> *Lord, have mercy.*
>
> From The Prayers of the People
> *The Book of Common Prayer*, pp. 384-385

Teacher: Let us go forth in the name of Christ.
Students: Thanks be to God.

TEACHER'S ASSESSMENT

Are the students able to identify the essential elements of the Great Thanksgiving? In what ways do they demonstrate awareness of both the personal and community participation in Holy Communion?

LOOKING AHEAD

In the next session, the focus is on going forth from the Holy Communion to serve God in the world. Reflect on what it is like for you when you leave a service at your church. Be aware of your responses.

EUCHARIST: SHARED LIFE

SESSION 5
GOING FORTH INTO THE WORLD

FOCUS

The people of God give thanks for the benefits of the Eucharist. Their prayer is followed by a blessing, a dismissal, and a closing hymn. They are to go forth into the world to live out the good news proclaimed as they were gathered at the Lord's Table. The students should be able to state why Christian liturgy is closely connected to the everyday lives of the people.

GETTING READY

In the service of Eucharist, the Great Thanksgiving is followed by the Lord's Prayer. Then comes the breaking of the bread, sometimes accompanied by an anthem (said or sung):

"Christ our Passover is sacrificed for us;
Therefore let us keep the feast."

These words remind the congregation that Christ died for each person. As beneficiaries of Christ's sacrifice, all who receive Holy Communion are obliged to be his servants. This theme is apparent in each form of the final prayer of thanksgiving by Celebrant and people:

"... we humbly beseech thee, O heavenly Father, so to assist us with thy grace, that we may continue in that holy fellowship, and do all such good works as thou hast prepared for us to walk in; ..." (Rite I, BCP, p. 339.)

Or, "Send us now into the world in peace, and grant us strength and courage to love and serve you with gladness and singleness of heart; through Christ our Lord." (Rite II, p. 365.)

Or, "And now, Father, send us out to do the work you have given us to do, to love and serve you as faithful witnesses of Christ our Lord." (Rite II, p. 366.)

Communicants are given a mission by the risen Lord who meets us at the Holy Table again and again. Note that three of the Sacrament's four forms of dismissal stress the word "go." (BCP, pp. 339-340, 366.) The letters of the apostle Paul underscore repeatedly the necessity for Christians to rejoice in the Lord, and let the love of God show in our lives. See, for example, *Philippians 4:4-7.*

Almighty God our heavenly Father, you declare your glory and show forth your handiwork in the heavens and in the earth: Deliver us in our various occupations from the service of self alone, that we may do the work you give us to do in truth and beauty and for the common good; for the sake of him who came among us as one who serves, your Son Jesus Christ our Lord, who lives and reigns with you and the Holy Spirit, one God, for ever and ever. *Amen.*

For Vocation in Daily Work
The Book of Common Prayer, p. 261

TEACHING TIP

Intermediate-age students do not have to wait until they are old enough to carry out acts of Christian witness. They can volunteer for meaningful participation in many areas of the church. Consider the mission projects of your own congregation in which they can participate. Do not overlook other forms of service in the larger community that may be open to young persons.

GATHERING

As students enter the classroom, give them an index card and a pencil or pen. Ask them to write down one thing that they could do for someone else—a friend or family member—that day. When they are finished, ask them to put their cards in a brown sack.

At the dismissal, put the sack in the center or front of the group as an offering to God. Tell students that the work of Christians begins as they carry the Good News from church to their homes and communities. Remind them to complete the task that they wrote on the cards at the Gathering.

When everyone is present, say:

Let us pray. (Use the Collect "For Vocation in Daily Work," above, or a prayer of your own choosing.)

The chosen student lector reads from the class Bible (NRSV):

A Reading from the Epistle to the Philippians, chapter 4, verses 4 through 7.

Rejoice in the Lord always; again I will say, Rejoice. Let your gentleness be known to everyone. The Lord is near. Do not worry about anything, but in everything by prayer and supplication with thanksgiving let your requests be made known to God. And the peace of God, which surpasses all understanding, will guard your hearts and minds in Christ Jesus.

Reader: The Word of the Lord.
Response: Thanks be to God.

INTRODUCING THE STORY
(Time: 10 minutes)

The student newspaper, *Community Times* (Unit III, Issue 5), includes several short stories about people's missions and ministries within and outside of the church. Tell one of these stories in your own words or describe your ministry or the work of someone in your congregation. For example, you might describe volunteer work in a community setting or within the church.

Invite the students to locate in their Bibles *Philippians* 4:4-7. Ask: What does the apostle Paul remind us to do? How are his words related to our mission as Christians?

Briefly discuss the cards the students wrote for the Gathering activity. Paul tells us to let the love of God show in our lives by what we do and say. How should we act when we do something for others?

Remind students that we are sent out into the world at the end of the Communion service. Review the movement of the service of Holy Eucharist, from the entrance rite to the dismissal. (You may want to copy, on a chalkboard or newsprint, the general outline provided in the *Chalice Year Treasurebook* or the student newspaper, *Community Times*.)

Call attention to the final set of words on the placard on Poster No. 13 in the Teacher's Packet: MISSION (MISSIO). Explain that the word "mission" comes from the Latin *missio*, which means "sending out." The word "dismiss" literally means "to send forth." When the words of dismissal are spoken at the end of the service of Holy Eucharist, the people are being sent into the world to do the work of Christians as servants of the living Lord.

Describe the Sacrament of Holy Communion as a gathering of Christ's baptized people who receive spiritual nourishment at the Holy Table. They pray for the courage and strength to be faithful servants of God in the world.

EXPLORING
(Time: 15–20 minutes)

Option 1. Mission Project

Plan a class mission project to be accomplished in the congregation or the community. Ahead of time, solicit suggestions and assistance from clergy and vestry members to assure that the project is manageable in scope and more than busywork. (Possibilities: A spring cleaning job, indoors or outside; Easter season visits to homes of confined elderly persons; providing food for a homeless shelter.)

Define the project clearly and work out the details as a group. Remind the students that Christian mission is continuous and does not end with any specific project's completion.

Option 2. Going Into the World

Bring in an assortment of household items, such as a pail, broom, sewing kit, can of food, pencil, hammer, and nail. Be sure to have enough items for each student.

Pass out the items or let each student select one. Arrange the chairs in a circle, and ask students to hold their items so that everyone can see them.

Explain that the group is going to create a mission story using the items they are holding. Give them a moment to think of ways their items could be used to help others. Point to someone to begin the story. For example, a student with a broom could say it would be used to clean up after a church dinner. The next person in the circle then recaps what the first person said and adds to the story. The story continues in a similar fashion.

Encourage students to be creative in finding ways to use their items to make the story more interesting. By the end of the game, the plot will probably be confusing. As the last person recounts the entire story, write down on newsprint each of the ways the items are used.

Briefly discuss the tasks described in the story. Ask: How many of these things could you do?

Option 3. Word Puzzle

Turn in the student newspaper, *Community Times*, Unit III, Issue 5, to the word puzzle titled "Going Forth." Students may work alone, in pairs, or as a total group.

MUSIC
(Time: 10 minutes)

Introduce and sing "Go forth for God" *(The Hymnal 1982*, 347*)*. Listen to the words of all four stanzas on the *Children Sing!* tape.

CONNECTING/SPEAKING OUT
(Time: 15–20 minutes)

Option 1. Group Discussion

Discuss the connections between the celebration of the Holy Eucharist and our daily lives. Ask: What do we receive from our participation in Holy Eucharist? What do we take from it? How does attending worship affect the rest of our lives?

On a piece of newsprint, list student responses to the question: What does God ask us to do? Refer back to the Gathering exercise. Remind students that our service for others is service for God.

Option 2. Current Events

Point out that both adults and youth in the Church may be hesitant about speaking of their Christian beliefs to people outside the Christian community. Ask: What keeps us from sharing our faith? Why isn't it a natural thing to do?

These questions may open the door for the students to talk about prayer in schools. Use this opportunity to talk about maintaining Christian values even though court rulings may prohibit formal religious expression in public schools and community-wide gatherings. Remind students that God is always with them and hears their prayers no matter where they are.

REFLECTING
(Time: 10 minutes)

Lead a guided meditation on the sights and sounds of leaving your church after a service of Holy Eucharist. Encourage students to describe their own departures. Ask: How do you feel when the service is over? Do you stop and talk to people? What are you thinking about?

Ask the students to close their eyes and sit quietly. Tell them to think about the last time they had Holy Communion. Ask: Did you feel the presence of Christ? Were you prepared to serve others when you left? What could you do to make this service more meaningful?

Allow a brief time of silence. Ask: What helped you to think about serving God? serving other people? What do you like about attending and leaving the Holy Eucharist?

LEARNING SKILLS
(Time: 10–15 minutes)

Option 1. Class Memory Challenge

Invite the students to take another step in their walk through the Nicene Creed. Begin by reciting the portion already learned in previous sessions.

Introduce the section that begins "he ascended into heaven. . . ." and ends "his kingdom will have no end." Note the key words, "ascended into heaven" and "will come again." The Church has always affirmed its belief that Jesus Christ will appear again for the final establishment of God's reign.

Repeat these two clauses of the Creed in unison.

Option 2. Learning Scripture

Ask any students who have memorized verses suggested in the previous session to place ribbons, cards, and student symbols on the chalice.

Ask class members to memorize *Ephesians 3:20-21* or *Philippians 4:5* before the next class session. See "Learning Scripture" in the student newspaper, *Community Times*.

ONGOING PROJECT
(Time: 5–10 minutes)

Ask the planning group to complete its work on designing a service bulletin for a chosen Sunday, as described in previous sessions. At this meeting, consider the following:

1. If the liturgy is Rite II, which of the final prayers will be used (BCP, pp. 365 or 366)? The prayer for Rite I is on page 339.

2. Which words of dismissal will be used? (BCP, pp. 339-340 or 366)? Note, for the Sundays of Easter, that "Alleluia, alleluia" may be added.

3. What will be the final hymn? Will it be used in recession?

Appoint a committee to prepare the service

bulletin, incorporating all the decisions made from the beginning. Who will receive copies? Consider whether the group's work could be shared with your congregation's worship planners and possibly become the order used on the chosen Sunday.

SYMBOL CARD and TREASUREBOOK

Card 23 shows a crosslet, a verse of Scripture, and an explanation on the back.

Ask students to ready Part III, Section 5, in the *Chalice Year Treasurebook*, which emphasizes practical ways of responding to the good news of Christ reenacted in the sacrament of Holy Communion. Encourage the group to think about their own ministries as young Christians in the world.

GOING FORTH

Gather the group for the dismissal. The leader will say the following, pausing for the response of "Lord, have mercy":

> For our Bishop, and for all the clergy and people, let us pray to the Lord.
> *Lord, have mercy.*
>
> For this city (town, village, ____), for every city and community, and for those who live in them, let us pray to the Lord.
> *Lord, have mercy.*
>
> That we may end our lives in faith and hope, without suffering and without reproach, let us pray to the Lord.
> *Lord, have mercy.*
>
> For _____ [learners may add their own petitions], let us pray to the Lord.
> *Lord, have mercy.*
>
> From The Prayers of the People
> *The Book of Common Prayer*, pp. 384-385

Teacher: Let us go forth in the name of Christ.
Students: Thanks be to God.

TEACHER'S ASSESSMENT

How would you assess the students' awareness that they are "witnesses" who can share the good news of Jesus Christ? How did they respond to the idea of going forth into their community as Christians?

LOOKING AHEAD

The next four sessions of this Unit will examine closely the events of Holy Week and Easter. We do not leave the theme of Eucharist behind, for it echoes through all that happens in the last days of Jesus. Session 6 is devoted to the time block of Palm Sunday through Maundy Thursday. What do you feel about the annual drama of Holy Week?

EUCHARIST: SHARED LIFE
SESSION 6
HOLY WEEK BEGINS

FOCUS

Palm Sunday begins Holy Week. On Maundy Thursday, with his words and actions at the Last Supper, Jesus instituted the sacrament of Holy Eucharist. He predicted a betrayal and a denial. Using the *Gospel of Mark*, the students should be able to describe the events of Holy Week—from the triumphant arrival in Jerusalem to the Last Supper and Peter's denial of Jesus.

GETTING READY

The sweep of emotions evoked by Jesus' last days on earth carries us from the exuberant "Hosannas" of Palm Sunday, through the deep despair of the crucifixion on Good Friday, and on to the joyous "Alleluias" of Easter Day. The next four sessions of this Unit are devoted to selected events from the story of Holy Week.

In this session the focus is on the events preceding and immediately following the Last Supper. The *Gospel of Mark* presents a vivid series of "word pictures" conveying mood and setting, along with memorable phrases:

- Procession with palms into Jerusalem *(Mark 11:1-11)*
- Jesus cleanses the temple *(Mark 11:15-19)*
- Jesus teaches in the temple *(Mark 12, 13)*
- The Last Supper *(Mark 14:12-31)*
- Jesus prays in the Garden of Gethsemane *(Mark 14:32-42)*
- The betrayal *(Mark 14:43-50)*
- The trial before the high priests *(Mark 14:53-65)*
- Peter's denial *(Mark 14:66-72)*

Jesus and his friends entered Jerusalem in the week of Passover, a sacred meal celebrating the Hebrews' deliverance from slavery in Egypt. After his triumphant arrival, Jesus made his presence known in Jerusalem by his actions in the temple and his teaching of the crowd who gathered around him.

On Thursday, Jesus instructed two disciples to find and prepare a place for the Passover meal. He and the Twelve gathered in an upper room of a local house.

Jesus' words and actions at the meal are filled with meaning and prophecy: "one of you will betray me," "I will never again drink of the fruit of the vine," and "you will deny me three times."

Every time we gather for Holy Eucharist, we remember this fateful event. We picture the exhausted disciples falling asleep as Jesus prayed in the Garden of Gethsemane.

From there, the action moves swiftly with the ironic intimacy of Judas' kiss of betrayal; the frenzied, false testimony before the high priests; and Peter's denial, heart-rending for him as he realized what he had done.

Jesus, deserted by friends, journeyed on to the humiliation and agony of his crucifixion.

> Almighty Father, whose dear Son, on the night before he suffered, instituted the Sacrament of his Body and Blood: Mercifully grant that we may receive it thankfully in remembrance of Jesus Christ our Lord, who in these holy mysteries gives us a pledge of eternal life; and who now lives and reigns with you and the Holy Spirit, one God, for ever and ever. *Amen.*
>
> Maundy Thursday
> *The Book of Common Prayer*, p. 221

TEACHING TIP

Liturgy helps us understand and become a part of events that occurred long ago. Intermediate-age students will better understand the importance of the final week of Christ's life if they take part in the services that lead up to Easter. Describe services at your church scheduled for Holy Week and encourage students to attend especially Palm Sunday, Maundy Thursday, Good Friday, and Easter Vigil.

GATHERING

Display the Palm Sunday picture from Poster No. 14 in the Teacher's Packet. Nearby, on a large sheet of paper, post selected lines from *Mark 11:1-11*. Ahead of time, photocopy a simple face and a blank cartoon-like balloon (for inserting words) for each person in the class.

As students arrive, give them the cartoons and markers. Ask them to write words of welcome for Jesus that would be appropriate for Palm Sunday. Decide on a way to tape the completed greetings around the quotations from *Mark*.

When everyone is present, say:

Let us pray. (Use the Collect "Maundy Thursday," above, or a prayer of your own choosing.)

The chosen student lector reads from the class Bible (NRSV):

A Reading from the Gospel of Mark, chapter 14, verses 16, 22 through 25, and 28 through 31.

So the disciples set out and went to the city, and found everything as (Jesus) had told them; and they prepared the Passover meal. . . .

While they were eating, (Jesus) took a loaf of bread, and after blessing it he broke it, gave it to them, and said, "Take; this is my body." Then he took a cup, and after giving thanks he gave it to them, and all of them drank from it. He said to them, "This is my blood of the covenant, which is poured out for many. Truly I tell you, I will never drink again of the fruit of the vine until that day when I drink it new in the kingdom of God. . . ."

"But after I am raised up, I will go before you to Galilee." Peter said to him, "Even though all become deserters, I will not." Jesus said to him, "Truly I tell you, this day, this very night, before the cock crows twice, you will deny me three times." But (Peter) said vehemently, "Even though I must die with you, I will not deny you." And all of them said the same.

Reader: The Word of the Lord.
Response: Thanks be to God.

INTRODUCING THE STORY
(Time: 10–15 minutes)

Invite the students to assist in retelling the events of Holy Week. Organize this activity as round-robin storytelling. Prepare eight large sheets of paper to serve as story titles; on each sheet write the title of the particular event on one side, and attach a copy of the appropriate Scripture on the backside. The events are listed in Getting Ready (above), and are included in the game in the student newspaper, *Community Times*, Issue 6.

Distribute the story sheets to teams or individuals. Ask the students to number the sheets in the correct order. Give Group 4 the Teacher's Packet poster of the Last Supper to accompany their part of the story. Set a time limit for preparation.

Encourage each team to read the Scripture and then use their own words to tell about the people, places, and actions of their segment of Holy Week. Suggest they read the stories about Holy Week events in the student newspaper, *Community Times* (Unit III, Issue 6), for storytelling ideas.

Signal the time to start, and gather in a circle. As teams conclude their stories, place each title sheet (along with the Last Supper poster) in a display on a bulletin board or wall.

If there is time, look in the *Gospel of Mark* for a description of a betrayal and a denial by two disciples. Ask the student to look in their Bibles at *Mark 14:43-50* and *66-72*. Who are the disciples? Was Jesus surprised by their actions?

EXPLORING
(Time: 15–20 minutes)

Option 1. Hosanna

Plan a drama about the events of Palm Sunday. Begin by making props for your play. Assign one group of students to make palm leaves and "leafy branches" to be waved by the crowd and placed on Jesus' path. Ask another group of students to find a way to depict Jesus riding a colt. Another group could make a roadway using available chairs and tables.

After the props are ready, reread *Mark 11:1-11*. Assign roles, including the crowd. Ask them to quickly memorize the passage in *Mark 11:9b-10* of the words the crowd shouted. The drama will end when Jesus reaches the temple.

Talk about how the people felt on Palm Sunday. Ask: Have you ever been a part of an excited crowd at a parade, rally, or sports event? What was that like? What caused the people to change their minds about Jesus during the week?

Option 2. Last Supper Pictures

Invite the students to draw their own versions of the scene in the Upper Room at the Last Supper. Provide drawing paper, pencils, and fine-tip markers.

Before beginning, ask the students to discuss some of the details they think should be included to illustrate the story (table, Jesus, twelve disciples, bread, cup of wine). You may want to keep a written record of the students' comments about the Last Supper.

Option 3. Word Puzzle

Turn in the student newspaper, *Community Times*, Unit III, Issue 6, to the puzzle titled "Events of Holy Week." Students may work alone, in pairs, or as a total group.

MUSIC
(Time: 10 minutes)

Listen on the *Children Sing!* tape to the spiritual, "Were you there when they crucified my Lord" *(The Hymnal 1982*, 172; *We Sing of God*, 32*)*, and then sing it together. It will be sung again at the next session.

CONNECTING/SPEAKING OUT
(Time: 15–20 minutes)

Option 1. Group Discussion

Jesus did not slip unnoticed into Jerusalem and then remain hidden away. His was a triumphant, celebrated arrival. During his days in Jerusalem he continued to teach. Among other actions, he threw the money changers out of the temple *(Mark 11:15-19)*.

After reading the passage, ask the students to put themselves in the position of the religious authorities. The practice of selling animals to be offered at the temple was an accepted custom. People often traveled many miles to be at the temple during Passover. Many were unable to bring their own animals and needed to buy an appropriate sacrifice. Money changers were available to help in making these transactions.

Ask: How would you (as a temple official) respond to Jesus' actions? What would you have said or done to Jesus? Why? Do you think Jesus was a "troublemaker"?

Option 2. Current Events

The account of the Last Supper in the *Gospel of John* focuses almost entirely on Jesus' washing the feet of his disciples. In many churches, the Maundy Thursday liturgy includes symbolic footwashing. If this is true in your own congregation, or in other churches of your community, discuss how it is done. Who does the washing? Whose feet are washed? What do people say about this action? Why is it considered important? Would you feel comfortable participating in a foot washing? Would you rather be the recipient or the person who washes the feet? Why?

REFLECTING
(Time: 10 minutes)

Help the students understand Peter's denial of Jesus during a time of reflection. Begin by reading the story of the denial in *Mark 14:66-72*. Encourage students to share their images of this scene in the courtyard of the high priest. Who would be there at this early hour? What would be happening? What sounds would be heard?

Now ask the students to silently think about a time of denial they have experienced. For example, a friend who was with another group of students may not have acknowledged them, or perhaps they were the ones who ignored one of their friends. Ask them to try to remember how it feels to have someone ignore or deny you or to be the person who ignores or denies someone else.

Then ask them to talk to God about this experience. Ask: Do you need to ask for forgiveness? Do you need to forgive someone? Did Jesus forgive Peter?

LEARNING SKILLS
(Time: 10–15 minutes)

Option 1. Class Memory Challenge

Recite all the lines of the Nicene Creed that have been learned in previous sessions. Then introduce the two sentences on the Holy Spirit, beginning "We believe . . . ." and ending "through the Prophets."

Point out that this section affirms the Church's belief in the Trinity. The Holy Spirit is worshiped together with the Father and the Son. Note also that the Creed reminds us the Holy Spirit spoke through the prophets of Hebrew tradition.

(Decide whether to share the fact that believers have disagreed on whether to retain the words "who proceeds from the Father and the Son." In some Christian churches, this phrase is rejected because of the belief that the Holy Spirit proceeds only from the Father.)

Repeat the two sentences in unison.

Option 2. Learning Scripture

Add ribbons, cards, and symbols to the chalice for any verses students have learned from suggestions in previous sessions.

Invite the class members to choose one or both of the following verses to be committed to memory before the next class session: *Mark 11:9b* or *Mark 14:72b*, or *c*. See "Learning Scripture" in the student newspaper, *Community Times*.

ONGOING PROJECT
(Time: 5–10 minutes)

For the last four sessions of this Unit, suggest that the students work together to design and produce individual announcement sheets for services of Holy Week and Easter: Maundy Thursday, Good Friday, the Easter Vigil, and the Fifty Days of Easter. They can make line drawings and compose text related to these liturgies, including the dates and times, participants, and the like (including choir presentations or other elements of the services).

At this session, prepare the announcement for Maundy Thursday. If time permits, you may want to make photocopies of the finished product to send home with the students.

SYMBOL CARD and TREASUREBOOK

Card 24 shows a rooster, a verse of Scripture, and an explanation on the back.

Students may read Part III, Sections 4-5, of the *Chalice Year Treasurebook* which shows the link between the sacrament of Holy Eucharist and the Last Supper.

GOING FORTH

Gather the group for the dismissal. The leader will say the following, pausing for the response of "Lord, have mercy":

> For our Bishop, and for all the clergy and people, let us pray to the Lord.
> *Lord, have mercy.*

For this city (town, village, ____), for every city and community, and for those who live in them, let us pray to the Lord.
Lord, have mercy.

That we may end our lives in faith and hope, without suffering and without reproach, let us pray to the Lord.
Lord, have mercy.

For _____ [learners may add their own petitions], let us pray to the Lord.
Lord, have mercy.

> From The Prayers of the People
> *The Book of Common Prayer*, pp. 384-385

Teacher: Let us go forth in the name of Christ.
Students: Thanks be to God.

TEACHER'S ASSESSMENT

From your observations, do the students see the sequence of the events in Holy Week? Can they connect the Last Supper and our celebrations of Holy Eucharist? Do they know about Holy Week services and events in your church?

LOOKING AHEAD

The next session looks at the drama of the crucifixion. Read *Mark 15:16-39* and reflect on the mental images that come to mind as you read this account. What emotions does it arouse in you? Consider why we call this the Passion.

EUCHARIST: SHARED LIFE

SESSION 7
THE PASSION OF CHRIST

FOCUS

The crucifixion of Jesus is described in just four paragraphs in the *Gospel of Mark*. At the end, it is the centurion (Roman guard) who declares that Jesus was the Son of God. The students should be able to tell the story of the Passion in their own words.

GETTING READY

The earliest Gospel account of Jesus' passion is found in *Mark 15:16-39*. The story falls into three sections:

The mocking (verses 16-20). Once condemned, Jesus had no rights, so the soldiers were free to do with him what they wanted. The whole battalion ("consort" in the NRSV) contained about 600 soldiers. Their mock homage was an episode of brutal horseplay. It was not a part of the punishment dictated by Pilate, for Jesus had already been scourged. The soldiers stripped Jesus, clothed him in purple (to mark him as "king"), and later re-clothed him in his own garments.

The crucifixion (verses 21-32). Some scholars believe that the original source of Mark's narrative was the women who were Jesus' followers (verse 40), or possibly the centurion (verse 39), who may have been a Christian. Certainly, the details of this day would have been shared totally for years by those who were eyewitnesses.

Crucifixion was ordinarily a punishment for slaves. The victim was nailed to a crossbar which was later hoisted and attached to a vertical post. His feet were nailed or bound to the upright piece.

Tradition holds that Simon of Cyrene was an African. He was seized by the soldiers and forced to carry Jesus' cross. The name Golgotha for the place of crucifixion means "skull" in the Aramaic language. It was located north of Jerusalem.

The drink offered to Jesus was possibly meant to deaden the pain. Mark reports that Jesus refused it. Because people were crucified naked, the soldiers could do as they wished with Jesus' clothing. The two men who were crucified with Jesus may have been involved in an insurrection against the government.

Death on the cross (verses 33-39). Jesus was on the cross six hours (from approximately nine o'clock until three o'clock). This was a comparatively short time; many victims lived for two days or so. Jesus' death was preceded by three hours of darkness, beginning at noon.

Only *Mark* includes mention of Elijah (verses 35-36). It is unlikely that the soldiers would have known about the prophet.

For Mark, the "loud cry" (verse 37) was probably a shout of victory and triumph rather than a voice of despair or pain.

O God, by the passion of your blessed Son you made an instrument of shameful death to be for us the means of life: Grant us so to glory in the cross of Christ, that we may gladly suffer shame and loss for the sake of your Son our Savior Jesus Christ; who lives and reigns with you and the Holy Spirit, one God, for ever and ever. *Amen.*

Tuesday in Holy Week
The Book of Common Prayer, p. 220

TEACHING TIP

Intermediate-age students may vary considerably in their emotional reactions to the pain and suffering portrayed in stories of the crucifixion of Jesus. However, most class members will want to know the details of Jesus' death on the cross, including the nails, the pain, and the thirst. Their curiosity and questioning are normal and deserve responses that are honest and sensitive. Avoid over-dramatizing the agony of the event.

GATHERING

Display the set of four crucifixion pictures provided in the Teacher's Packet on Poster No. 16. You may want to gather and exhibit other prints of the scene.

As the students arrive, point out that this is one of the most common themes in Christian art. Encourage them to compare the pictures and make their own observations about the differing artists' perceptions. Help class members appreciate the variations in style.

When everyone is present, say:

Let us pray. (Use the Collect "Tuesday in Holy Week," above, or a prayer of your own choosing.)

The chosen student lector reads from the class Bible (NRSV):

A Reading from the Gospel of Mark, chapter 15, verses 25 through 39.

It was nine o'clock in the morning when they crucified him. The inscription of the charge against him read, "The King of the Jews." And with him they crucified two bandits, one on his right and one on his left. Those who passed by derided him, shaking their heads and saying, "Aha! You who would destroy the temple and build it in three days, save yourself, and come down from the cross!" In the same way the chief priests, along with the scribes, were also mocking him among themselves and saying, "He saved others; he cannot save himself. Let the Messiah, the King of Israel, come down from the cross now, so that we may see and believe." Those who were crucified with him also taunted him.

When it was noon, darkness came over the whole land until three in the afternoon. At three o'clock Jesus cried out with a loud voice, "Eloi, Eloi, lema sabachthani?" which means, "My God, my God, why have you forsaken me?" When some of the bystanders heard it, they said, "Listen, he is calling for Elijah." And someone ran, filled a sponge with sour wine, put it on a stick, and gave it to him to drink, saying, "Wait, let us see whether Elijah will come to take him down." Then Jesus gave a loud cry and breathed his last. And the curtain of the temple was torn in two, from top to bottom. Now when the centurion, who stood facing him, saw that in this way he breathed his last, he said, "Truly this man was God's Son!"

Reader: The Word of the Lord.
Response: Thanks be to God.

INTRODUCING THE STORY
(Time: 10–15 minutes)

Read the story of the crucifixion told from the viewpoint of the centurion in the student newspaper, *Community Times* (Unit III, Issue 7). Find a similar way to retell the story in your own words. For example, you could be one of the people "looking on from a distance."

Use the outline of events from the *Mark 15* passage and the notes provided in the Getting Ready (above) in telling your story.

Ask the students to turn in their Bibles to the four Gospels to compare the accounts of Jesus' last words. Ask individuals or groups to look up *Matthew 27:46, Mark 15:34, Luke 23:46,* and *John 19:30*. Ask: What are the differences? Have you ever disagreed with someone who witnessed the same event but saw it differently?

Mention the references to Jesus' death during the service of Holy Eucharist, in the Creed, and in the Great Thanksgiving. The Christian faith rests on the reality of Christ's sacrifice for the sake of the whole world. We celebrate this precious gift at every celebration of Holy Communion.

EXPLORING
(Time: 15–20 minutes)

Option 1. Passion Cross

Invite the students to create a cross decorated with symbols of Christ's passion, using a large sheet of butcher paper or newsprint.

Outline a simple cross composed of four rectangles vertically and three rectangles horizontally. Make each rectangle 9 by 12 inches.

As a group, identify several symbols of the Passion, such as: crown of thorns, nails, whip, robe, cross, torn curtain, three crosses on a hill, sponge and vinegar, dice. Working as individuals, in pairs, or in teams, students can choose and draw one symbol to be placed in each rectangle of the cross. Use crayons, markers, fabric, and construction paper to provide color for the symbols.

Option 2. Passion Collages

Use charcoal, soft lead pencils, or colored chalk—along with torn pieces of paper and cloth—to create collages symbolizing the mood of the Passion story. Large sheets of white or gray construction paper can be used for background. Be sure to have glue on hand.

Consider adding nails and small sticks to form a cross.

Option 3. Crossword Puzzle

Turn in the student newspaper, *Community Times*, Unit III, Issue 7, to the crossword titled "The Cross." Students may work alone, in pairs, or as a total group.

MUSIC
(Time: 10 minutes)

Sing along with the *Children Sing!* tape "Were you there when they crucified my Lord" *(The Hymnal 1982,* 172; *We Sing of God*, 32*)*.

CONNECTING/SPEAKING OUT
(Time: 15–20 minutes)

Option 1. Group Discussion

Suggest that the class members work in teams to compare Mark's passion account with the parallels in the other Gospels: *Mark 15:21-41; Luke 23:26-49; Matthew 27:32-56; John 19:17-30.*

On a piece of newsprint, write down the major events in each Gospel. Ask students to find actual quotes from Jesus in these accounts. Many churches plan dramas or prayers around the "last words" of Jesus spoken from the cross. In all, the four Gospels recall seven of these sayings. What are they, and in which Gospel(s) is each one found?

Option 2. Current Events

At the trial of Jesus before Pilate, the crowd shouted "Crucify, crucify him!" Even after Pilate suggested that Jesus be beaten and released, the people continued to shout loudly that he should be crucified. This seems to be an example of mob psychology, in which a climate of hatred takes over and everyone participates.

Ask: Why do people sometimes act differently in a crowd from the way they might act as individuals? When do crowds join in cruelty and violence? Encourage the class members to cite not only events they know about from history or the news but also the times in their own lives when they may have seen groups acting in a mob-like way. Point out the harm and destructiveness of such behavior.

REFLECTING
(Time: 10 minutes)

Suggest that the students consider what it would have been like to be a witness at the crucifixion of Jesus. How would they have felt about Jesus? About the others crucified with him? About the people responsible for what was happening?

Ask the class members to remain quiet a few moments and think about an experience of loss. For example, the death of a grandparent, the loss of a beloved pet, or a time that a close friend moved away. Encourage them to try to remember how they felt at that time.

Then remind them that many of Jesus' close friends and family members felt a similar loss when Jesus died. Ask them to pray for people who are experiencing loss at this time. If students know of someone in particular, encourage them to include this person's name during the prayers at the dismissal.

LEARNING SKILLS
(Time: 10–15 minutes)

Option 1. Class Memory Challenge

As the class members continue learning and reciting the Nicene Creed, focus on the two sentences, "We believe in one holy catholic and apostolic Church," and "We acknowledge one baptism for the forgiveness of sins." Underscore the theme of Christian unity in the Creed (one God, one Lord, one Church, one baptism). Note the similarity to *Ephesians 4:1-6.*

Say the section in unison.

Option 2. Learning Scripture

Ask students who have memorized verses assigned at previous sessions to add ribbons, cards, and student symbols to the chalice.

Suggest that the class members choose one of the following to memorize before the next session: *Mark 15:24* or *Mark 15:39*. See "Learning Scripture" in the student newspaper, *Community Times*.

ONGOING PROJECT
(Time: 5–10 minutes)

Continue the project to design and make individual announcement sheets for services of Holy Week and Easter, as described in Session 6. Include the essential facts and appropriate illustrations.

For this session, prepare the announcement for Good Friday. You may want to make photocopies to send home with the students.

SYMBOL CARD and TREASUREBOOK

Card 25 shows the Greek letters INRI, a verse of Scripture, and an explanation on the back.

In the *Chalice Year Treasurebook*, Part III, Section 6, is a retelling of the story behind the words of our Eucharistic acclamation, "Christ has died." What did Jesus accomplish by his death on the cross?

GOING FORTH

Gather the group for the dismissal. The leader will say the following, pausing for the response of "Lord, have mercy":

> For our Bishop, and for all the clergy and people, let us pray to the Lord.
> *Lord, have mercy.*
>
> For this city (town, village, ___), for every city and community, and for those who live in them, let us pray to the Lord.
> *Lord, have mercy.*
>
> That we may end our lives in faith and hope, without suffering and without reproach, let us pray to the Lord.
> *Lord, have mercy.*
>
> For _____ [learners may add their own petitions], let us pray to the Lord.
> *Lord, have mercy.*
>
> From The Prayers of the People
> *The Book of Common Prayer,* pp. 384-385

Teacher: Let us go forth in the name of Christ.
Students: Thanks be to God.

TEACHER'S ASSESSMENT

From your observations, in what ways did the students experience the story of Jesus' mocking and crucifixion? What questions did they have? What did their comments and emotional reactions reveal about their understanding of these events?

LOOKING AHEAD

The next session resounds with the good news and joy of Jesus' resurrection. In what ways are you anticipating Easter?

EUCHARIST: SHARED LIFE

SESSION 8
THE RESURRECTION OF CHRIST

FOCUS

The final chapter of Mark's Gospel tells the story of Jesus' rising from the dead. When three women were told by an angel that Jesus had been raised from the dead, they fled in terror, telling no one. The students should be able to retell the story of the resurrection from *Mark 16:1-8*.

GETTING READY

Jesus' body was laid in a tomb provided by Joseph of Arimathea. A faithful and prominent Jew, Joseph was a member of the Sanhedrin and apparently a secret follower of Jesus. He boldly asked Pilate for permission to take the body, which he wrapped in a linen cloth he had purchased. Then he had the body placed in his own newly made tomb. A large slab of stone was rolled against the hewn rock tomb.

The day following the crucifixion was the Sabbath. The next morning, Mary Magdalene, Mary the mother of James, and Salome went to the tomb to anoint the body. The account of what happened when they arrived is found in *Mark 16:1-8*. They did not see their risen Lord, but an angel, a young man dressed in white, gave them the astonishing news of the resurrection. Mark reports that the women were so afraid that they "said nothing to anyone" (verse 8).

Ancient Greek texts of the New Testament offer different endings for the *Gospel of Mark*. Some of these conclude with chapter 16:8. Others provide a shorter ending that adds two sentences after verse 8. Still others include a longer ending with verses numbered 9-20. This longer ending also varies in content. These differences are shown clearly in the New Revised Standard Version of the Bible.

If the original text of *Mark* did not say that the risen Jesus appeared to the disciples and others, it is important to emphasize that the early Christians had no doubt that he had done so. Years before Mark wrote his Gospel, the apostle Paul had written about appearances of the resurrected Christ. (*I Corinthians 15:3-8*). The very existence of the Church rested on the certainty of the Easter news, "Christ is risen." (*Mark 16; John 20:11-18*)

Almighty God, who through your only-begotten Son Jesus Christ overcame death and opened to us the gate of everlasting life: Grant that we, who celebrate with joy the day of the Lord's resurrection, may be raised from the death of sin by your life-giving Spirit; through Jesus Christ our Lord, who lives and reigns with you and the Holy Spirit, one God, now and for ever. *Amen.*

Easter Day
The Book of Common Prayer, p. 222

TEACHING TIP

Most intermediate-age students have watched cartoons and movies in which characters come back to life. Storytellers expect their audiences to suspend belief in order to enjoy the tale. The story of Christ, however, asks that we accept the resurrection on faith because of our belief in God. Help young people distinguish between modern stories about life after death and the resurrection of Jesus—a fundamental belief of the Christian faith.

GATHERING

Display Poster No. 17 from the Teacher's Packet showing three women who went to the empty tomb. Ask: What are the women doing? Why have they come to this place? Who is in the background?

When everyone is present, say:

Let us pray. (Use the Collect "Easter Day," above, or a prayer of your own choosing.)

The chosen student lector reads from the class Bible (NRSV):

A Reading from the Gospel of Mark, chapter 16, verses 1 through 8.

When the sabbath was over, Mary Magdalene, and Mary the mother of James, and Salome brought spices, so that they might go and anoint him. And very early on the first day of the week, when the sun had risen, they went to the tomb. They had been saying to one another, "Who will roll away the stone for us from the entrance to the tomb?" When they looked up, they saw that the stone, which was very large, had already been rolled back. As they entered the tomb, they saw a young man, dressed in a white robe, sitting on the right side; and they were alarmed. But he said to them, "Do not be alarmed; you are looking for Jesus of Nazareth, who was crucified. He has been raised; he is not here. Look, there is the place they laid him. But go, tell his disciples and Peter that he is going ahead of you to Galilee; there you will see him, just as he told you." So they went out and fled from the tomb, for terror and amazement had seized them; and they said nothing to anyone, for they were afraid.

Reader: The Word of the Lord.
Response: Thanks be to God.

INTRODUCING THE STORY
(Time: 10 minutes)

Begin by inviting the students to join in the ancient Easter versicle:
Teacher: Alleluia. Christ is risen.
Students: The Lord is risen indeed. Alleluia.

Remind the class members that Christians all over the world celebrate the resurrection of Jesus Christ. Easter is a great festival of joy at the good news of our Lord's victory over sin and death. We sing and shout "Alleluia" (a word of Hebrew origin, meaning "praise to God").

Tell the story of Christ's resurrection from the *Gospel of Mark* and from information in Getting Ready (above). The student newspaper, *Community Times* (Unit III, Issue 8), tells the story as if it were written by a reporter from the first century. You could also tell the story from the viewpoint of one of the women.

Then ask the students to turn in their Bibles to *Mark 16* to examine the different endings. (Some Bibles include footnotes. The New Revised Standard Version gives a clear explanation that could be photocopied for study.) Speculate about why the ancient manuscripts are different.

Remind students that few people had access to books or documents at that time. Briefly mention other New Testament witnesses to the resurrection. Point out that the earliest references to Jesus' appearing to the disciples and others is found in the apostle Paul's first letter to the church at Corinth. (You may want to read aloud *I Corinthians 15:3-8*.) Each of the four Gospels tells the story of the empty tomb in a different way. Mark's account is the shortest, and surprisingly it does not include an actual appearance of the risen Jesus. No doubt Mark simply assumes that his readers know the story that had been shared among Christians for years.

EXPLORING
(Time: 15–20 minutes)

Option 1. Sharing the Good News

Easter is a wonderful time to share the Good News of Christ. Bring in tubes of icing gel and enough plain sugar cookies for everyone in the class and for younger students in another class. Let the teachers of the younger class know that your group will be providing snacks toward the end of the church school period.

Before decorating the cookies, talk about appropriate symbols for Easter, such as a lily, the letters "INRI," the word "Alleluia," and an empty cross. Use the gel to add the symbols to the cookies.

You may wish to plan some simple games to play while the cookies are being decorated. Tell the students that as Christians we are expected to tell others of the good news of Christ's victory over death. As a group, take the cookies to the other classroom to share with the younger students.

Option 2. Easter Cross Mosaics

Ask each class member to prepare a cross, using brown, black, or gray squares of construction paper large enough to add paper mosaic "tiles." Provide paste or glue and several stacks of brightly colored paper cut into small squares and rectangles. Invite each student to choose a stack and take several pieces from it.

The students will then design and cut out simple flowers, making several additional ones for exchanging and trading with others. All can then add flowers to their mosaic crosses. Vary this activity by providing stacks of foil, tissue, or other material for flowers.

Option 3. Word Search

Turn in the student newspaper, *Community Times*, Unit III, Issue 8, to the word search titled "Resurrection."

Students may work alone, in pairs, or as a total group.

MUSIC
(Time: 10 minutes)

Introduce the hymn "Come, ye faithful, raise the strain" *(The Hymnal 1982, 199, 200)*. Listen to it on the *Children Sing!* tape while working on a project.

CONNECTING/SPEAKING OUT
(Time: 15–20 minutes)

Option 1. Group Discussion

Invite the students to compare the actions and reactions of the women in the resurrection stories in the four Gospels: *Mark 16:1-8, Matthew 28:1-10, Luke 24:1-11*, and *John 20:1-18*. Ask them to focus particularly on Mary Magdalene. Ask: What does each Gospel say about her? How do the stories differ in describing what she did?

Then ask the students to think about all that the women had witnessed in the week just ended. They had all witnessed the death of Christ and probably watched his broken body placed in the tomb. What feelings and emotions had they experienced? What were they worried about? Why would they wonder what to do after seeing and hearing the young man at the empty tomb? Why would they be afraid?

Option 2. Current Events

In most places in the United States, the celebration of Easter coincides with the beginning of spring. Even in warmer climates, there are changes in nature at this time of year.

Talk about other renewals that we experience at this time. Ask: What changes do you observe in the foliage? Have you noticed more or different kinds of birds in the area?

Easter egg hunts are also a part of many celebrations. Why is the egg associated with this season? Why do we decorate the church with lilies?

Talk about the different symbols for Easter and spring. Why does it seem natural to celebrate Easter when bulbs that were dormant all winter suddenly burst into flower? In many areas, the joy we feel as Christians is reflected in nature.

REFLECTING
(Time: 10 minutes)

Ask the students to think about what it was like for the three women who made their plans to go to the tomb of Jesus. How were they feeling about the events of the last few days? What would they talk about as they prepared the spices?

Invite the class members to close their eyes and sit quietly. Tell them to think about a time when they were waiting for something, but were unsure of the outcome. For example, the moment before they found out if their entry in the science fair that had taken so much time had won a prize. Or, waiting for the times to be posted at a swim meet or track event. Or, watching a doctor approach to tell the family news about a loved one.

Think about your emotions as you waited with uncertainty. You want to find out what happened, but you still feel hesitant. Is this how the women felt as they approached the tomb?

Remember that God is always with you, especially during these times. Share with God both your fears and your joy in the coming weeks.

LEARNING SKILLS
(Time: 10–15 minutes)

Option 1. Class Memory Challenge

Recite all the sections of the Nicene Creed that have been memorized in previous sessions, then introduce the final lines: "We look for the resurrection of the dead, and the life of the world to come. Amen."

Note aloud that the Creed ends on a strong note of hope for the future. Christians believe Jesus Christ has opened to us the way to life after death.

Say the closing sentence in unison, including the "Amen."

Option 2. Learning Scripture

Add ribbons, cards, and student symbols to the chalice for any verses students have memorized since the last session.

For the next session, ask class members to learn *Mark 16:6b, c* or *Luke 14:5c*. See "Learning Scripture" in the student newspaper, *Community Times*.

ONGOING PROJECT
(Time: 5–10 minutes)

Work again on designing individual announcement sheets for services of Holy Week and Easter, as described in Session 6.

For this session, prepare a sheet announcing an Easter Vigil service. Include the time, place, and other essentials. You may want to list other Easter events, such as sunrise services or Easter breakfasts. Add appropriate illustrations, and decide whether to make photocopies for sharing.

SYMBOL CARD and TREASUREBOOK

Card 26 shows a phoenix, a verse of Scripture, and an explanation on the back.

Suggest that students read in the *Chalice Year Treasurebook*, Part III, Section 7, about the glad story we acclaim when we say "Christ is risen." What difference does it make that Jesus Christ rose from the dead?

GOING FORTH

Gather the group for the dismissal. The leader will say the following, pausing for the response of "Lord, have mercy":

> For our Bishop, and for all the clergy and people, let us pray to the Lord.
> *Lord, have mercy.*
>
> For this city (town, village, ____), for every city and community, and for those who live in them, let us pray to the Lord.
> *Lord, have mercy.*
>
> That we may end our lives in faith and hope, without suffering and without reproach, let us pray to the Lord.
> *Lord, have mercy.*
>
> For _____ [learners may add their own petitions], let us pray to the Lord.
> *Lord, have mercy.*
>
> From The Prayers of the People
> *The Book of Common Prayer,* pp. 384-385

Teacher: Let us go forth in the name of Christ.
Students: Thanks be to God.

TEACHER'S ASSESSMENT

What evidence did you gather that the students sense the joy of Easter? How well are they able to distinguish between the Church's celebration of Jesus' resurrection and the general culture's emphasis on springtime, bunnies, baby chicks, and new clothes?

LOOKING AHEAD

The next session focuses on Jesus' post-resurrection appearance to the disciples fishing in the Sea of Galilee. The disciples recognize Jesus in the breaking of the bread. Reflect on the centrality of Jesus' presence at every Holy Eucharist we celebrate.

EUCHARIST: SHARED LIFE

SESSION 9
BREAKFAST BY THE SEA

FOCUS

In a post-resurrection appearance by the Sea of Tiberias (Galilee), the living Christ made himself known to seven disciples who had been fishing. Jesus prepared an early-morning breakfast, and the men were certain he was the Lord. The students should be able to tell this story in their own words and explain its significance for Christians.

GETTING READY

The *Gospel of John*, the last of the four accounts of Jesus' life, is markedly different from the first three (known as "Synoptics" because of their close relationship). The final third of the *Gospel of John* (chapters 13-21) is devoted to the period from the Last Supper through the resurrection appearances. The portion composed of chapters 14-17 tells of Jesus' farewell statement and a concluding prayer.

John's account of the risen Christ's appearing is the most vivid in the New Testament. In addition to offering more details about the empty tomb and the linen cloths lying within, John shares two stories found nowhere else: Jesus' revealing himself to Thomas, who doubted *(John 20:24-29)*, and the breakfast by the Sea of Galilee *(John 21:1-14)*.

In that story, several disciples had gone fishing, but had caught nothing. When Jesus called from the shore and told them where to cast their net, their nets were filled with fish. "That disciple whom Jesus loved" was the first to recognize Jesus and shout, "It is the Lord!" (verse 7). We may assume that this beloved disciple is John himself.

The breakfast prepared by Jesus reinforced the disciples' certainty that he was indeed risen and present with them. This meal is a parallel to the supper shared with the two followers on the road to Emmaus *(Luke 24:28-35)*. Both stories are linked with the early Church's understanding of Christ's presence in the sacred meal of Holy Eucharist.

Almighty God, whom truly to know is everlasting life: Grant us so perfectly to know your Son Jesus Christ to be the way, the truth, and the life, that we may steadfastly follow his steps in the way that leads to eternal life; through Jesus Christ your Son our Lord, who lives and reigns with you, in the unity of the Holy Spirit, one God, for ever and ever. *Amen.*
Fifth Sunday of Easter
The Book of Common Prayer, p. 225

TEACHING TIP

Intermediate-age students often separate things that happen at church from the rest of their lives. However, Jesus chose everyday images and events to help us see that God dwells in every part of our lives. The image of a meal is used over and over—the Eucharist itself is based on Jesus' last meal with his disciples. Help students see that the best way to find Jesus is to look for him in the people we see each day and the ordinary things we do.

GATHERING

Display Poster No. 18 of the risen Jesus at the breakfast by the Sea of Galilee, found in the Teacher's Packet. Hang a piece of newsprint next to the picture with the heading, "How I Spend My Time." As students arrive, ask them to list on the newsprint the three activities that take up most of their time.

When everyone is present, say:

Let us pray. (Use the Collect "Fifth Sunday of Easter," above, or a prayer of your own choosing.)

The chosen student lector reads from the class Bible (NRSV):

Unit III. Eucharist: Shared Life—Session 9
Chalice Year Intermediate—Copyright © 2000 Virginia Theological Sminary and Morehouse Publishing

A Reading from the Gospel of John, chapter 21, verses 1 through 14.

After these things Jesus showed himself again to the disciples by the Sea of Tiberias; and he showed himself in this way. Gathered there together were Simon Peter, Thomas called the Twin, Nathanael of Cana in Galilee, the sons of Zebedee, and two others of his disciples. Simon Peter said to them, "I am going fishing." They said to him, "We will go with you." They went out and got into the boat, but that night they caught nothing.

Just after daybreak, Jesus stood on the beach; but the disciples did not know that it was Jesus. Jesus said to them, "Children, you have no fish, have you?" They answered him, "No." He said to them, "Cast the net to the right side of the boat, and you will find some." So they cast it, and now they were not able to haul it in because there were so many fish. That disciple whom Jesus loved said to Peter, "It is the Lord!" When Simon Peter heard that it was the Lord, he put on some clothes, for he was naked, and jumped into the sea. But the other disciples came in the boat, dragging the net full of fish, for they were not far from the land, only about a hundred yards off.

When they had gone ashore, they saw a charcoal fire there, with fish on it, and bread. Jesus said to them, "Bring some of the fish that you have just caught." So Simon Peter went aboard and hauled the net ashore, full of large fish, a hundred fifty-three of them; and though there were so many, the net was not torn. Jesus said to them, "Come and have breakfast." Now none of the disciples dared to ask him, "Who are you?" because they knew it was the Lord. Jesus came and took the bread and gave it to them, and did the same with the fish. This was now the third time that Jesus appeared to the disciples after he was raised from the dead.

Reader: The Word of the Lord.
Response: Thanks be to God.

INTRODUCING THE STORY
(Time: 10 minutes)

Look at the activities the students listed on the newsprint during the Gathering. Briefly talk about the way they spend their time. Then explain that many of the disciples had been fishermen before they joined Jesus. After his death, they went back to the thing that they knew best.

In your own words, tell the story about the seven disciples who were fishing in the early morning on the Sea of Galilee when Jesus appeared *(John 21:1-14)*. Use the article on page 1 of the student newspaper, *Community Times* (Unit III, Issue 9), for ideas in telling the story.

Discuss the significance of the risen Jesus eating with his disciples. They would always associate this story with the sacred meal of the Holy Eucharist instituted by Christ the night before his crucifixion.

In addition to the story of Jesus' appearance to the fishermen at the Sea of Galilee, the writer tells of three other appearances of the risen Christ:

• to Mary Magdalene outside the empty tomb *(John 20:11-18)*;
• to the disciples gathered behind closed doors *(John 20:19-23)*;
• to Thomas, who insisted on touching the scars on Jesus' body before he would stop doubting *(John 20:24-29)*.

Divide the class members into four groups and assign to each group one of the resurrection appearances from *John 20-21* (listed above). Call on each group to report briefly what John's Gospel shares about these occasions.

Call the students' attention to the Great Fifty Days between Easter Day and the Day of Pentecost. On the seven Sundays of Easter, the Church's worship is a continuing celebration of the resurrection of Jesus Christ. The readings from the Bible invite us to rejoice in the good news of our Lord's victory over death.

EXPLORING
(Time: 15–20 minutes)

Option 1. Words for a Chalice

Work with the entire group to brainstorm an extended list of words related to the events of Holy Week through Easter Day. Record the words on a chalkboard or large sheet of newsprint for all to see.

Provide each class member with a 9 by 12 sheet of drawing paper. Direct the students to use pencils or fine-tipped markers to draw the outline of a chalice (symbol card No. 22 for the Chalice Year provides an easy pattern).

Students can then choose words from the class list to be arranged on the chalice outlines. Let the words flow with the contour of the chalice.

A line from Scripture or from *The Book of Common Prayer* may be chosen as a caption.

Option 2. The Last Days of Christ

Beforehand, make a list of the events that occurred in the last days of Christ, beginning with Palm Sunday and ending with his ascension. For example, gathering of palms, washing feet, prayers in the garden, betrayal by Judas, trial before Pilate, darkness over the land, appearance to Mary Magdalene, appearance behind closed doors, and breakfast at Galilee. Make sure there is one event for each student.

Write the events on index cards, one to a card. Shuffle the cards. Using masking tape, attach one card to each student's back. Announce to the class that first they must discover which event is described on their cards. They must circulate around the room asking only questions that can be answer by saying yes or no.

After everyone has discovered the event on his or her card, tell the group that they must now line up in the order that the events occurred in the Bible. (Be sure you have a master list with the events in the correct order.) When the students are ready, ask them to read their cards in the correct order. Celebrate their success by passing around a bowl of fish-shaped crackers.

Option 3. Crossword

Turn in the student newspaper, *Community Times*, Unit III, Issue 9, to the crossword puzzle titled "By the Sea of Galilee." Students may work alone, in pairs, or as a total group.

MUSIC
(Time: 10 minutes)

Listen again to "Come ye faithful, raise the strain" *(The Hymnal 1982, 200)* on the *Children Sing!* tape.

CONNECTING/SPEAKING OUT
(Time: 15–20 minutes)

Option 1. Group Discussion

Talk with the students about Jesus' post-resurrection appearances as a time for the disciples to discover how the events of his death and resurrection fulfilled all that he had taught them. They began to understand better the meaning of Jesus' parables and teachings.

Ask the students if they like to read mysteries or watch movies that have unexpected endings. Encourage one or more class members to share their favorite mysteries—without telling the endings.

Talk about how endings help us understand things that happened earlier. For example, in the movie *Jurassic Park*, small problems that seem only inconvenient early in the story later become major obstacles.

In the same way, the followers of Jesus had a better understanding of his teachings after his resurrection and later appearances. Earlier, they had not understood his references to his own death. Ask: If you had been a disciple, what would you say to him after the resurrection? What would you like to ask him?

Option 2. Current Events

Refer to the article on page two of the student newspaper, *Community Times*, about how Orthodox Christians celebrate Easter. If possible, bring in newspaper articles and books (available at public libraries) about the different ways Christians commemorate this festival.

Note that the date for Easter in the Orthodox Church is determined by the Jewish festival of Passover, since the biblical accounts of Holy Week occur at that time.

Brightly colored eggs displaying symbols of the Resurrection are made using natural dyes and wax. Special breads are baked and adorned with a dyed red Easter egg.

During Easter Vigil, at midnight, all the lights are extinguished. The priest appears with an icon of the Resurrection and three lighted candles. From these, candles held by members of the congregation are lit. The people carefully guard the tiny flame until they arrive home and use it to light a Vigil Light that remains burning throughout Easter Day.

After looking at books and articles, talk about customs the group finds interesting. Explore the possibility of incorporating one of the ideas during the Easter season.

REFLECTING
(Time: 10 minutes)

Invite the students to think quietly about the story of the risen Lord's appearance at the Sea of Galilee. Refer to Poster No. 18 and note that these disciples were doing a task that they understood and had done many times.

Ask the students to close their eyes and think back to the Gathering activity and the three activities they listed. Suggest that they select one, and visualize themselves doing that activity. How would Jesus appear to them? How would they recognize him? What would he say? How would they feel? Will you act differently in his presence?

Suggest that the next time they are doing this activity to remember that Jesus is there.

LEARNING SKILLS
(Time: 10–15 minutes)

Option 1. Class Memory Challenge

In turn, each section of the Nicene Creed has been introduced for the students' reflection and memorization. At this final session of the Unit, invite the class members to stand together and recite the Creed without the text or any prompting. Point out that this memory task is for a lifetime, since the words will be said in unison by every congregation at all Sunday Eucharists and other Major Feasts of the Church.

Option 2. Learning Scripture

Add ribbons, cards, and student symbols to the chalice described in Session 1 and used throughout this Unit for verses students learned since the last session. Encourage the students to learn *John 20:21* or *John 21:12a*. See "Learning Scripture" in the student newspaper, *Community Times*.

Discuss with the group what to do with the chalice and its ribbons. Perhaps it could be put on display where others in the congregation would see it.

In Unit IV, another group of verses will be introduced, along with a different procedure for recording each one that has been learned.

ONGOING PROJECT
(Time: 5–10 minutes)

Conclude this project for designing announcement sheets, as described in Session 6. For this session, prepare information about services and events in your congregation during the Fifty Days of Easter. Include all the essential facts and add appropriate illustrations. Decide whether to make photocopies for sharing.

SYMBOL CARD and TREASUREBOOK

Card 27 shows three fish in a circle, with a verse of Scripture, and an explanation on the back.

Suggest that students read the *Chalice Year Treasurebook*, Part III, Section 8, that describes Jesus' post-resurrection appearances and shares the promise, "Christ will come again." Why does the Church expect Jesus to come again? Encourage students to review all of Part III and identify the sections they found most meaningful.

GOING FORTH

Gather the group for the dismissal. The leader will say the following, pausing for the response of "Lord, have mercy":

> For our Bishop, and for all the clergy and people, let us pray to the Lord.
> *Lord, have mercy.*
>
> For this city (town, village, _____), for every city and community, and for those who live in them, let us pray to the Lord.
> *Lord, have mercy.*
>
> That we may end our lives in faith and hope, without suffering and without reproach, let us pray to the Lord.
> *Lord, have mercy.*
>
> For _____ [learners may add their own petitions], let us pray to the Lord.
> *Lord, have mercy.*
>
> From The Prayers of the People
> *The Book of Common Prayer,* pp. 384-385

Teacher: Let us go forth in the name of Christ.
Students: Thanks be to God.

TEACHER'S ASSESSMENT

Did the students understand the significance of Jesus' post-resurrection appearances? How would they respond to being called "Easter people?" Consider the ways in which the students' knowledge and understanding of the liturgy of the Holy Eucharist has grown during this Unit.

Note: The following letter is for teachers and parents of children in the Intermediate level of church school. These pages can be reproduced or used as a model for a personalized letter.

Episcopal Children's Curriculum
Unit IV: THE CATECHISM

Dear Parents and Guardians,

Each time we renew our baptismal covenant, we say again what we believe about God and the practice of our faith as Christians. Indeed, we spend our whole lives reflecting on our beliefs, moving on in our faith journeys as we gain new and deeper insight.

During this Unit of the Chalice Year, students will look at "An Outline of the Faith," commonly called the Catechism, which is found in *The Book of Common Prayer*, pp. 845-862. It is a summary of the Church's teaching and is intended to provide a means for teaching what we believe.

The purpose of this Unit is to introduce intermediate-age students to the Catechism. Eight of the sessions are designed to teach students the traditional ways of expressing what God has done for us through Jesus Christ.

Spend some time talking to your child about what he or she is learning. You can do this by reading the Scripture identified below, discussing the Symbol Cards and *Community Times* sent home each week, and by reading together Part IV of the *Chalice Year Treasurebook*, which includes information that is related to the sessions of this Unit.

As a whole, all these sources provide elaboration on the Catechism sections chosen for study.

Following are summaries of the Unit's sessions:

Session 1: "The New Covenant" is about the new relationship between God and humankind that came from the life, death, and resurrection of Jesus Christ. We begin with this section of the Catechism because the gospel message is the reason for our existence as a worshiping and serving people. Students will learn that the New Covenant does not replace the Old; rather, it is a fulfillment of what God began in giving the law to Moses. (*John 13:31-35*)

Session 2: "The Trinity" is an overview of God the Father, God the Son, and God the Holy Spirit. An understanding of the Trinity was worked out in the early centuries of the Church's history. The Nicene Creed of 325 CE was a decisive statement of beliefs as found in the New Testament. Students will be encouraged to find their own understanding of the Trinity in relation to the Church. (*Jude 17-21*)

Session 3: "The Church" illustrates several ways to view the life of God's baptized people in the world. We refer to the Church as "one," but we recognize the varied names and forms of government that are observed among Christian congregations throughout the world. The New Testament portrays the Church as "Christ's body." All members of that body are valued and respected. (*I Corinthians 12:20-28*)

Session 4: "The Creeds" introduces the debate at the Council of Nicaea about whether Christ was "of one Being with the Father." From that Council came the Creed known as the "Nicene Creed." We use it at all Sunday Eucharists and on other special days. In the previous Unit, students had an opportunity to memorize the Nicene Creed. This session helps them better understand what we believe as people of God. (*John 20:26-31*)

Session 5: "Sin and Redemption" invites students to think about human beings as sinners. Like sheep who wander away from their shepherd, we stray from God's intentions for us. The good news of the Christian faith is that God has acted through Jesus to forgive us. When we faithfully confess our sins, God forgives us. (*Romans 3:21-26*)

Session 6: "Prayer and Worship" is about our response to all that God has done for us—both as individuals and as a community of believers. Prayer is "responding to God by thought and by deeds, with or without words." Students will explore seven kinds of prayer as listed in the Catechism. (*Romans 12:12-18*)

Session 7: "Ministry" is an introduction to the four orders described in the Catechism: lay persons, bishops, priests, and deacons. In this session, the students are challenged to consider their own roles as people of God. All baptized persons take on specific tasks of Christian ministry. All orders share a common responsibility to "represent Christ and his Church" in the world. (*Ephesians 4:11-13*)

Session 8: "Christian Hope" is the last of the sessions on the Catechism. Student will be encouraged to think deeply about the meaning of their lives and the source of their hope. The most important emphasis will be on the certainty that nothing, not even death itself, can separate us from the love of God in Jesus Christ. This assurance is found in the New Testament and in the words of our prayers. (*Romans 8:31-39*)

Session 9: "Celebrating Pentecost" will be used either just before or after the Feast of Pentecost. The session focuses on Peter's sermon following the Holy Spirit's descending on the apostles. The disciples emerged from a period of doubt and uncertainty to undertake the great commission to go into all the world and preach the good news of Jesus Christ. Students will be encouraged to reaffirm the presence of the Holy Spirit in the Church today and in their lives. (*Acts 2:14-17*)

Yours in Christ,

Church School Teachers

THE CATECHISM
SESSION 1
THE NEW COVENANT

FOCUS

Our faith cannot be contained in words alone, but it is helpful for Christians to have an outline and a summary of the Church's teaching. *The Book of Common Prayer* contains "An Outline of the Faith," commonly called the Catechism. The section titled "The New Covenant" describes what Jesus Christ brings to us all and what he asks of us. The students should be able to explain the purpose of the Catechism and to summarize the section on The New Covenant.

GETTING READY

A catechism is a list of questions and answers designed to outline the beliefs of the Church. The use of printed catechisms began in the Protestant Reformation of the sixteenth century. Martin Luther prepared a Short Catechism which was later revised and used in the Church of England. From 1549, the Prayer Book has included brief catechisms. The latest version is the longest and most complete, containing sections that were developed in recent years.

For this session, we look at "The New Covenant" (the Catechism, pp. 850-851). This is the covenant in Jesus Christ, the Messiah. From the Scriptures and the creeds of the Church, we discern that the New Covenant is not a replacement or substitute for the Old. It is a fulfillment or a completion of the covenant God initiated in giving the Law (the Ten Commandments) to Moses. (See "The Old Covenant," the Catechism, pp. 847-848.)

The vision of a "new covenant" was shared by the Hebrew prophet Jeremiah. He wrote of a future relationship between God and human beings in which the law would be written in hearts rather than on tablets of stone. (See *Jeremiah 31:31*.) Christians see Jesus Christ as this promised new covenant. Through him we have been welcomed into the household of God. By his death on the cross, his resurrection, and ascension, we are saved from sin and death. Through him we have the promise of eternal life.

Jesus summarized the Law in two commandments: "You shall love the Lord your God . . . , and "You shall love your neighbor as yourself." Before his death, Jesus gave his disciples a new commandment: "Love one another." (*John 13:34-35*) This mutual love (more than simply keeping a law) is to be modeled on the love that Jesus showed to his disciples. Love for one another is a powerful sign of true Christian discipleship.

> O God the Father of our Lord Jesus Christ, our only Savior, Prince of Peace: Give us grace seriously to lay to heart the great dangers we are in by our unhappy divisions; take away all hatred and prejudice, and whatever else may hinder us from godly union and concord; that, as there is but one Body and one Spirit, one hope of our calling, one Lord, one Faith, one Baptism, one God and Father of us all, so we may be all of one heart and of one soul, united in one holy bond of truth and peace, of faith and charity, and may with one mind and one mouth glorify you; through Jesus Christ our Lord. *Amen.*
> For the Unity of the Church
> *The Book of Common Prayer*, p. 818

TEACHING TIP

The word "love" has been overused in our culture from casual references to deeply felt emotional responses between two people. Intermediate-age students are able to express love for family members, but are hesitant about talking about love for friends. They also interact primarily with persons of the same sex. Be sensitive to their reluctance to talk about love. Help them find appropriate ways to show their respect for one another.

GATHERING

Ahead of time, arrange copies of *The Book of Common Prayer* in a work area where all students can have space to look at it. Prepare a number of questions on slips of paper in a basket, or list them on a chalkboard or newsprint. Ask questions related to the section of the Catechism dealing with the New Covenant (pp. 850-851). Examples: What is a promise in the New Covenant? What is the New Commandment?

As the students arrive, challenge them to find the answers to the questions in the Prayer Book.

When everyone is present, say:

Let us pray. (Use the prayer "For the Unity of the Church," above, or a prayer of your own choosing.)

The chosen student lector reads from the class Bible (NRSV):

A Reading from the Gospel of John, chapter 13, verses 31 through 35.

When he had gone out, Jesus said, "Now the Son of Man has been glorified, and God has been glorified in him. If God has been glorified in him, God will also glorify him in himself and will glorify him at once. Little children, I am with you only a little longer. You will look for me; and as I said to the Jews so now I can say to you, 'Where I am going, you cannot come.' I give you a new commandment, that you love one another. Just as I have loved you, you also should love one another. By this everyone will know that you are my disciples, if you have love for one another."

Reader: The Word of the Lord.
Response: Thanks be to God.

INTRODUCING THE STORY
(Time: 10 minutes)

Begin by telling the story of Jesus giving the two great commandments, also called the summary of the law, to his followers. For ideas of how to present the story, read the article on page 1 of the student newspaper, *Community Times* (Unit IV, Issue 1).

Ask if any of the students found these commandments during the Gathering activity. Where in the Prayer Book did you find this information? Invite class members to find "An Outline of the Faith commonly called the Catechism," beginning on p. 845.

Print the word "catechism" on a chalkboard or a sheet of newsprint while you pronounce it. Point out that it comes from Greek words that mean "echo." Define it in the following way: A catechism usually consists of a set of questions and answers that outline the principal beliefs of Christians.

Read the questions from the Gathering activity, and ask students to provide the answers. Note that the "Law" refers to the Ten Commandments and all the rules and regulations that grew out of them.

Remind students that a "covenant" is an agreement between God and humans. The Old Covenant under Moses involved the Ten Commandments. The New Covenant is the new relationship with God given through Jesus Christ. It is a fulfillment and not a replacement for the Old Covenant.

If there is time, help students discover references to the two great commandments in the Bible and the Prayer Book. Write each of the following six references on separate index cards: *The Book of Common Prayer*, p. 851; *The Book of Common Prayer*, p. 324; *Matthew 22:37-40; Mark 12:28-31; Luke 10:27; Deuteronomy 6:5*. Ask the students to work in teams to find these references and look for similarities and differences.

EXPLORING
(Time: 15–20 minutes)

Option 1. Answers and Questions

Ask students to think of a series of questions and answers for a game based on the television show "Jeopardy." Begin by agreeing on several categories, such as famous Americans, sports trivia, and Bible knowledge. Then assign pairs to come up with a series of answers and questions, such as:

George Washington. (Who was our first President?)

Love your neighbor as yourself. (What is the second Great Commandment given by Jesus?)

Then play several rounds of the game, with the "host" giving the answers while two or three students have the opportunity to respond with the appropriate question. The student who rings a bell or claps his or her hands first gets to reply. Be sure students are not given the same categories they worked on earlier. Ask: How is this game similar to the Catechism?

Option 2. The New Commandment

Supply large sheets of drawing paper with crayons and markers. Invite the class members to make their own illuminations or illustrations to accompany the text of *John 13:34*. If possible, bring in several samples of illustrated manuscripts from the library for students to see. Each student may design a way to include the words on the sheet.

Option 3. Crossword

Turn in the student newspaper, *Community Times*, Unit IV, Issue 1, to the crossword puzzle titled "New Covenant." Students may work alone, in pairs, or as a total group.

MUSIC
(Time: 10 minutes)

Listen on the *Children Sing!* tape to "Jesu, Jesu, fill us with your love" *(The Hymnal 1982, 602; We Sing of God, 93)*. How do the words relate to the commandments of Jesus?

CONNECTING/SPEAKING OUT
(Time: 15–20 minutes)

Option 1. Group Discussion

Review the meaning of "covenant" as a solemn promise from God. Ask the students to work individually or in teams to look up God's covenant with Noah *(Genesis 9:8-13)*; with Abraham *(Genesis 15:18-21)*; and with Moses *(Exodus 19:1-6)*.

Many Christians call the covenant God made with Moses and the Ten Commandments the Old Covenant. With this in mind, ask the students to look at the definition given in answer to the first question under the section, "The New Covenant" in the Prayer Book Catechism, p. 850.

Option 2. Current Events

Engage the class members in discussing Jesus' Summary of the Law: Love God, and love your neighbor as yourself. Ask: What do you think Jesus meant by "loving" one's neighbor? How do we go about doing this? Consider times when it might be hard to love others—in areas of high crime; in places where violence occurs; in times of war.

At the students' own level of experience, talk together about situations in their lives that make it difficult to obey Jesus' command to love: during an argument with a friend, when a family quarrels, when someone accuses or punishes us unfairly. Suggest that love and justice go together. Christians are called to work for justice and peace as a way of extending love to others.

REFLECTING
(Time: 10 minutes)

For this Unit, invite students to prepare a series of reflections about their beliefs—a personal version of the Catechism. These are to be private statements, saved in a booklet format, and placed in envelopes for privacy.

At this first session, use construction paper or posterboard to make individual booklet covers, approximately 9 x 12 inches in size. Supply large paper fasteners or notebook rings to secure the booklets, and markers for adding students' names. Supply an envelope for each student to store their booklet. Keep writing paper of an appropriate size for the booklets.

At this session on the New Covenant, ask the students to write or draw their own interpretations of Jesus' commandments.

When students have finished, ask them to insert their work in their booklets, and place the booklets in envelopes with their names on the outside. Keep the envelopes in a safe place.

LEARNING SKILLS
(Time: 10–15 minutes)

Option 1. Class Memory Challenge

The memory challenge for this Unit is the structure and content of *The Book of Common Prayer*. Each student should have a copy of the Prayer Book.

At this session, ask the students to turn to the three-page Table of Contents, and identify the main sections that are printed in bold-face type, beginning with the Daily Office. Explain that the Prayer Book can be analyzed in three "orders": 1. prayers that follow the order of the *day*, from Morning Prayer to Compline (nighttime); 2. prayers and services that follow the order of the liturgical *year*, Advent through the season after Pentecost; and 3. services that follow the order of a *life*, from infancy (Holy Baptism) through death (Burial Service).

Ask the students to find examples from all three orders (above) and call out the name and page number of a prayer or liturgy. Note briefly the content of pages 8-33, which include introductory statements and the Calendar of the Church Year. Then encourage the students to focus on the Daily Office.

Invite the group to work in teams to memorize contents of the Daily Office, including the following: Morning Prayer, Evening Prayer, Noonday Prayer, Compline, and Daily Devotions for Individuals and Families.

Option 2. Learning Scripture

To keep track of the students' progress in learning Scripture during this Unit, prepare a Scripture Tree to which branches and leaves can be added each session. For this session, construct a sturdy tree trunk from brown or black construction paper. Write each Scripture verse given throughout the Unit on a separate branch. As students memorize each verse, they can add leaves along the corresponding branch. By the end of the Unit, the tree should have many branches and leaves.

For this session, invite the students to learn *John 13:34; John 15:10;* or *John 20:31*. See "Learning Scripture" in the student newspaper, *Community Times*.

ONGOING PROJECT
(Time: 5–10 minutes)

As an ongoing project for this Unit, invite the students to create a large picture book that follows the order of the Catechism in *The Book of Common Prayer*. Use twenty sheets of light-colored posterboard (22 x 28 inches), two to serve as covers and eighteen as the book's pages. Supply pencils and colored markers or crayons.

At each session, the group will place Catechism section headings at the top of the book pages, in large block letters. It will be the class members' task to design, draw, and color illustrations that suggest the content of the Catechism sections.

For this session, the students can work in teams to do the following:

Decorate the front cover with the title, "Our Catechism in Pictures."

Prepare the first two book pages: "Human Nature" and "God the Father." Label them pages 1 and 2. The students will need to read the questions and answers under each section of the Catechism (BCP, pp. 845-846) for images to add. Possible pictures for the two sheets might be a person extending hands as if reaching for God or a view of the world with light streaming upward.

Leave room for holes on the left-hand side of each posterboard sheet so that all the book "pages" can be laced together with ribbon or yarn.

SYMBOL CARD and TREASUREBOOK

Card 28 has a Prayer Book with a Latin cross, a verse of Scripture, and an explanation on the back.

Ask the students to read, in *Chalice Year Treasurebook*, Part IV, Section 1 about the purpose of the Catechism in *The Book of Common Prayer*. How do we describe the relationship between the Old and the New Covenants?

GOING FORTH

Gather the group for the dismissal. The leader will say:

I ask your prayers for peace; for goodwill among nations; and for the well-being of all people.
Pray for justice and peace.
Silence

I ask your prayers for the poor, the sick, the hungry, the oppressed, and those in prison.
Pray for those in any need or trouble.
Silence

[Learners may add their petitions.]

I ask your prayers for all who seek God, or a deeper knowledge of him.
Pray that they may find and be found by him.

From The Prayers of the People
The Book of Common Prayer, p. 386

Teacher: Let us go forth in the name of Christ.
Students: Thanks be to God.

TEACHER'S ASSESSMENT

From your observations, how well do the students understand the meaning and purpose of the New Covenant? Can they describe the role of the Catechism?

LOOKING AHEAD

The next session focuses on the Catechism sections on God the Father, God the Son, and God the Holy Spirit. Reflect on what the concept of the Trinity, God as three persons, means to you. In what ways does this image of God enrich your understanding and faith?

THE CATECHISM
SESSION 2
THE TRINITY

FOCUS

The Catechism of *The Book of Common Prayer* includes separate sections on the three Persons of the Trinity: God the Father, God the Son, and God the Holy Spirit. The doctrine of the Trinity is implied in the New Testament but spelled out only in the creeds of the Church. The students should be able to express in their own ways the traditional Christian concept of God as three-in-One, and to recognize several symbols for the Trinity.

GETTING READY

The term Trinity denotes the Christian doctrine that God is a unity of three Persons: Father, Son, and Holy Spirit. The Church preserves its understanding of the Trinity through its creeds. The New Testament does not speak explicitly on this subject. In *II Corinthians 13:13*, we discover the earliest hint of the Trinity. See also *Matthew 28:19*.

Three Catechism sections spell out primary claims about each Person:

- "God the Father" (BCP, p. 846) defines God as creator of heaven and Earth and everything in them. God sustains and directs all that has been created. Our role as human beings is to enjoy and care for every creature "in accordance with God's purposes."

- "God the Son" (BCP, pp. 849-850) describes Jesus as the perfect image of God the Father. He shows us that God is love. His saving work for our benefit is expressed in the language of the creeds. Finally, we share in Jesus' "victory over sin, suffering, and death" when we are baptized into the New Covenant as members of Christ's body, the Church.

- "God the Holy Spirit" (BCP, pp. 852-853) identifies the third Person as "God at work in the world." In the Old Covenant, the Holy Spirit is the "giver of life" who spoke through the prophets. Christians recognize the Spirit's presence in their lives as they confess Jesus Christ as Lord and "are brought into love and harmony with God, with ourselves, with our neighbors, and with all creation."

As the Catechism affirms, all our beliefs about the Persons of the Trinity are tested against what is said in the Bible. The Church asks continually: Are we being true to what is revealed in Holy Scripture?

> Almighty God, you have revealed to your Church your eternal Being of glorious majesty and perfect love as one God in Trinity of Persons: Give us grace to continue steadfast in the confession of this faith, and constant in our worship of you, Father, Son, and Holy Spirit; for you live and reign, one God, now and for ever. *Amen.*
>
> Of the Holy Trinity
> *The Book of Common Prayer*, p. 251

TEACHING TIP

Understanding the concept of the Trinity is difficult at any age. Keep in mind that most intermediate-age students are not yet ready to think in abstract terms. They can best understand new ideas expressed in concrete terms that are based on their own experiences. For example, you may wish to describe yourself as a three-in-one person: a church school teacher, a parent, and an employee in the workforce.

GATHERING

Ahead of time, obtain three large sheets of paper and copy the following Scripture passages: Sheet 1, *Genesis 1:1, 31*; Sheet 2, *Isaiah 9:6-7; Luke 2:1-7*; Sheet 3, *Acts 2:1-4*. Also provide three large placards, each containing the name of one Person of the Trinity: God the

Father, God the Son, and God the Holy Spirit. As the class members arrive, invite each one to match the three placards with the Scripture sheets.

When everyone is present, say:

Let us pray. (Use the Collect "Of the Holy Trinity," above, or a prayer of your own choosing.)

The chosen student lector reads from the class Bible (NRSV):

A Reading from the Letter of Jude, verses 17 through 21.

But you, beloved, must remember the predictions of the apostles of our Lord Jesus Christ; for they said to you, "In the last time there will be scoffers, indulging in their own ungodly lusts." It is these worldly people, devoid of the Spirit, who are causing divisions. But you, beloved, build yourselves up on your most holy faith; pray in the Holy Spirit; keep yourselves in the love of God; look forward to the mercy of our Lord Jesus Christ that leads to eternal life.

Reader: The Word of the Lord.
Response: Thanks be to God.

INTRODUCING THE STORY
(Time: 10 minutes)

Begin by telling a story about the central issue debated at the Council of Nicaea that resulted in our Nicene Creed. Use the article in the student newspaper, *Community Times* (Unit IV, Issue 2), as a model.

Arius, a parish priest, had been preaching that Jesus was not God. He believed Jesus was like God, but had been created by God. Because he could cry and feel pain, he was human just like us.

Athanasius, a deacon and assistant to the bishop who came from Alexandria in Egypt, argued that Jesus was both truly God and truly human. If Jesus is not one with God, he said, then we could not be saved by Christ. Athanasius believed that ideas like those of Arius were dangerous to the Church.

The debate over this issue resulted in the Church's first great Council in 325 CE. The document that was produced, the Nicene Creed, affirmed that Jesus Christ is "one Being with the Father"—a fully equal person in the three-in-one God. The argument of Athanasius successfully opposed other views about Jesus.

Show the class members Poster No. 19 in the Teacher's Packet that is filled with Trinity symbols.

Ask: Which symbols are you familiar with? Have you seen any of the symbols in our church? Where?

Explain that the Trinity is a central doctrine of the Church, developed over many years but based on Scripture. The word "trinity" does not appear in the New Testament, but it is clear that the apostle Paul and the Gospel writers had a strong sense of the threeness of God as Father (Creator), Son (Redeemer), and Holy Spirit (Sanctifier).

Explain that the Catechism contains separate sections of God the Father, God the Son, and God the Holy Spirit. In your own words, share the summaries from Getting Ready (above).

Ask students to look up *Matthew 28:19-20* and compare these verses with the words said as a person is baptized (*The Book of Common Prayer*, p. 307). This passage is called the Baptismal formula.

EXPLORING
(Time: 15–20 minutes)

Option 1. Examining the Catechism

Ahead of time, prepare a number of paper slips on which are written descriptive words or phrases connected with the Persons of the Trinity, taken from the Catechism sections: *The Book of Common Prayer*, pp. 846, 849-50, and 852-53. Examples: "creator of heaven and earth" (Father); "image of the Father" (Son); "One who spoke through the prophets" (Holy Spirit). Place the slips in a basket or other container.

On a bulletin board or large piece of posterboard print the following headings:

God the Father   God the Son   God the Holy Spirit

Ask students to draw slips, then pin or tape them under the appropriate headings. When all the slips have been placed, review the Catechism sections and rearrange the words and phrases in the order of their appearance. Celebrate those placed correctly.

Option 2. Trinity Symbols

Invite the students to create new Trinity symbols. Provide each person a 9 x 12-inch sheet of paper. The sheet may be folded into thirds so that it will stand. A different symbol may be drawn on each panel. Use markers and pens to add color to the chosen symbols. For ideas, refer to the student newspaper, *Community Times*, Unit IV, Issue 2, and to Poster No. 19 in the Teacher's Packet.

Option 3. Word Puzzle

Turn in the student newspaper, *Community Times*, Unit IV, Issue 2, to the word puzzle titled "The Trinity." Students may work alone, in pairs, or as a total group.

MUSIC
(Time: 10 minutes)

Sing or listen on the *Children Sing!* tape to one or more stanzas of the Trinity hymn, "Holy, holy, holy! Lord God Almighty!" (*The Hymnal 1982,* 362; *We Sing of God,* 56). Point out examples of "threeness" in the stanzas, such as: Holy, holy, holy; wert, art, evermore shall be; power, love, purity; earth, sky, sea.

CONNECTING/SPEAKING OUT
(Time: 15–20 minutes)

Option 1. Group Discussion

Using the Sunday Lectionary of *The Book of Common Prayer*, ask the students to locate Trinity Sunday (the next Sunday after the Day of Pentecost). Call attention to the fact that it is a Principal Feast of the Church (BCP, p. 15).

Note that the word "trinity" has a very prominent place in the Church's liturgies. Ask the students to work individually or in teams to locate examples in the Prayer Book. (You may want to assist by listing the following page numbers: 148, 176, 199, 228, 251, 347, 380, 460, 463, 548, 852.)

Point out that this important Christian doctrine is a *mystery*. Invite the students to create their own statements about each Person: Father, Son, and Holy Spirit. How do our statements differ? In what ways are they alike?

Option 2. Current Events

Offer one or two examples from the following list to suggest concrete ways of conveying the sense of unity-in-threeness we can observe around us:
- water, steam, ice (moisture)
- yesterday, today, tomorrow (time)
- daughter, mother, sister (one woman)
- beginning, middle, end (of a story or action)
- water, land, sky (physical world)
- core, flesh, skin (of an apple)
- root, stem, flower (plant)

Encourage the class members to come up with their own ways of expressing the ways in which one substance can have three parts. Invite comparison to the doctrine of the Trinity, but remind the group that the mystery of God's three-in-Oneness is a far deeper and greater mystery than any of our concrete examples can suggest.

REFLECTING
(Time: 10 minutes)

Use the process of reflecting outlined in Session 1, with students adding a sheet on the topic of the Trinity. (Note: Students can make booklet covers and begin writing personal statements at any session.)

Distribute the booklets and encourage the students to reflect on the three Persons of the Trinity—God the Father, God the Son, and God the Holy Spirit. Suggest that they write or draw their own ways of thinking about the unity of the three.

When the work is completed, ask the students to insert their sheets into the booklets and place them in the envelopes for storage.

LEARNING SKILLS
(Time: 10–15 minutes)

Option 1. Class Memory Challenge

Continue the task of learning the structure and content of *The Book of Common Prayer* as described in Session 1. At this session, ask the group to make a list of headings under the Daily Office, working from memory. Consult the student newspaper, *Community Times,* to correct any errors or omissions.

Turn to the Great Litany and the Collects (Traditional and Contemporary). Note the directions on page 148 for use of the Great Litany. Explain briefly how the Collects are used during the Church Year (p. 158). Practice locating the Collects to be used in your congregation in the weeks ahead. Compare the traditional and contemporary language for these prayers. Challenge the class members to memorize the locations of the Great Litany and the Collects.

Option 2. Learning Scripture

Ask students to report on verses learned since the previous session. Add branches to the Scripture Tree, as described in Session 1. Use one branch of the tree for each Bible verse. Class members who have memorized verses can add a leaf to each corresponding branch.

Encourage the students to memorize, before the next session, *II Corinthians 13:13* or *Galatians 4:6b*. See "Learning Scripture" in the student newspaper, *Community Times.*

ONGOING PROJECT
(Time: 5–10 minutes)

Begin or continue work on the catechism book described in Session 1. Check the supply of pencils and markers. The posterboard sheets for this session are to be labeled "The Old Covenant" (page 3) and "The Ten Commandments" (page 4). Ask the students to form teams to read these sections in the Catechism (BCP, pp. 846-848) and decide how to illustrate them. Possible pictures: Hand of God and hand of a person reaching toward each other in a covenant relationship; tablets of stone for the Commandments.

Punch holes in the pages so they can be added to the book.

SYMBOL CARD and TREASUREBOOK

Card 29 shows a Trinity shield, with a verse of Scripture, and an explanation on the back.

Ask the students to read in the *Chalice Year Treasurebook*, Part IV, Section 2, about the Church's concept of God in three Persons. Why do we call ourselves "Trinitarians"?

GOING FORTH

Gather the group for the dismissal. The leader will say:
I ask your prayers for peace; for goodwill among nations; and for the well-being of all people.
Pray for justice and peace.
Silence

I ask your prayers for the poor, the sick, the hungry, the oppressed, and those in prison.
Pray for those in any need or trouble.
Silence

[Learners may add their petitions.]

I ask your prayers for all who seek God, or a deeper knowledge of him.
Pray that they may find and be found by him.

From The Prayers of the People
The Book of Common Prayer, p. 386

Teacher: Let us go forth in the name of Christ.
Students: Thanks be to God.

TEACHER'S ASSESSMENT

In what ways did the class members respond to the Trinity? What did they find most helpful as they struggled with the mystery? In your judgment, are they able to sense the relatedness and oneness of the three Persons?

LOOKING AHEAD

The next session focuses on the Catechism section on the Church. The creeds describe the Church as "one, holy, catholic, and apostolic." Reflect on what each of these words means for you.

THE CATECHISM
SESSION 3
THE CHURCH

FOCUS

The Catechism offers names and descriptions for the Church that are found in the Bible and in the creeds. It also defines the Church's mission, which is carried out by all its members. The students should be able to explain what is meant by the Church as "the Body of Christ," and cite the four words from the creeds that describe the Church (one, holy, catholic, and apostolic).

GETTING READY

The English word "church" comes from the Greek word "kuriakon." It means "of the Lord (kurios)." The Scottish word "kirk" (church) shows a closer resemblance to the same root.

The New Testament word for Church is the Greek "ekklesia," which means "assembly" or "gathering." The Church is viewed as a community gathered by God, through Jesus Christ. God called this community of baptized believers into being, dwells in it, rules over it, and works through the lives of its people as they live out their faith in the world.

Turn to *I Corinthians 12:12-26* for a New Testament image of the Church used by the apostle Paul. He called it "the body of Christ," composed of many members (just as a human body has various parts). In this picture, every member of the Church honors all the other members, and if "one member suffers, all suffer together" (verse 6).

This image of the "body" is used also by the writer of *Ephesians 4:1-16*. Each member has gifts and abilities to be shared in the Church's mission of proclaiming the good news of Christ to the world.

The Catechism defines the Church as "the community of the New Covenant," and lists additional images from the Bible and the creeds. Four words in particular are emphasized: one, holy, catholic, and apostolic. All are explained more fully in answer to short questions (Prayer Book, p. 854). Three concluding questions (BCP, p. 855) address the Church's mission.

> Almighty and everlasting Father, you have given the Holy Spirit to abide with us forever: Bless, we pray, with his grace and presence, the bishops and the other clergy and the laity here assembled in your Name, that your Church, being preserved in true faith and godly discipline, may fulfill all the mind of him who loved it and gave himself for it, your Son Jesus Christ our Savior; who lives and reigns with you, in the unity of the Holy Spirit, one God, now and for ever. *Amen.*
>
> For a Church Convention
> *The Book of Common Prayer,* p. 255

TEACHING TIP

People use the word "church" to refer to Christians, organized religion, and local congregations. This is a good time to help intermediate-age students understand that the Church is something far greater than their own congregation. Begin with a biblical view of the Church, using concrete images in describing its various aspects. Be ready to distinguish between the word "catholic," which refers to all Christians in the universal Church, and the Roman Catholic Church.

GATHERING

Ahead of time, prepare a collection of paper shapes in varied colors (triangles, rectangles, circles, squares)—large enough to accommodate writing or drawing.

As the students arrive, ask each one to choose a shape. Challenge them to add words or illustrations related to the word "church," such as priest, stained glass, buildings, and Eucharist. Work together to arrange the shapes in a display.

When everyone is present, say:

Let us pray. (Use the Collect "For a Church Convention," above, or a prayer of your own choosing.)

The chosen student lector reads from the class Bible (NRSV):

A Reading from the First Epistle to the Corinthians, chapter 12, verses 20 through 28.

As it is, there are many members, yet one body. The eye cannot say to the hand, "I have no need of you," nor again the head to the feet, "I have no need of you." On the contrary, the members of the body that seem to be weaker are indispensable, and those members of the body that we think less honorable we clothe with greater honor, and our less respectable members are treated with greater respect; whereas our more respectable members do not need this. But God has so arranged the body, giving the greater honor to the inferior member, that there may be no dissension within the body, but the members may have the same care for one another. If one member suffers, all suffer together with it; if one member is honored, all rejoice together with it.

Now you are the body of Christ and individually members of it. And God has appointed in the church first apostles, second prophets, third teachers, then deeds of power, then gifts of healing, forms of assistance, forms of leadership, various kinds of tongues.

Reader: The Word of the Lord.
Response: Thanks be to God.

INTRODUCING THE STORY
(Time: 10 minutes)

Look at the display the students made during the Gathering of the words and illustrations related to the word "church." Talk about the different ways the group defines church.

Ask the students to work individually or in teams to locate Paul's image of the Church as "the body of Christ" in *I Corinthians 12:12-26* and the reference to the Church's unity as a body in *Ephesians 4:1-16*.

Discuss Paul's powerful image of the Church as a body with each member serving a special purpose. You may want to introduce Paul's description with background information about the passage from the student newspaper, *Community Times* (Unit IV, Issue 3). Paul appears to be responding to reports that there had been divisions and arguments among members of the Christian church in Corinth.

To illustrate the interdependence described by Paul, invite four volunteers from the class to become a "body," with each person assigned a role: one to be eyes and brain; one to be mouth; one to be the right arm; and one to be the left arm.

Arrange the body with "mouth" kneeling, "eyes and brain" standing above, and the "left arm" and "right arm" in position. Set up rules: Only the mouth can talk, but only as the brain whispers what to say. Arms can do only what the mouth tells them to do.

Give the body one or more of these tasks: Locate, read, and copy a verse from Scripture. Write a short note, and put it into an envelope. Wrap a package, and tie a ribbon around it. Here are more challenging but messier tasks: Open a can of soda, pour it into a cup, and drink. Open a container of peanut butter, and use a knife to spread some of it on crackers.

As a group, talk about the importance of each person that is a member of the "body of Christ." When one member is injured in any way, all the members are affected.

EXPLORING
(Time: 15–20 minutes)

Option 1. Parts of the Whole

Beforehand, write words or phrases describing the Church from the questions in the Catechism (*The Book of Common Prayer*, p. 854-855) on both sides of a piece of posterboard. The front and back should look almost alike. Then cut the poster up in enough pieces for every student in the class. The pieces should be similar to make the task of putting them back together more difficult.

Shuffle the puzzle pieces and pass them out to the students. Tell them that the goal is to put the puzzle together as quickly as possible. To make the activity more interesting, hold back one or two key pieces.

Afterwards, talk about the experience. Ask: What was the hardest part of the task? How did you decide which side of the puzzle to work on? How did the puzzle look with pieces missing? (If you held pieces back, put them in the puzzle at this time.)

Option 2. Posters Describing the Church

Provide each class member with a large sheet of posterboard, pencils, and markers. The second question of the Catechism's section, "The Church," provides a list of biblical images of the Church. Suggest that the students form teams to locate these references in the New Testament:

- the Body of which Jesus Christ is the Head *(Colossians 2:19; Ephesians 1:22-23; 4:15).*
- baptized persons *(Romans 12:4-5; I Corinthians 6:15, 12:12; Ephesians 4:25,30)*
- the People of God *(I Peter 2:9)*
- the New Israel *(Galatians. 6:16)*
- a holy nation *(I Peter 2:9)*
- a royal priesthood *(I Peter 2:5,9)*
- the pillar and the ground of truth *(I Timothy 3:15)*

Challenge students to design a poster incorporating the biblical images that they found. They may wish to make a collage of the images or to select one to illustrate. A small group could also make a booklet that includes each image.

Option 3. Word Search

Turn in the student newspaper, *Community Times*, Unit IV, Issue 3, to the word search titled "What is the Church?" Students may work alone, in pairs, or as a total group.

MUSIC
(Time: 10 minutes)

Introduce and sing "The Church's one foundation" *(The Hymnal 1982, 525)* or listen to it on the *Children Sing!* tape. Encourage the students to listen for phrases that describe the Church—such as "new creation by water and the word" (stanza 1) or "elect (chosen) from every nation."

CONNECTING/SPEAKING OUT
(Time: 15–20 minutes)

Option 1. Group Discussion

Ahead of time, label circles with the following simple names: congregation, diocese, province, national Episcopal Church, worldwide Anglicans; universal Church. Suggest that the students give the circles more specific labels: name of your church; name of your Diocese; name of your Province; full name of the Episcopal Church (The Protestant Episcopal Church in the United States of America); the worldwide Anglican Communion; the universal Church (one, holy, catholic, and apostolic Church).

Discuss how it feels to think of each congregation's place in the larger picture of the Church of Jesus Christ in the world. How do Paul's words about the Church as the Body of Christ relate to our own Episcopal (Anglican) churches?

Option 2. Current Events

Talk about the concept of "mission" in the last three questions of the Catechism section of The Church (BCP, p. 855). Ask the group to brainstorm specific tasks that are done by the Church in pursuing its mission and list them on a piece of newsprint.

On a separate piece of newsprint, ask the group to list everything their church does to pursue its mission. Use the answers in the Catechism for ideas. Be sure to include ministries to people inside and outside of your church.

If there is interest, identify an activity the students already do or could participate in to help the church carry out its mission. For example, if people in the church serve food to the homeless, the group could provide dessert. Talk about who will be responsible for contacting the people in charge, what each person needs to contribute, and when the work will take place. Emphasize the importance of each person in the group (the body) sharing the workload.

REFLECTING
(Time: 10 minutes)

Distribute the students' catechism booklets and invite them to add another entry. (See Session 1 for a description of this process, which can be started at any session.)

Encourage the class members to think about the Church, how we describe it, and its mission in the world. Suggest that they prepare entries for their booklets entitled "How I View the Church." They may write or draw. Use the display from Gathering for ideas.

When the work is completed, ask the students to insert the sheets into the booklets and place them in the envelopes. Put them in a place for safekeeping.

LEARNING SKILLS
(Time: 10–15 minutes)

Option 1. Class Memory Challenge

As described in Session 1, the memory challenge for this Unit is the structure and content of *The Book of Common Prayer*. Review the work accomplished thus far, then look together at the section titled Proper Liturgies for Special Days. Note that the six services are for the period from Ash Wednesday through the Great Vigil of Easter.

Call attention to distinctive characteristics of each liturgy, such as: imposition of ashes on Ash Wednesday (p. 265); distribution of palms (p. 270) and reading of the Passion narrative on Palm Sunday (pp. 272-273); the possibility of a foot washing on Maundy Thursday (p. 274); the Solemn Collects and Anthems of Good Friday (pp. 277-282); the absence of the Eucharist on Holy Saturday (p. 283); and the lighting of the Paschal Candle at the Easter Vigil (pp. 285-286).

Invite the class members to remember what is special about each of the liturgies.

Option 2. Learning Scripture

For each new verse students have learned since the previous session, write the appropriate citations on a branch, and tape it to the Scripture Tree (as described in Session 1). Individual students may add leaves to the corresponding branches for each verse they have memorized.

Invite the students to learn before the next session *Matthew 16:18; I Corinthians 3:16;* or *I Corinthians 12:27.* See "Learning Scripture" in the student newspaper, *Community Times.*

ONGOING PROJECT
(Time: 5–10 minutes)

Continue working on the picture book as described in Session 1. Label three new pages: "Sin and Redemption," "God the Son," and "The New Covenant." Ask the students to read these sections in the Catechism (BCP, pp. 848-851), then work in groups to prepare pages 5-7 in the large book. Possibilities for the three illustrations, in order: human figure bent over to show separation from God; head or symbol for Jesus Christ; picture of a New Testament (Scripture).

Punch holes to add the pages to the large book.

SYMBOL CARD and TREASUREBOOK

Card 30 shows a Cross of Triumph, a verse of Scripture, and an explanation on the back.

Suggest that students read in the *Chalice Year Treasurebook,* Part IV, Section 3, about how the Catechism defines the Church. What is a "great danger" described in the prayer for Church unity?

GOING FORTH

Gather the group for the dismissal. The leader will say:
I ask your prayers for peace; for goodwill among nations; and for the well-being of all people.
Pray for justice and peace.
Silence

I ask your prayers for the poor, the sick, the hungry, the oppressed, and those in prison.
Pray for those in any need or trouble.
Silence

[Learners may add their petitions.]

I ask your prayers for all who seek God, or a deeper knowledge of him.
Pray that they may find and be found by him.
From The Prayers of the People
The Book of Common Prayer, p. 386

Teacher: Let us go forth in the name of Christ.
Students: Thanks be to God.

TEACHER'S ASSESSMENT

How would you describe the students' approach to this session's study of the Church? Which of the images appealed to them most? How well are they able to articulate the relationship between their own congregation and the worldwide Church?

LOOKING AHEAD

The creeds of the Church are the focus of the next session. What comes to mind when you say the words, "I believe . . . ." Why?

THE CATECHISM
SESSION 4
THE CREEDS

FOCUS

Creeds of the Church are statements of our beliefs about God. The statements bind Christians together even when they are separated into different churches and denominations. The students should be able to describe how creeds came into being and to explain how creeds are used in the Church.

GETTING READY

In the early Church, candidates for Holy Baptism were required to confess their faith in the presence of a congregation. A person being baptized would declare, "I believe that Jesus Christ is the Son of God." Eventually, short and simple confessions of faith developed into what we now know as the Apostles' Creed. We use this Creed just before the prayers in the Daily Office (Morning and Evening Prayer). Each time we say it, we are reminded of our own baptisms. The Baptismal Covenant (BCP, p. 304) begins with three questions about the Persons of the Trinity, and the answers are the articles of the Apostles' Creed concerning the Father, the Son, and the Holy Spirit.

A second purpose of a written creed is to clarify the Church's teaching about the Christian faith. The prime example is the Nicene Creed, produced by the Council of Nicaea in 325 CE. (Nicaea was a city located in present-day Turkey.) The scholar Athanasius strongly influenced the outcome of the Council by persuading its members to declare that Jesus Christ is "of one Being with the Father." Thus the Church took its stand against any notion that Jesus did not share the divinity of God.

The Nicene Creed is said at Holy Eucharist immediately following the sermon. When we say this Creed in worship, we are confessing the faith of the whole Church, not just our personal affirmations.

In *The Hymnal 1982*, the tune for the Trinity hymn, "Holy, holy, holy! Lord God Almighty!" (362) is titled *Nicaea*.

The Catechism refers also to "an ancient document" known as the Athanasian Creed (BCP, pp. 864-865). This statement is believed to have originated in southern France in the fifth century. It bears the name of Athanasius since it is clearly consistent with his teaching. This Creed is not used in public worship. It is included in our Prayer Book because of its strong reaffirmation of the doctrine of the Trinity.

> I believe in God, the Father almighty,
> creator of heaven and earth.
> I believe in Jesus Christ, his only Son, our Lord
> He was conceived by the power of the Holy Spirit
> and born of the Virgin Mary.
> He suffered under Pontius Pilate,
> was crucified, died, and was buried.
> He descended to the dead.
> On the third day he rose again.
> He ascended into heaven,
> and is seated at the right hand of the Father.
> He will come again to judge the living and the dead.
> I believe in the Holy Spirit,
> the holy catholic Church,
> the communion of saints,
> the forgiveness of sins,
> the resurrection of the body,
> and the life everlasting. Amen.
>
> The Apostles' Creed
> *The Book of Common Prayer*, p. 96

TEACHING TIP

The beliefs stated in the creeds have withstood the test of time. Even though they were written long ago, the creeds are still relevant to us now. Help students appreciate the value of our creeds in preserving our distinctive beliefs as Christ's people in the world.

GATHERING

Tape a long length of butcher paper to a wall. Place markers nearby.

In various places on the sheet of paper, write: "I believe . . ." Leave plenty of space. As students arrive, encourage them to complete the statements in as many ways as they care to. To help them get started, enter a few examples, such as "I believe in mothers," "I believe in being fair," or "I believe children should be in school." (You may want to add a controversial example or two, such as "I believe television is a bad influence," or "I believe no one should have to eat anything that doesn't taste good."

When everyone is present, say:

Let us say what we believe. (Use the Apostles' Creed, above, or the Nicene Creed, if you choose.)

The chosen student lector reads from the class Bible (NRSV):

A Reading from the Gospel of John, chapter 20, verses 26 through 31.

A week later his disciples were again in the house, and Thomas was with them. Although the doors were shut, Jesus came and stood among them and said, "Peace be with you." Then he said to Thomas, "Put your finger here and see my hands. Reach out your hand and put it in my side. Do not doubt but believe." Thomas answered him, "My Lord and my God!" Jesus said to him, "Have you believed because you have seen me? Blessed are those who have not seen and yet have come to believe."

Now Jesus did many other signs in the presence of his disciples, which are not written in this book. But these are written so that you may come to believe that Jesus is the Messiah, the Son of God, and that through believing you may have life in his name.

Reader: The Word of the Lord.
Response: Thanks be to God.

INTRODUCING THE STORY
(Time: 10 minutes)

Refer to the "I believe. . ." statements that emerged at the Gathering (above). Not all class members will agree with everything written. Take a few minutes to try to work out a statement of beliefs the whole class can accept.

Point out that Christians through the centuries have had their differences when they compared their beliefs about God as Father, Son, and Holy Spirit. It has always been very important for the Church's people to search the Scriptures and pray in order to come to closer agreement. The Church's creeds are careful statements that came about through serious thought and debate. In the Christian tradition, Creeds are extremely important as the foundation for the Christian life.

Distribute copies of *The Book of Common Prayer*, and ask the students to turn to the Catechism section, "The Creeds" (pp. 851-852), and read the answers to the five questions. Review these facts alongside Poster No. 20 in the Teacher's Packet that compares Creeds.

• At the left is the Apostles' Creed, used at Holy Baptism and in Morning and Evening Prayer.

• At the right is the Nicene Creed, adopted by a great Church Council that met in the city of Nicaea in 325 CE. It is used in Holy Eucharist.

Ask: What is similar in the two Creeds? What is different? Which do you prefer?

The Catechism section adds a definition of the Athanasian Creed, as an ancient document on the Trinity. Encourage the students to find it in the Prayer Book, pp. 864-865. (Note the additional information under Getting Ready.)

Other background information about the Creeds can be found in the student newspaper, *Community Times* (Unit IV, Issue 4). Also included are summaries of the Creeds and a story about Thomas.

If you have time, ask students to look up *I Corinthians 15:1-11* to read what the apostle Paul wrote to the Christians in Corinth. Ask: How many words or phrases in these verses are similar to the Apostle's Creed?

EXPLORING
(Time: 15–20 minutes)

Option 1. Identification Game

Divide the class into two teams. One team is responsible for the Apostles' Creed, the other for the Nicene Creed. Ask each group to copy its Creed, phrase by phrase, on a large piece of paper, allowing blank space after each copied line. Encourage the group members to take turns, so that one person does not have to do all the writing.

When the Creeds are copied, cut the two sheets into strips so that only one phrase appears on each piece. Fold the strips, one by one, and place them in a basket or bag.

One at a time, a student will draw out a slip of paper. The team then has 30 seconds to identify which Creed it comes from. (Encourage students to try saying the phrase that comes before and the one after the words on each strip.) Continue until all the paper strips have been used.

A variation would be to involve the whole class in trading their phrases and taping them onto a display board, until both Creeds are reconstructed in their entirety.

Option 2. The Trinity

Refer to Poster No. 20 used during the Introducing the Story segment. Ask the students to look at the symbols of the Trinity used in the borders. Note that each comes from either a triangle or circle, or some combination of the two.

Pass out rulers, compasses, pencils, markers, and paper. Encourage students to make up their own symbols or copy the ones from the poster. Suggest they fill the paper by overlapping the different symbols. When they are finished, see if any new symbols have emerged.

Encourage them to add color to the drawings if they had not done so before. Display the art until this Unit is completed.

Option 3. Acrostic

Turn in the student newspaper, *Community Times*, Unit IV, Issue 4, to the acrostic titled "Words from the Creeds." Students may work alone, in pairs, or as a total group.

MUSIC
(Time: 10 minutes)

Listen to "We know that Christ is raised and dies no more" *(The Hymnal 1982, 296)* on the *Children Sing!* tape. Point out that this is a modern hymn sometimes sung at Holy Baptism. Ask: Which words and phrases of the hymn remind us of beliefs found in the Apostles' Creed?

CONNECTING/SPEAKING OUT
(Time: 15–20 minutes)

Option 1. Group Discussion

Remind the students that the Creeds of the Church tell the story of Jesus. Refer to Poster No. 20 that shows a comparison of the Creeds. How do the Creeds describe him? What are the essential facts about God's Son that are spelled out in the Apostles' Creed? in the Nicene Creed? What is promised in each Creed?

Encourage the group to discuss the central place of Jesus Christ in our life and worship. This is why the Creeds are at the center of our liturgies.

Option 2. Current Events

Engage the students in talking about their own beliefs as Christians. Which parts of the Creeds are easiest to accept? Which are hardest? Why? (Poster No. 20 may help the class members assess their reactions to each Creed's content.)

Ask: How would you respond to someone who said, "I don't believe everything in your church's Creeds"? It may be helpful to point out that individual members of a church may not believe in the same ways, but when we say the Creed together in our liturgy, we are speaking for the Church as a whole.

REFLECTING
(Time: 10 minutes)

Continue with (or arrange to begin) the method of reflecting suggested in Session 1. Hand out the envelopes with the students' booklets and invite them to add another entry.

Ask the students to think about the Creeds of the Church and to reflect on "Why I Say the Creed."

Suggest that the students choose a section, line, or phrase from either the Apostles' Creed or the Nicene Creed. Encourage them to express their ideas and feelings about what they selected—either in writing or by drawing illustrations. Or they could do a series of "I believe . . ." statements.

When they have finished, ask the students to add their work to their booklets and place them inside the envelopes.

LEARNING SKILLS
(Time: 10–15 minutes)

Option 1. Class Memory Challenge

Continue the memory work on the structure and content of *The Book of Common Prayer*. Begin by reviewing what has been accomplished in previous sessions, then move on to Holy Baptism (pp. 299-313) and The Holy Eucharist (pp. 316-409).

Concentrate on the directions for these Sacraments (Baptism, pp. 298 and 312-314; Eucharist, pp. 322 and

406-409). Ask the students to work as individuals or as teams to discover at least one aspect of these liturgies that they had not known or thought about before.

Encourage the class members to add Holy Baptism and Holy Eucharist to their memorized outline of *The Book of Common Prayer*.

Option 2. Learning Scripture

Add paper branches for verses students have memorized to the Scripture Tree, as described in Session 1, placing written citations on each new branch. Those who have learned verses may add leaves to the corresponding branches for each Scripture.

Challenge the class members to memorize before the next session, *John 3:16* or *Hebrews 11:1*. See "Learning Scripture" in the student newspaper, *Community Times*.

ONGOING PROJECT
(Time: 5–10 minutes)

Work may proceed on the catechism book as described in Session 1. For this session, ask the students to work in teams to prepare pages 8-10: "The Creeds," "The Holy Spirit," "The Holy Scriptures." Ask the students to read these sections in the Catechism (BCP, pp. 851-854) and decide on appropriate illustrations. Some possibilities, in order: Prayer Book opened to the Nicene Creed; a descending dove to symbolize the Spirit; a scroll or a modern Bible.

Punch holes to add pages to the large book.

SYMBOL CARD and TREASUREBOOK

Card 31 shows the Apostles' shield, with a line from *The Book of Common Prayer*, and an explanation on the back.

Encourage the students to read about the creeds in the *Chalice Year Treasurebook*, Part IV, Section 4. Why was the Nicene Creed adopted? When was it adopted?

GOING FORTH

Gather the group for the dismissal. The teacher or a student will say:

I ask your prayers for peace; for goodwill among nations; and for the well-being of all people.
Pray for justice and peace.
Silence

I ask your prayers for the poor, the sick, the hungry, the oppressed, and those in prison.
Pray for those in any need or trouble.
Silence

[Learners may add their petitions.]

I ask your prayers for all who seek God, or a deeper knowledge of him.
Pray that they may find and be found by him.

From The Prayers of the People
The Book of Common Prayer, p. 386

Teacher: Let us go forth in the name of Christ.
Students: Thanks be to God.

TEACHER'S ASSESSMENT

As students explored the significance of each Creed, what feelings did they express? What evidence did you gather that the students view the Creeds as statements of their own beliefs? How would they explain the relationship between the Creeds and the Bible?

LOOKING AHEAD

The next session focuses on the Church's teachings about human nature and sin and redemption. What do these terms mean for you? Reflect on why it is important for the church to address these concepts.

THE CATECHISM
SESSION 5
SIN AND REDEMPTION

FOCUS

Questions and answers in the Catechism outline our human situation under God. We are created in God's image, to live in peace and harmony. But we rebel and misuse our freedom. God in Christ acts to redeem us, freeing us from the power of evil, sin, and death. The students should be able to express these Christian teachings in their own words.

GETTING READY

As human beings, how are we related to God? What has the Lord Jesus Christ done to change that relationship?

The answers to these two questions can be summed up in one sentence: We are sinners who have been redeemed.

• In the beginning, we were created "in the image of God" *(Genesis 1:26-27)*. As the Catechism puts it, "this means that we are free to make choices: to love, to create, to reason, and to live in harmony with creation and with God" (BCP, p. 845). It is God's will that we should live in such a relationship to our Creator.

• However, we have broken our relationship with God by not living up to our part of the covenant. We seek to do our own will instead of the will of God. We rebel against our Creator, distorting all our relationships. This condition is *sin*. None of us is free from this flaw, for "all we like sheep have gone astray . . . ." *(Isaiah 53:6)*.

• God has reached out to us in Jesus Christ to redeem us—to make us whole again and restore us to a right relationship with our Creator. The Hebrew prophets prepared us for the redemptive work of the Messiah, God's only Son. Through his life, death, and resurrection, we have been set free from "the power of evil, sin, and death" (BCP, p. 849).

We still commit sins because we are human. Only God is perfect and without sin. We do our best, with God's help, to return to God's will for our lives and ask forgiveness.

Throughout our lives we ponder the wonderful mystery of God's loving action in redeeming humankind. Intermediate-age students, on the edge of adolescence, are beginning to experience new ways to rebel. They are also able to understand the good news that God reaches out to us to offer forgiveness for our sin.

Almighty and everlasting God, whose will it is to restore all things in your well-loved Son, the King of kings and Lord of lords: Mercifully grant that the peoples of the earth, divided and enslaved by sin, may be freed and brought together under his most gracious rule; who lives and reigns with you and the Holy Spirit, one God, now and for ever. *Amen.*
Of the Reign of Christ
The Book of Common Prayer, p. 254

TEACHING TIP

Young people often equate sin with extremely negative behavior, such as armed robbery and murder. Because they do not rob banks or kill people, they do not believe they are really sinners. They need help in understanding that sin occurs when we turn away from God or when we hurt others, both intentionally and accidentally. By recognizing our sins, we are able to accept God's forgiveness.

GATHERING

Ahead of time, clip several headlines and stories from newspapers and magazines to make a bulletin board display showing varying sides of the human condition. Look for accounts that emphasize brokenness and distorted relationships, along with stories with positive images of people engaged in unselfish, neighborly deeds. If possible, find some stories that involve young people.

Mix up the stories and spread them on a table. As students arrive, ask them to examine the stories and headlines and separate them into two piles: Broken Acts and Wholeness. Encourage class members to talk about the stories as they work.

When everyone is present, say:

Let us pray. (Use the Collect "Of the Reign of Christ," above, or a prayer of your own choosing.)

The chosen student lector reads from the class Bible (NRSV):

A Reading from the Epistle to the Romans, chapter 3, verses 21 through 26.

But now, apart from law, the righteousness of God has been disclosed, and is attested by the law and the prophets, the righteousness of God through faith in Jesus Christ for all who believe. For there is no distinction, since all have sinned and fall short of the glory of God; they are now justified by his grace as a gift, through the redemption that is in Christ Jesus, whom God put forward as a sacrifice of atonement by his blood, effective through faith. He did this to show his righteousness, because in his divine forbearance he had passed over the sins previously committed; it was to prove at the present time that he himself is righteous and that he justifies the one who has faith in Jesus.

Reader: The Word of the Lord.
Response: Thanks be to God.

INTRODUCING THE STORY
(Time: 10 minutes)

Begin by referring to the clippings used at the Gathering (above). Ask: How would you describe the contrasts among the stories and headlines? After reading through these items, what could we say about human beings? In a discussion of the stories, help students draw a distinction between the troubling news that people behave badly toward one another and the positive images that show people are capable of goodness.

In your own words, tell the story from the student newspaper, *Community Times* (Unit IV, Issue 5), about the boy who deserted his friend on a buddy hike during a church school retreat. After a fight on their way to the retreat, the boys were paired for the hike. The first boy hid from his friend, and came back to camp alone. When he realized his friend was really lost, he realized that he had let everyone down. After his friend was found, he asked everyone and God for forgiveness. You could tell a similar story from your own experience.

Identify the sin and its consequences. Stress the importance of seeking, accepting, and sharing forgiveness.

Ask the students to turn in *The Book of Common Prayer* to the Catechism sections, "Human Nature" (p. 845) and "Sin and Redemption" (pp. 848-849). Draw on the material provided in Getting Ready (above) to assist the class members in defining the Church's understanding of our human condition and what God has graciously done in our behalf through Jesus Christ.

Listen for any evidence that the students are using "sin" only to name specific actions like lying, stealing, and hurting others. Work toward an understanding that sin is turning away from God.

Encourage the students to find and read *Isaiah 53:1-6*, which describes the Messiah's mission. Ask: How does this poetry remind us of Jesus? In verse 6, what does Isaiah say about us?

EXPLORING
(Time: 10–20 minutes)

Option 1. Role Plays

Invite students to participate in a series of role plays to help them understand the concept of sin. Divide into several groups and ask each group to act out one of the following situations or one of their own choosing:

After church, a group of intermediate-age students decides to skip church school since they think it's boring and God doesn't care anyway.

A class member who is different from the rest of the group tries to join a group. The other students make it clear that this person is not wanted.

As a group you go to a convenience store for drinks. As you walk back to the church, several students toss empty cups on the side of the road.

After the role plays talk about how the students felt, especially the person who was left out. Add new endings to the plays that include forgiveness.

Option 2. Watercolor Impressions

Invite the class members to create their own watercolor impressions of the phrase, "in harmony with God, within ourselves, with our neighbors, and with all creation" (BCP, p. 849).

After their work has dried, the students may wish to use permanent markers for adding the phrase below their pictures.

Option 3. Crossword

Turn in the student newspaper, *Community Times*, Unit IV, Issue 5, to the crossword titled "Redemption." Students may work alone, in pairs, or as a total group.

MUSIC
(Time: 10 minutes)

Introduce the hymn, "Just as I am, without one plea" *(The Hymnal 1982, 693)*, and then listen to it on the *Children Sing!* tape. Focus on stanzas 2-3, and make a list of words and phrases that describe our human condition (such as conflict, doubt, fighting, fear, poor, wretched, blind). To whom does the hymn point as the source of pardon and cleansing from human sin?

CONNECTING/SPEAKING OUT
(Time: 15–20 minutes)

Option 1. Group Discussion

Discuss with the students the concept of human freedom. Refer to the Catechism (BCP, p. 845). Ask: In what way are we created "free"? What has gone wrong in our use of freedom?

Note that God gives us the freedom to make choices. Why do we make choices that are wrong? What keeps us from seeing the consequences of wrong choices?

Distribute copies of *The Book of Common Prayer* and say together one of the Confessions of Sin used in Morning Prayer or the Holy Eucharist. Choose the form most frequently used in your congregation's worship. (See pp. 62 or 79, or pp. 331 or 360.) Notice that each of these forms of confession is followed by a prayer of forgiveness and absolution.

Ask: How do these confessions remind us of the Catechism discussions on sin and redemption? What are some wrong choices mentioned in the prayers? What do we ask God to do about these? Why do we ask for God's help of forgiveness?

Option 2. Current Events

Ask students to think about times they have hurt friends and family members. Invite them to share some of these experiences if they wish.

Pass out stationery and envelopes. Encourage students to write a letter to someone they have hurt or a person they are angry with. In the letter, suggest that they admit any wrongdoing and ask for forgiveness.

When everyone is finished, tell students to put their letters in the envelopes and seal them. Students can either take the letters home and mail them, or the letters could be collected in a basket and presented at the dismissal as a thanksgiving for God's forgiveness. If the letters are used as an offering, ensure class members that no one will read them.

REFLECTING
(Time: 10 minutes)

Distribute the envelopes with the reflection booklets. (See Session 1 for details on how to begin this activity.) Ask the students to prepare another entry.

Suggest that the group recall the session's discussion on human sin and redemption.

Invite the class members to write personal reflections on "How It Feels to Be Forgiven." Ask: When, in your own life, have you felt the greatest need to be forgiven for thinking only about yourself? for making a choice that was wrong?

When the writing is completed, ask the students to add their entries to their booklets and place them inside the envelopes for safekeeping.

LEARNING SKILLS
(Time: 10–15 minutes)

Option 1. Class Memory Challenge

As the students return to the task of learning the structure and content of *The Book of Common Prayer*, focus on Pastoral Offices (pp. 413-507). Copy major headings from the student newspaper, *Community Times*, onto newsprint or a chalkboard, and ask the group to comment on what they expect to find under each of these. Then invite the students to scan the Pastoral Offices, concentrating on Confirmation, Marriage, Reconciliation of a Penitent, Ministration to the Sick, and Burial of the Dead.

Remove the displayed list and challenge the class members to reconstruct it from memory.

Option 2. Learning Scripture

Ask students to share any verses they have memorized since the previous session. Prepare branches with citations and add them to the Scripture Tree, as described in Session 1. Encourage students who have learned these and other verses to add leaves to the appropriate branches.

Before the next session, the students may memorize one or both of the following: *Luke 6:37* or *Romans 3:24*. See "Learning Scripture" in the student newspaper, *Community Times*.

ONGOING PROJECT
(Time: 5–10 minutes)

Ask the students to continue developing the catechism book, as described in Session 1. For this session, the class members may form two teams to prepare pages 11-12, labeled "The Church" and "The Ministry." Invite the group to read these two sections in the Catechism (BCP, pp. 854-856) and choose ways to illustrate the respective pages. Possibilities: Church building with people entering or leaving; a scene showing a bishop, a priest, a deacon, and a lay person.

Punch holes in the posterboard sheets and add them to the large book.

SYMBOL CARD and TREASUREBOOK

Card 32 shows a thistle, with a verse of Scripture, and an explanation on the back.

Comments about sin and redemption are offered in *Chalice Year Treasurebook*, Part IV, Section 5. What do Christians mean when they speak about sin and about being forgiven?

GOING FORTH

Gather the group for the dismissal. The teacher or a student will say:

I ask your prayers for peace; for goodwill among nations; and for the well-being of all people.
Pray for justice and peace.
Silence

I ask your prayers for the poor, the sick, the hungry, the oppressed, and those in prison.
Pray for those in any need or trouble.
Silence

[Learners may add their petitions.]
I ask your prayers for all who seek God, or a deeper knowledge of him.
Pray that they may find and be found by him.

From The Prayers of the People
The Book of Common Prayer, p. 386

Teacher: Let us go forth in the name of Christ.
Students: Thanks be to God.

TEACHER'S ASSESSMENT

As you reflect on the students' reactions to this session, which concepts seemed most meaningful to them? Can they distinguish between "sin" as a general condition of the human race and the particular sins of individuals? What did you learn about their attitudes toward freedom and the opportunity for personal choices?

LOOKING AHEAD

In the next session, the focus is on the several types of prayer outlined in the Catechism. Reflect on what it means to pray. What part does prayer play in your daily routines?

THE CATECHISM
SESSION 6
PRAYER AND WORSHIP

FOCUS

The Catechism defines Christian prayer and describes seven kinds of prayer. The students should be able to list these and compose one or more prayers.

GETTING READY

Prayer is defined in the Catechism as "responding to God, by thought and by deeds, with or without words" (BCP, p. 856). Opportunities to pray are as constant as the events of every single day. All that happens to us, all that we do, can be a form of communication with God.

Although the Catechism proceeds to list and define seven different kinds of prayer, it is possible to speak of all our praying as *praise* or *petition*.

• The term "praise" can include adoration and thanksgiving. We turn to God with hearts and minds uplifted—not seeking anything except to enjoy the presence of God, to express God's great worth, and to acknowledge our gratitude for every blessing.

• The word "petition" (asking for something) can include prayers of penitence, oblation (an offering of ourselves), and intercession. We ask forgiveness, we ask God to use our life and labor for good purposes, and we bring to God our own needs and the needs of others.

It is helpful to have the Catechism's careful distinctions among the principal kinds of prayer. But it is important to recognize that our turning to God in prayer is usually a general mixture of all these. We pour out our hearts to the Creator (through Jesus Christ and in the power of the Holy Spirit), with the assurance that God truly hears us.

In the New Testament, Jesus is our model and instructor with respect to prayer. Jesus teaches that prayer should be private, brief, earnest, and faith-filled. Prayer is to be offered with a spirit of forgiveness. Major prayers attributed to Jesus are the Lord's Prayer *(Luke 11:2-4)* and the High Priestly Prayer *(John 17)*.

We are called to pray both alone and alongside others in corporate worship.

> Almighty God, who hast promised to hear the petitions of those who ask in thy Son's Name: We beseech thee mercifully to incline thine ear to us who have now made our prayers and supplications unto thee; and grant that those things which we have faithfully asked according to thy will, may effectually be obtained, to the relief of our necessity, and to the setting forth of thy glory; through Jesus Christ our Lord. *Amen.*
>
> For the Answering of Prayer
> *The Book of Common Prayer,* p. 834

TEACHING TIP

Intermediate-age students like to do things with others and to develop close friendships. But as preadolescents, they also need times and places where they can retreat for privacy. This may be especially true in regard to prayer. Avoid pressing class members to offer personal prayers aloud unless they wish to do so.

GATHERING

Display Poster No. 21 titled "Prayer," by Thomas Hart Benton, found in the Teacher's Packet. As the students arrive, invite them to view the painting from a variety of angles. Ask: What do you think the painter had in mind? What event did he portray?

Encourage the group to look at the hands of the figures in the painting. What do they suggest?

When everyone is present, say:

Let us pray. (Use the prayer "For the Answering of Prayer," above, or a prayer of your own choosing.)

Unit IV. The Catechism—Session 6
Chalice Year Intermediate—Copyright © 2000 Virginia Theological Sminary and Morehouse Publishing

The chosen student lector reads from the class Bible (NRSV):

A Reading from the Epistle to the Romans, chapter 12, verses 12 through 18.

Rejoice in hope, be patient in suffering, persevere in prayer. Contribute to the needs of the saints; extend hospitality to strangers.

Bless those who persecute you; bless and do not curse them. Rejoice with those who rejoice, weep with those who weep. Live in harmony with one another; do not be haughty, but associate with the lowly; do not claim to be wiser than you are. Do not repay anyone evil for evil, but take thought for what is noble in the sight of all. If it is possible, so far as it depends on you, live peaceably with all.

Reader: The Word of the Lord.
Response: Thanks be to God.

INTRODUCING THE STORY
(Time: 10 minutes)

Begin by sharing a story about prayer from your own experience or from someone you know. For ideas, see the article on page 1 of the student newspaper, *Community Times* (Unit IV, Issue 6) about a young person's involvement in a closing service. She was asked to write a prayer and read it at the service.

Invite students to look at the definition of prayer in the Catechism under the heading "Prayer and Worship" on p. 856. Then guide the group in using a simple, three-part pattern to compose a prayer.

Address (such as "Almightly God," "O God Eternal," or Dear Lord");

What is declared or asked (a statement, request, or plea);

Closing (such as "through Jesus Christ our Lord," or "in Jesus' name.").

When the prayer is completed, look more carefully at the Catechism and the seven principal kinds of prayer: adoration, praise, thanksgiving, penitence, oblation, intercession, and petition (BCP, pp. 856-857). Be sure they understand the meaning of words such as oblation. Write each type on a chalkboard or piece of newsprint, with notes about each type of prayer.

Invite the students to work individually or in pairs to look up the Lord's Prayer (*Luke 11:2-4*) and Jesus' prayer (*John 17*). Which words and phrases of these prayers of Jesus express adoration? intercession and petition? Which of the prayers includes a note of penitence?

Ask the group to analyze the prayer they composed together. What principal kind of prayer was it? Why do they think so? (Note that the prayer may prove to be a mixture of several kinds.) Find out if students would like to add to or refine parts of their prayer.

When class members are satisfied with their work, ask a volunteer to write it on newsprint large enough for the class to read. Say it one time together; consider using it again at the dismissal.

EXPLORING
(Time: 15–20 minutes)

Option 1. Scavenger Hunt

Divide the class members into pairs and give each pair a Prayer Book. Announce that they are going on a Prayer Scavenger Hunt in *The Book of Common Prayer*. Briefly go through the list of prayer types on the chalkboard that you compiled in the Introducing the Story activity.

Challenge each pair to find at least one example of each prayer type in the Prayer Book. Give them paper and pencils to write down citations (name of prayer and page number). Remind them that many or even most prayers combine two or more types.

When everyone is finished, check the work as a group. Which prayers were easiest to find? Which were most difficult? Did they find a prayer that they particularly liked? Why?

Option 2. Framed Call to Prayer

Provide rectangles of posterboard or heavy paper (approximately 9 x 12 inches), strips of construction paper, pencils and markers. Suggest that each student make a framed, illuminated "call to prayer." Any one of the following Scripture quotations would be appropriate, or class members may compose their own texts:

"Hear my prayer, O Lord"
"Give ear to my prayer, O God."
"To you, O Lord, I lift up my soul."
"Pray without ceasing."

The words may be printed in block letters and decorated with various colors and decorative designs. Glue construction paper strips around the edges to form frames. The students may want to hang these in their homes.

Option 3. Matching Exercise

Turn in the student newspaper, *Community Times*, Unit IV, Issue 6, to the matching exercise titled "Forms of Prayer." Students may work alone, in pairs, or as a total group.

MUSIC
(Time: 10 minutes)

Listen on the *Children Sing!* tape to the prayer of praise titled "Morning has broken" *(The Hymnal 1982*, 8; *We Sing of God*, 6*)*. It has been said, "Those who sing, pray twice." With this in mind, invite the students to find examples of prayer among the hymns of *The Hymnal 1982*. Begin by scanning the first lines in the index at the back. Look especially for instances of praise, thanksgiving, and petition. Here are some examples:

"Now thank we all our God," 396 (thanksgiving)
"Praise to the Lord, the Almighty," 390 (praise)
"Take my life, and let it be," 707 (oblation)
"Help us, O Lord, to learn," 628 (petition)

CONNECTING/SPEAKING OUT
(Time: 15–20 minutes)

Option 1. Group Discussion

Refer again to the painting from Poster No. 21 in the Teacher's Packet displayed at the Gathering. Call the students' attention to the three figures in the scene whose hands are placed like the picture of "Praying Hands," by Albrecht Durer. Artist Thomas Hart Benton included the ship on the sea in the background, along with the hat on one of the men, to suggest the arrival and settlement of the American Pilgrims.

Invite the class members to imagine they are with the group in the painting. Ask: What would you be praying for? Why?

Option 2. Current Events

Ask class members to begin listing all the different times and places they have prayed or heard prayer outside of church. Write down their ideas on a piece of newsprint.

Suggest they begin thinking about prayer in their homes, for example at meals or before bed. Then go through a typical day. Do they pray in the morning before school? Although formal prayers cannot be said in public schools, students can call on God at any time. For example, before a difficult test, they can ask God to help them stay calm and remember facts they know. If they are shut out of a conversation or forced to eat lunch alone, they can ask God to help them get through that difficult moment. Prayers may also be a part of extracurricular activities, such as scouting.

Encourage students to make prayer a part of every day. Ask them to identify times and places they can find a moment to talk to God.

REFLECTING
(Time: 10 minutes)

Distribute the students' reflection envelopes and booklets and invite them to continue commenting on the topics of the Catechism. (See Session 1 for a description of this process of reflecting.)

To spark ideas for this session's entry, ask the students to think about their own praying. Ask: What do you think is the most important kind of praying you do? Why?

Students may wish to conclude their entry with a prayer.

When the writing is completed, ask the students to insert their entries and place the booklets in envelopes for safekeeping between sessions.

LEARNING SKILLS
(Time: 10–15 minutes)

Option 1. Class Memory Challenge

As the class members continue memorizing the structure and content of *The Book of Common Prayer*, ask them to find Episcopal Services. These are services at which a Bishop must always preside. What are the six headings? Urge the group to compare the three Ordination liturgies. What is distinctive about each one? (Note the differing words of The Examination in the three services.) What do all the ordinations have in common? (Note the presentations, the laying on of hands, and the use of the Litany for Ordinations, p. 548.)

Ask: When would a congregation use the service for Celebration of a New Ministry? Or the service for the Consecration of a Church or Chapel? Encourage the students to learn the names of the services listed under the heading, Episcopal Services.

Option 2. Learning Scripture

Suggest that the students memorize before the next session, *Psalm 32:6a* or *Romans 12:12*. See "Learning Scripture" in the student newspaper, *Community Times*.

Add branches to the Scripture Tree for the new Scripture citations. Students who have memorized previous verses can add leaves as appropriate.

ONGOING PROJECT
(Time: 5–10 minutes)

The catechism book project, described in Session 1, may continue. For this session, ask the students to form teams to label and illustrate pages 13-14 in the book: "Prayer and Worship," and "The Sacraments." The class members will need to read these two sections in the Catechism (BCP, pp. 856-859). Possible pictures, respectively: worshippers kneeling; shell and chalice (to represent Holy Baptism and Holy Eucharist).

Punch holes in the posterboard sheets to add them to the large book.

SYMBOL CARD and TREASUREBOOK

Card 33 shows praying hands with a verse of Scripture, and an explanation on the back.

Suggest that students read in *Chalice Year Treasurebook*, Part IV, Section 6 about the principal kinds of prayer. Ask them to think about what prayer means to them and how they could make it more meaningful.

GOING FORTH

Gather the group for the dismissal. The leader will say:
I ask your prayers for peace; for goodwill among nations; and for the well-being of all people.
Pray for justice and peace.
Silence

I ask your prayers for the poor, the sick, the hungry, the oppressed, and those in prison.
Pray for those in any need or trouble.
Silence
[Learners may add their petitions.]

I ask your prayers for all who seek God, or a deeper knowledge of him.
Pray that they may find and be found by him.
From The Prayers of the People
The Book of Common Prayer, p. 386

Teacher: Let us go forth in the name of Christ.
Students: Thanks be to God.

TEACHER'S ASSESSMENT

Based on what you have observed in this session, how do your students approach prayer? Are they reverent in settings where people pray? In what ways can prayer become more consciously a part of their daily lives?

LOOKING AHEAD

The next session considers the orders of ministry in the Church. As members of the laity, all Christians are called to be witnesses for Christ in all that we do each day. Reflect on situations in which you have the opportunity to minister to others.

THE CATECHISM
SESSION 7
MINISTRY

FOCUS

Four orders of Christian ministry are defined in the Catechism: lay persons, bishops, priests, and deacons. Each of these is vital to the building up of the Church—and all share the same duty to follow Christ in their worship, work, and stewardship. The students should be able to identify and describe the four orders of ministry, and to state how they serve the Lord in their own lives.

GETTING READY

In the original meaning of the word, a "minister" is a person who serves as an agent or representative for another. We use the term similarly in the Church. In the Catechism section on Ministry (BCP, pp. 855-856), each of the named groups of ministers is said "to represent Christ and his Church." Lay persons, bishops, priests, and deacons all have their special forms of service within the Body of Christ.

The four roles of Christian ministry are called "orders." Bishops, priests, and deacons are members of Holy (Sacred) Orders. But all forms of Christian service, both ordained (clergy) or non-ordained (lay), are honored in the Church. Indeed, every baptized person promises to take on specific tasks of Christian ministry.

The New Testament offers no fixed definitions of the roles of bishops priests, and deacons. The tradition of priesthood in the Church was derived from our Hebrew roots. Offices of bishop (overseer) and deacon (servant) had their parallels in the Greek culture.

Recognition of the laity as an order of ministry is affirmed in the Prayer Book. All believers are regarded as a "holy priesthood" by the New Testament writer in *I Peter 10:4-10*. The same idea is implied in the apostle Paul's letters to churches.

The leaders of the Protestant Reformation endorsed the "priesthood of all believers"—the concept that all Christians function as one body, God's priest to the world. Such a vision of our role was said to fulfill God's call to the people of Israel to be "a kingdom of priests and a holy nation" *(Exodus 19:6)*.

God our Father, you see your children growing up in an unsteady and confusing world: Show them that your ways give more life than the ways of the world, and that following you is better than chasing after selfish goals. Help them to take failure, not as a measure of their worth, but as a chance for a new start. Give them strength to hold their faith in you, and to keep alive their joy in your creation; through Jesus Christ our Lord. *Amen*.

For Young Persons
The Book of Common Prayer, p. 829

TEACHING TIP

Intermediate-age students, who have many talents and abilities, are capable of responsible roles in the congregation. It is important that they see their service to the Church and the larger community as ministry or service offered in the name of Jesus Christ. Help young people recognize their contributions in the church and in activities at school, clubs, teams, and organizations. Also recognize tasks they have performed as individuals.

GATHERING

Display Posters No. 22 and 23 from the Teacher's Packet that picture individuals in the roles of lay persons, bishops, priests, and deacons. As the students arrive, invite them to study the pictures closely. Ask: What is significant about the ways various individuals are dressed? What actions are symbolized in the pictures? On paper placed near the posters, ask students to write captions for each of the groupings. Encourage them to draw on their own experiences or those of people they know in describing each situation.

When everyone is present, say:

Let us pray. (Use the prayer "For Young Persons," above, or a prayer of your own choosing.)

The chosen student lector reads from the class Bible (NRSV):

A Reading from the Epistle to the Ephesians, chapter 4, verses 11 through 13.

The gifts he gave were that some would be apostles, some prophets, some evangelists, some pastors and teachers, to equip the saints for the work of ministry, for building up the body of Christ, until all of us come to the unity of the faith and of the knowledge of the Son of God, to maturity, to the measure of the full stature of Christ.

Reader: The Word of the Lord.
Response: Thanks be to God.

INTRODUCING THE STORY
(Time: 10 minutes)

Begin by asking the students to turn in their Bibles to *Ephesians* 4:4-7, 11-13. How does the writer describe people in the Church? What are the names given to the different leaders? What is the purpose of their work?

Next look at the captions written next to Posters No. 23 and 24 during the Gathering exercise. Did the students use any of the words found in *Ephesians*? How were the actions described?

Drawing on information provided in the Getting Ready, in the Catechism (BCP, pp. 855-856), and in the student newspaper, *Community Times* (Unit IV, Issue 7), make a brief presentation on the four kinds of ministers in the Church: lay persons, bishops, priests, and deacons.

Divide the group into four teams, and share the following assignments:

Team 1. Read The Examination in the service for the ordination of a Bishop, p. 517, and the article on page 1 of *Community Times*. What is a bishop asked to do in the Church?

Team 2. Read The Examination in the service for the ordination of a Priest, p. 531. What are the tasks a priest is called to undertake?

Team 3. Read The Examination in the service for the ordination of a Deacon, p. 543. What are the duties of a deacon in the Church?

Team 4. Think about the work of lay people in the church and the larger community. For ideas, read the promises made at Confirmation or the article about the ministry of lay persons on page 2 of *Community Times*. Why is our role a ministry? (You may also want to share a copy of *The Book of Occasional Services*, with its "Commissioning for Lay Ministers in the Church," p. 175.)

Call for a brief report from each of the groups. Then ask the class members to turn to the Catechism (BCP, p. 855) and read the answer to the question, "What is the ministry of the laity?" Ask: In what way(s) are the ministries of lay persons similar to those of bishops, priests, and deacons? How are the ministries different?

EXPLORING
(Time: 15–20 minutes)

Option 1 Ministers We Know

Ahead of time, gather a variety of materials to create a display depicting the four kinds of ministry that are named in the Catechism (BCP, p. 855). It may take the form of a bulletin board, posters, or a set of simple dioramas. Look for pictures, shields, and other information. You may want to take photographs of such items as a bishop's chair (seat), vestments, and a chalice.

Encourage the students to work together as they prepare the exhibit. Urge them to include persons they actually know—beginning with themselves and adding (by name) bishops, priests, deacons, and other active lay persons. Decide on captions to add to the segments of the display (possibly phrases from the Catechism).

Option 2. Vestments for Ministers

Use clothespins or pipe cleaners to fashion a simple figure each student can clothe with appropriate vestments. They can choose to do one or more of the four orders of ministry: lay persons, bishops, priests, and deacons. Use small scraps of fabric, ribbon, or bits of soft paper (tissue, foil), along with markers and glue, to fashion the vestments. When the figure(s) are completed, tape them to sturdy sheets of background paper, and label each one.

The pictures on Posters No. 22 and 23 in the Teacher's Packet posters provide helpful hints for designing the vestments.

Option 3. Message

Turn in the student newspaper, *Community Times*, Unit IV, Issue 7, to the hidden message titled "Gifts for Ministry." Students may work alone, in pairs, or as a total group.

MUSIC
(Time: 10 minutes)

Listen to "Lord you give the great commission" *(The Hymnal 1982,* 528*)* on the *Children Sing!* tape. Then read each stanza in unison. Ask: What kinds of ministry are described? As we sing this prayer, what are we asking the Lord to do?

CONNECTING/SPEAKING OUT
(Time: 15–20 minutes)

Option 1. Group Discussion

Ask the students to assume that they are attending a Holy Eucharist, Rite II, where persons from all four orders of ministry (laity, a bishop, a priest, and a deacon) are present.

Invite the group to use *The Book of Common Prayer* to find the answers to the questions below. They may consult page 354, "Concerning the Celebration," and also the rubrics (the italicized directions within the service, pp. 355-366).

Who is the principal celebrant? (Bishop or a priest named by the bishop.) Who reads the Gospel lesson? (Deacon.) Who may read the other lessons? (Lay persons.) Who leads the Confession of Sin? (Deacon.) Who says the words of absolution, beginning "Almighty God have mercy on you, . . ."? (Bishop.) Who leads the Prayers of the People? (Lay person.)
Who prepares the Holy Table? (Deacon.) Who brings the offerings to the altar? (Lay persons.) Who blesses the people at the end of the service? (Bishop.) Who preaches the gospel? (Bishop or another clergy person.) Who serves the bread at Holy Communion? (Bishop and other clergy.) Who may serve the people the chalice (wine)? (Clergy and licensed lay persons.)

Talk about the ways that people in each of the orders contribute to the service. Ask: Which order does an acolyte belong in? Why?

Option 2. Current Events

Focus specifically on the ministry of the laity in your own congregation. If possible, provide current copies of church bulletin announcements and newsletters. Consider in turn each of the various activities carried out by the church's members—such as visiting persons who are ill or unable to attend corporate worship, food and clothing programs for the needy, and other special ministries. Ask: Which of these tasks can also involve members of the class? Challenge the group to think of specific types of service they could undertake.

REFLECTING
(Time: 10 minutes)

Continue with the method of reflecting suggested in Session 1. Hand out the envelopes with booklets to class members and invite them to add another entry.

For this session, suggest that the students write about "My Ministry." Ask: When does a person begin ministry in the Church? When did you begin some kind of Christian ministry? What kinds of service could you offer to the Church, to your family, to friends, and to others in the community?

When their work is completed, ask the students to add their entries to the booklets, place them in the envelopes, and store them in a safe place.

LEARNING SKILLS
(Time: 10–15 minutes)

Option 1. Class Memory Challenge

Continue working on the structure and content of *The Book of Common Prayer.* Begin by recalling the general headings: The Daily Office; The Great Litany; The Collects; Proper Liturgies for Special Days; Holy Baptism; The Holy Eucharist; Pastoral Offices; Episcopal Services. Ask the students to call out what they remember about each of these sections.

At this session, look together at the Psalter, Prayers and Thanksgivings, and An Outline of the Faith, or Catechism (pp. 585-862).

The Psalms and the Prayers and Thanksgivings are especially valuable for individual worship. Point out, for example, the prayer For a Birthday (p. 830), and Grace at Meals (p. 835). Encourage students to locate other prayers they value.

Option 2. Learning Scripture

Ask students to add paper branches and leaves to the Scripture Tree for verses they have learned since the last session, as described in Session 1.

Assign, for the next session, *Romans 12:6* or *Ephesians 4:12.* See "Learning Scripture" in the student newspaper, *Community Times.*

ONGOING PROJECT
(Time: 5–10 minutes)

Prepare pages 15-16 in the large picture book about the Catechism, as described in Session 1. For this session, ask the class members to label and illustrate the two pages: "Holy Baptism" and "The Holy Eucharist." Read over these sections in the Catechism (BCP, pp. 858-860). Possible images: font and shell, for Baptism; chalice and paten, for bread and wine of Holy Communion.

Punch holes in the posterboard sheets to add them to the large book.

SYMBOL CARD and TREASUREBOOK

Card 34 shows the shield of Simon the Zealot, with a verse of Scripture, and an explanation on the back.

Ask the students to read *Chalice Year Treasurebook*, Part IV, Section 7, about the four orders of Christian ministry. Who are Christ's ministers in today's Church? What are they called to do?

GOING FORTH

Gather the group for the dismissal. The teacher or a student will say:
  I ask your prayers for peace; for goodwill among nations; and for the well-being of all people.
  Pray for justice and peace.
  Silence
  I ask your prayers for the poor, the sick, the hungry, the oppressed, and those in prison.
  Pray for those in any need or trouble.
  Silence
  [Learners may add their petitions.]

  I ask your prayers for all who seek God, or a deeper knowledge of him.
  Pray that they may find and be found by him.
      From The Prayers of the People
      The Book of Common Prayer, p. 386

  Teacher: Let us go forth in the name of Christ.
  Students: Thanks be to God.

TEACHER'S ASSESSMENT

Which aspects of this session seemed meaningful to the students? What evidence did you gather that the students are beginning to think of themselves as ministers in the Church? What more could be done to encourage them to be fully involved?

LOOKING AHEAD

The next session is on the final section of the Catechism, "Christian Hope." Where do you find your own source of hope? In what ways is Christian hope different from all other forms of viewing the future?

THE CATECHISM
SESSION 8
CHRISTIAN HOPE

FOCUS

Christians live in the sure and certain hope of everlasting life, believing that nothing can separate us from the love of God in Christ Jesus—not even death. The final section of the Catechism outlines the Christian understanding of final judgment, heaven and hell, resurrection, the communion of the saints, and everlasting life. The students should be able to describe Christian hope in their own words.

GETTING READY

In his ministry, Jesus Christ proclaimed that the kingdom or reign of God is at hand. In our own time, God continues to redeem and empower humankind with the gifts of faith and love. Jesus also pointed to a future day when the will of God would prevail in all our relationships. The richest promises of the Hebrew prophets were to be fulfilled, and the nations of the world would dwell in peace.

The reign of God is both now and not yet. In Christ we have hope that is a contemporary reality and at the same time an expectation for the future. It has been the faith of the Church all along that Jesus Christ will come again, and we shall know the eternal completion of God's kingdom.

In the Catechism of *The Book of Common Prayer*, Christian hope is defined as (p. 861): "to live with confidence in newness and fullness of life, and to await the coming of Christ in glory, and the completion of God's purpose for the world."

In answer to the last question, the Catechism speaks of our assurance as Christians (p. 862): "that nothing, not even death, shall separate us from the love of God which is in Christ Jesus our Lord."

Between these two affirmations (of hope and assurance), the Catechism includes questions about key words of our Creeds: heaven, hell, resurrection of the body, communion of saints, and everlasting life.

The challenge for teachers of intermediate-age students is to stop short of giving flat definitions of what our future will be like when our earthly lives have ended. The Catechism's answers help us explore the mystery of faith while providing hope and assurance.

O merciful Father, who has taught us in your holy Word that you do not willingly afflict or grieve your children: Look with pity upon the sorrows of these servants for whom our prayers are offered. Remember them, O Lord, in mercy, nourish their souls with patience, comfort them with a sense of your goodness, lift up your countenance upon them, and give them peace; through Jesus Christ our Lord. *Amen.*
For a Person in Trouble or Bereavement (adapted)
The Book of Common Prayer, p. 831

TEACHING TIP

It may be inevitable that intermediate students who are involved in discussions about last things and judgment will speculate about who goes to heaven and who goes to hell—even to the point of naming individuals. Some may be thinking anxiously about people they know who have died. Assure them that final judgment belongs to God, not us. We live with confidence in the goodness and mercy of God.

GATHERING

Arrange a graffiti board for the classroom on the topic of "hope." Use a chalkboard, newsprint easel, or other surface. Provide large markers for adding words and drawings.

Ahead of time, spatter the board with quotations like the following: Hope springs eternal. Hope against hope. I live on hope. Hope is always present. Where there is life, there is hope.

As the students arrive, invite them to read and comment on the graffiti, adding additional words and decorative touches to symbolize the concept of hoping (such as flowers, butterflies, and simple splashes of bright colors).

When everyone is present, say:

Let us pray. (Use the prayer "For a Person in Trouble or Bereavement, above, or a prayer of your own choosing.)

The chosen student lector reads from the class Bible (NRSV):

A Reading from the Epistle to the Romans, chapter 8, verses 31 through 39.

What then are we to say about these things? If God is for us, who is against us? He who did not withhold his own Son, but gave him up for all of us, will he not with him also give us everything else? Who will bring any charge against God's elect? It is God who justifies. Who is to condemn? It is Christ Jesus, who died, yes, who was raised, who is at the right hand of God, who indeed intercedes for us. Who will separate us from the love of Christ? Will hardship, or distress, or persecution, or famine, or nakedness, or peril, or sword? As it is written,

"For your sake we are being killed all day long;
we are accounted as sheep to be slaughtered."

No, in all these things we are more than conquerors through him who loved us. For I am convinced that neither death, nor life, nor angels, nor rulers, nor things present, nor things to come, nor powers, nor height, nor depth, nor anything else in all creation, will be able to separate us from the love of God in Christ Jesus our Lord.

Reader: The Word of the Lord.
Response: Thanks be to God.

INTRODUCING THE STORY
(Time: 10 minutes)

Make twin, vertical placards for the words "hope" and "assurance," and place them where all can see. Ask the students to turn to the Catechism section, "Christian Hope" (BCP, pp. 861-862), and pay particular attention to the first and the last questions.

Ask students to turn in their Bibles to *Romans 8:38-39* and reread the words of the apostle Paul. Ask class members to compare the phrases he used with the final question and answer in the Catechism section on Hope.

Note that the first and last questions in this section (on hope and assurance) are "bookends" for the section. Between the bookends are seven questions and answers about words and phrases Christians use in Creeds and in our discussions about what happens after we die: *heaven, hell, death, judgment, resurrection of the body, communion of saints,* and *everlasting life.*

Invite the students to locate the following words that appear in this section: *new, life, live, living, love, loving,* and *joy.* Point out that the ultimate intention of God is that we should enjoy a new, everlasting, and joyful existence in the kingdom of heaven. That is what Jesus Christ came to proclaim and promise. His own death and resurrection opened the door for us to hope, even in the face of the greatest sorrows, disappointments, injuries, and death.

Look again at the symbols and words class members added to the graffiti board during the Gathering activity on the topic of hope. Give students time to explain some of their entries. You may also wish to share information from the student newspaper, *Community Times* (Unit IV, Issue 8), especially the story on page about hope in the face of evil.

Conclude by reminding the students that the purpose of the Catechism is to provide an "outline" for learning about our beliefs as Christians. It is a brief summary of the Church's teaching—a "point to start from" in exploring our faith. The Catechism does not end our questioning. On the contrary, it encourages us to keep on thinking, studying, and listening throughout our lifetimes.

EXPLORING
(Time: 15–20 minutes)

Option 1. Reaching Out With Hope

Discuss with the students the importance of hope, especially during difficult times. Ask them to think of ways they could spread hope to others, such as smiling at someone who seems angry or distracted, offering to carry something for someone who is overburdened, or writing a note to someone who can no longer get around.

Using the words and phrases from the graffiti board and from the Catechism question about Christian Hope (BCP, pp. 861-862), design greeting cards for shut-ins.

The cards could be taken to a nursing home to be placed on food trays or sent to people in the parish who are unable to leave their homes.

Ask students to fold a piece of construction paper in half. After creating a design for the cover, ask students to write a personal message inside, such as "Thinking of You." Collect the cards and put them in a basket or small container. Present them at the dismissal as a thanksgiving for Christ's message of hope.

Option 2. Bookshelf of Hope

Encourage each student to design a sheet titled "Bookshelf of Hope." Provide drawing paper, strips of construction paper in various colors, black markers for labeling, scissors, and glue or paste.

First, draw a shelf and make a pair of bookends labeled "Christian Hope" and "Christian Assurance." Trim seven other strips to symbolize books for the shelf, and label them: Christ in Glory; Heaven and Hell; The Dead in God's Presence; Last Judgment; Resurrection of the Body; Communion of Saints; Everlasting Life. Students may want to add other "volumes" with words or phrases of their own or from the Gathering activity.

Glue the bookends and books in place. As the students work, continue discussing what the Catechism says about each topic the "books" represent.

Option 3. Word Puzzle

Turn in the student newspaper, *Community Times*, Unit IV, Issue 8, to the word puzzle titled "Christian Hope." Students may work alone, in pairs, or as a total group.

MUSIC
(Time: 10 minutes)

Sing the hymn, "Amazing grace! how sweet the sound" *(The Hymnal 1982, 671)* with the *Children Sing!* tape. Ask: What is the hope that is offered in this hymn's words?

CONNECTING/SPEAKING OUT
(Time: 15–20 minutes)

Option 1. Group Discussion

The apostle Paul wrote about hardships he had endured. Read aloud *II Corinthians 11:24-28*. Ask: If these things had happened to you, would you still be hopeful? Why, or why not? Point out that Paul must have had these experiences in mind when he wrote *Romans 8:35-39*.

Read again the answer to the question, "What is Christian hope?" (Catechism, BCP, p. 861). Appoint a class member to look up the word "confidence" in a dictionary and share the definition. Focus on the synonym "trust." The same trust that gave support and comfort to the apostle Paul in his times of trial are open to us all. The living Christ is always with us.

Option 2. Current Events

Ask the students to name some of the persons and groups in the world who may feel that they have no hope—such as the homeless, the destitute, the victims of violence, and the sick and depressed. Where do they turn for help and comfort? Ask also: Have there been times when you felt hopeless? What did you do?

Engage the class members in a discussion about why human suffering continues in the world. Refer to the article about hope in the student newspaper, *Community Times*. Turn again to the final answer in the Catechism of the Prayer Book (p. 862). How does this answer affect people today?

REFLECTING
(Time: 10 minutes)

Continue with the method of reflecting described in Session 1. Start by asking class members to open their envelopes and prepare to add another entry to their booklets.

Encourage the students to write on the topic, "Christian Hope." Ask: How do you use the word "hope"? Do you sometimes say, "I hope I pass this test" or "I hope we win this game"? What is the difference between this kind of hope and Christian hope? Where can you look for a deeper kind of hope that will help you face difficult times?

When the writing is completed, instruct the students to add their latest entries to their booklets, and then place them in the envelopes for safekeeping. (If this is the last session of the Unit, students may take their booklets home.)

LEARNING SKILLS
(Time: 10–15 minutes)

Option 1. Class Memory Challenge

In the continuing task of learning the structure and content of *The Book of Common Prayer*, ask the students to turn to the final pages, 863-1001. Here are found Historical Documents of the Church. Note that these Documents contain "Articles of Religion" (sometimes called the Thirty-Nine Articles), adopted in 1801. They form the basis for much discussion on Episcopal thought and practice through the generations.

Next comes Tables for Finding the Date of Easter and other Holy Days, together with the Lectionary (Sundays, Holy Days, Saints, and Various Occasions) and Daily Office Lectionary.

Encourage the class members to find the dates for Easter for the next two years. Ask: Once we know these dates, how can we calculate the dates for Ash Wednesday and Pentecost in the same years? (Count backward 40 days exclusive of Sundays for Ash Wednesday; count forward fifty days for Pentecost.)

Note that this session's work concludes the walk through the Prayer Book. Make plans for a review as suggested in Session 9.

Option 2. Learning Scripture

Add branches and leaves to the Scripture Tree for verses students have memorized, as described in Session 1.

Invite the students to learn, before the next session, *Romans 8:38-39* or *I Corinthians 13:13*. See "Learning Scripture" in the student newspaper, *Community Times*.

ONGOING PROJECT
(Time: 5–10 minutes)

Work on the final two pages of the large picture book developed during the Unit. For this session, prepare pages 17-18 and label them, respectively, "Other Sacramental Rites" and "The Christian Hope." Choose images to add after reading these sections of the Catechism (BCP, pp. 860-862). Suggested possibilities for the other sacramental rites: person being confirmed; a person being ordained; a couple being married; a person kneeling in confession; a sick person being anointed with oil. For Christian hope, the group may want to use a rainbow or an Easter symbol such as a butterfly.

Punch holes in the sheets to add them to the large book.

SYMBOL CARD and TREASUREBOOK

Card 35 shows an anchor, with a verse of Scripture, and an explanation on the back.

Suggest that the students read Part IV, Section 8, about the character of Christian hope. What makes a Christian person's hope different from hope in general?

GOING FORTH

Gather the group for the dismissal. The teacher or a student will say:

I ask your prayers for peace; for goodwill among nations; and for the well-being of all people.
Pray for justice and peace.
Silence

I ask your prayers for the poor, the sick, the hungry, the oppressed, and those in prison.
Pray for those in any need or trouble.
Silence

[Learners may add their petitions.]

I ask your prayers for all who seek God, or a deeper knowledge of him.
Pray that they may find and be found by him.
From The Prayers of the People
The Book of Common Prayer, p. 386

Teacher: Let us go forth in the name of Christ.
Students: Thanks be to God.

TEACHER'S ASSESSMENT

As you reflect on the students' work and discussion, what are the indications that they find hope in their faith in Jesus Christ? How well do they translate the concept of Christian hope into their own words?

LOOKING AHEAD

Session 9 on Pentecost can be used on the date most appropriate for your church's calendar. It has been designed independently of Sessions 1-8 and may be used at any time without disrupting the thematic flow of this Unit on the Church's Catechism. Find a way to relate activities to your congregation's plans for celebrating the Feast of Pentecost.

THE CATECHISM
SESSION 9
CELEBRATING PENTECOST

FOCUS

At the heart of the story of Pentecost is Peter's sermon, in which he says that the prophet Joel's words have been fulfilled in the pouring out of the Spirit upon the apostles. As the Church celebrates this great feast, we recall the Catechism's teaching about the Holy Spirit. The students should be able to retell the story of Pentecost and answer the question, "How do we recognize the presence of the Holy Spirit in our lives?"

GETTING READY

Pentecost (meaning "fiftieth day") is the Greek name for the Jewish Feast of Weeks, a celebration of thanksgiving that began seven weeks after the beginning of the barley harvest around the time of Passover. The Passover observance included a "waving of the barley sheaf," as described in *Leviticus 23:9-14*.

In later Judaism, the festival was observed as the anniversary of the giving of the Law to Moses on Mt. Sinai. Since the gift of the Holy Spirit to the Church occurred at Pentecost, the meaning of the feast was reinterpreted by Christians to reflect the beginning of the Church's life and mission.

The writer of *Acts* reports that there was a sudden sound "like the rush of mighty wind" from heaven, followed by "tongues of fire" distributed and resting on each one of the apostles. As a result, they began to speak in language that was miraculously understood by Jews and new converts to the Jewish faith, from many nations.

Following the outpouring of the Spirit, Peter proclaimed with power that Jesus had been raised from the dead. He declared that the last days had arrived, and he called for his hearers to repent and turn to the Lord. As a result of his Pentecost sermon, 3,000 people were baptized and added to the group of believers. (See *Acts 2*.) The events of Pentecost were a fulfillment not only of the prophecy of *Joel 2:8-32* but also of the promise of Jesus himself.

O God, who on this day taught the hearts of your faithful people by sending to them the light of your Holy Spirit: Grant us by the same Spirit to have a right judgement in all things, and evermore to rejoice in his holy comfort; through Jesus Christ your Son our Lord, who lives and reigns with you, in the unity of the Holy Spirit, one God, for ever and ever. *Amen*.
The Day of Pentecost: Whitsunday
The Book of Common Prayer, p. 227

TEACHING TIP

In many churches, people are invited to wear something red on the Day of Pentecost. This color symbolizes the faithful and courageous witness of apostles and martyrs. Encourage students to observe this custom as a part of their class observance of the festival.

GATHERING

Display the Pentecost picture on Poster No. 24 from the Teacher's Packet. As the students arrive, ask them to study the scene and describe what might be happening. Give them a hint that this event occurred after Jesus had ascended to heaven. (Be sure to cover the words at the bottom of the poster.) Ask: Who do you think is standing on the balcony? What could he be saying?

When everyone is present, say:

Let us pray. (Use the Collect "The Day of Pentecost: Whitsunday," above, or a prayer of your own choosing.)

The chosen student lector reads from the class Bible (NRSV):

A Reading from the Book of Acts, chapter 2, verses 14 through 17.

But Peter, standing with the eleven, raised his voice and addressed them, "Men of Judea and all who live in Jerusalem, let this be known to you, and listen to what I say. Indeed, these are not drunk, as you suppose, for it is only nine o'clock in the morning. No, this is what was spoken through the prophet Joel:
'In the last days it will be, God declares,
 that I will pour out my Spirit upon all flesh,
  and your sons and your daughters shall prophesy,
  and your young men shall see visions,
  and your old men shall dream dreams.'"

Reader: The Word of the Lord.
Response: Thanks be to God.

INTRODUCING THE STORY
(Time: 10 minutes)

Begin by asking the students if they could figure out why Peter was reassuring people that the disciples were not drunk in the Scripture passage. Ask the student to find the story of the Pentecost in *Acts 2*. Where does Peter's sermon begin? Where does he use the word of Joel, the prophet? What happened after he finished?

Using the article from the student newspaper, *Community Times* (Unit IV, Issue 9), as a guide, review the main events of the first Pentecost. Help students to describe the events in their own words. How many days had passed since the resurrection? Where were the believers gathered? Who was there in addition to the Twelve? (Note that Judas Iscariot had been replaced by Matthias.) What happened? How did people react?

Peter's sermon explained the significance of the Pentecost. He linked what had happened with the prophecy in *Joel 2:8-32*. Thousands responded by seeking baptism.

Recall what was said about the Holy Spirit, the third person of the Trinity, in Session 2 of this Unit. Ask the students to turn to the Catechism section, "The Holy Spirit" (BCP, p. 852-853). Ask them to look at the answer to the question, "How do we recognize the presence of the Holy Spirit in our lives?"

Ask: How would the new Christians at Pentecost have felt about that answer? What does the phrase "love and harmony" mean to you? How does a person live in love and harmony with God? with ourselves? our neighbors? all creation?

EXPLORING
(Time: 15–20 minutes)

Option 1. Pentecost Acrostic

Ask the class members to compose an acrostic with clues for Pentecost.

First, write the letters for Pentecost vertically on a large sheet of paper or chalkboard. Students may divide into teams to identify related words that can be placed horizontally across the letters. For example:

```
P
E
N
PeTer
E
C
HOly Spirit
S
bapTized
```

When the words have been selected, involve the whole group in developing clues for each one. Share the completed acrostic with other classes at your church.

Option 2. Spirit Spirals

Provide a large, sturdy sheet of paper for each class member, along with a black fine-tipped marker, and scissors. Ask the students to start in the middle of their paper sheets and use the marker to draw a continuous, ever-enlarging concentric circular line until they reach the edge of the paper. Then, starting in the center, write in the narrow spaces words and phrases from the Catechism, the prayers, and other sources that relate to Pentecost and the Holy Spirit. Some may wish to draw different pictures of the two symbols for Pentecost, tongues of fire and a descending dove. (See p. 3 of the student newspaper, *Community Times*, for descriptions of the symbols.)

Cut along the circular line to produce a spiral. Attach a paper fastener and long string to the innermost part. Pull gently to unwind the spiral so that it can be hung for all to see. (The larger the piece of paper used, the larger and longer the resulting spiral can be. Students may wish to write words on the other side of the spiral once it is cut.)

Option 3. Word Puzzle

Turn in the student newspaper, *Community Times*, Unit IV, Issue 9, to the word puzzle titled "Come, Holy Spirit." Students may work alone, in pairs, or as a total group.

MUSIC
(Time: 10 minutes)

Introduce and sing "Gracious Spirit, Holy Ghost" *(The Hymnal 1982,* 612; *We Sing of God,* 96*)*, or listen to it on the *Children Sing!* tape. Ask: Which words and phrases in this hymn remind us of the Pentecost story? of the Catechism section, "The Holy Spirit"?

CONNECTING/SPEAKING OUT
(Time: 15–20 minutes)

Option 1. Group Discussion

Review with the students the story of the apostle Peter. Recall the following events: Jesus called Simon Peter, a fisherman, to be one of his disciples *(Mark 1:16-18)*. After Peter proclaims Jesus to be "the Messiah, the Son of the living God," Jesus tells Peter that he is the rock on which Jesus shall build the Church *(Matthew 16:13-20)*. Following Jesus' arrest, Peter denied knowing him *(Mark 15:66-72)*. Following Jesus' resurrection, Peter pulled in a great catch of fish from the Sea of Galilee and rushed to meet the risen Lord *(John 21)*. At Pentecost, Peter preached a sermon of great power *(Acts 2)*.

Ask: How would you describe Peter? Why do you think he was chosen? What gave him the power to preach as he did? How do you think he lived after the events of Pentecost? How could you be like Peter?

Option 2. Current Events

Discuss your own church's celebration of Pentecost. What will make this Sunday different from others? (Call attention to the color red, the music, and other liturgical customs.) Ask: What are some of the activities and events in your congregation that suggest "love and harmony" among people and with God? How do these remind us of the Holy Spirit's presence in our lives? How can Christians take the ideas of love and harmony outside the church? Is it difficult to live in harmony when people treat you badly? How should you respond to these people?

REFLECTING
(Time: 10 minutes)

Continue with the procedure for reflecting suggested in Session 1. Distribute the envelopes with booklets to the students, and invite them to add an entry related to the Feast of Pentecost.

Ask: If Peter came to our church, what would he find? Do church members live in love and harmony by treating each other with respect? Do most people try to "grow in the likeness of Christ"? If Peter were preaching at worship services today, what would he talk about? Why?

When the writing is completed, ask the students to place their entries in their booklets. (If this is the final session of the Unit, remind the students to take their booklets home.)

LEARNING SKILLS
(Time: 10–15 minutes)

Option 1. Class Memory Challenge

To review the students' work in memorizing where to find the various sections of *The Book of Common Prayer,* divide the class into two groups. Appoint chairpersons, and invite each group to formulate a series of questions to ask of the opposite group. (If the class is large, two pairs of teams could be formed for this task.)

Encourage the groups to prepare practical questions, such as: Where do we look for the Baptism service? Where does Morning Prayer, Rite I, begin? Where would we find prayers for Grace at Meals?

When questions are finished, combine the groups and allow members to quiz one another. If time permits, the group may want to reconstruct from memory a general Table of Contents on a chalkboard or easel.

Option 2. Learning Scripture

The suggested verses to be learned following this session are *Acts 2:17a.* See "Learning Scripture" in the student newspaper, *Community Times.*

Continue with the Scripture tree, as described in Session 1, to track the students' accomplished memory tasks.

ONGOING PROJECT
(Time: 5–10 minutes)

Finish up the large picture book about the Catechism developed during this Unit. Suggest that the students go through the finished posterboard sheets and enter, in small letters at the bottom of each one, the matching page numbers in the Catechism of the Prayer Book. For example, on page 1, "Human Nature," write: *The Book of Common Prayer,* p. 845.

Lace the 18 pages and the covers with yarn or ribbon, so that they can be turned easily. As a group, decide on a way to share the book with others in the congregation—possibly as a display in a parish hall or as a traveling exhibit to be passed around in other church school classes. Choose class members to stay with the book and explain how it was developed from the Catechism.

SYMBOL CARD and TREASUREBOOK

Card 36 shows a Bethlehem cross with flames, a verse of Scripture, and an explanation on the back.

Ask the students to read the summary found in Part IV, Section 9, of *Chalice Year Treasurebook* that includes a statement about the Holy Spirit's leading of the Church. Suggest that they look through the entire book for references to the Holy Spirit. How does the Catechism help us to say what we believe?

GOING FORTH

Gather the group for the dismissal. The leader will say:
I ask your prayers for peace; for goodwill among nations; and for the well-being of all people.
Pray for justice and peace.
Silence

I ask your prayers for the poor, the sick, the hungry, the oppressed, and those in prison.
Pray for those in any need or trouble.
Silence

[Learners may add their petitions.]
I ask your prayers for all who seek God, or a deeper knowledge of him.
Pray that they may find and be found by him.

From The Prayers of the People
The Book of Common Prayer, p. 386

Teacher: Let us go forth in the name of Christ.
Students: Thanks be to God.

TEACHER'S ASSESSMENT

How well were the students able to recall the sequence of events in the story of Pentecost? What language did they use in describing the Holy Spirit? What are the indications that the class members consider the Holy Spirit to be active in their lives and in the world?

ECC
EPISCOPAL CHILDREN'S CURRICULUM

FOUNDATION PAPER

The following statement represents the theological foundation for Episcopal Children's Curriculum, a project of Virginia Theological Seminary, through its Center for the Ministry of Teaching, in collaboration with Morehouse Publishing. Adopted January, 1990.

The aim of Christian education in Episcopal Church parishes and congregations is to assist every member in living out the covenant made in Holy Baptism (BCP, p. 304). Hence, the common ministry of teachers and learners focuses on matters of both faith and practice:

Faith in God who made heaven and earth, in Jesus Christ the Son of God, and in the Holy Spirit who is Lord and giver of life.

Practice of worship and prayer, of repentance and obedience, of loving service to all persons, and of active pursuit of God's justice and peace in the world.

The content of our faith and practice is continually reexamined and corrected as we search Holy Scripture and the preserved tradition of the Church. All Christians have access to these sources and are invited to discover for themselves not only the record of God's action in former times but also God's living presence in our contemporary world; in that sense, every member of the church is engaged in theological reflection.

In every generation we consider afresh what it means to speak of the one God who created everything, who is still at work in Christ to "make all things new," that is always breaking into every dimension of our existence. Teachers of children, youth, and adults in the Church play a vital role in helping learners to approach all of life with an attitude of openness in order to discover and proclaim God's presence in relation to every event and movement. Our roles as teachers and learners require critical, discriminative thinking; Christian education's aim is to assist all members of the Church to discern the signs and spirits of the age and to bring sound theological judgment to bear upon what we observe and experience.

• We participate in worship with the prime intention of honoring God as transcendent. We acknowledge our sinfulness and confess our need of forgiveness. We give thanks for the good news of the gospel—that in Christ we receive pardon for all our offenses and are made worthy to stand before God.

In the liturgical life of the Church, we are confronted again and again with the story of God's creative and saving action in the world, revealed supremely in the life and work of Jesus Christ, our risen and ascended Lord. By continual participation in the prayers and rites of the Church, we are engrafted further into its holy fellowship and formed as the living church—glorifying God in the company of apostles and saints who have gone before us, and with all our brothers and sisters in Christ at home and throughout the world.

Participation in the Church's common life of worship is absolutely primary for effective Christian education. But so also is participation in Christ's ministry to individuals in need and to the structures of society when they produce oppression, discrimination, and misery rather than health and wholeness for all of God's people. Thus, we respond in our daily life and work to the saving gospel proclaimed by the church, and to the challenge to take part in carrying out the Church's mission throughout the world.

• At the same time, we engage in a constant process of explaining to ourselves and others where we came from, who we are as baptized persons gathered at the Lord's Table, and what we are called to be and to do in this present time.

We strive for greater knowledge of, and the ability to share:

- the whole story of God's revelation as we receive it from Holy Scripture;
- the lively and continuing tradition of the Church's history and heritage,
- and the practices that are morally and ethically appropriate among contemporary followers of Jesus Christ.

The Bible, Christian theology, church history, and current issues in the world are to be faithfully explored in our struggle to follow the leading of the Holy Spirit and to discover the will of God for our time.

There can be no substitute for serious efforts to teach and learn the Biblical narrative and the story of the Church in all their fullness.

The Church's ministry of teaching is an urgent endeavor undertaken by God's faithful people who renounce sin and evil, who turn to Christ as Savior, and who put their whole trust in the grace and love of God living together as redeemed sinners in the community of the thankful.

Our common life in the Church is not only the locus but also the vehicle of Christian education. Knowing that the Church is called to be a sign to the world of the reign of God that is to come, we engage in our work as teachers and learners so that we may become a people known to bear one another's burdens and to offer comfort and aid to all who suffer and are in need.

We seek also to foster well-informed and active membership in visible structures of the congregations and dioceses, as they pursue concrete acts of witness and mission to the world. We work together with our neighbors who are engaged in many kinds of work as they seek to serve the common good of humanity and to work for peace and justice.

Immersion in the Church's faith and practice through regular participation and repeated explanation becomes, therefore, the foundation for Episcopalians' work of Christian education.

The educative task in a parish or mission is a joint effort of clergy, parents, sponsors and others in the congregation. We cannot rely solely on organized classes for the instruction and nurture of individuals. With the help and support of the whole congregation, parents—by word and example, prayers and witness—seek to bring up their children in the Christian faith and way of life.

It is incumbent on a congregation to provide opportunities for children, youth, and adults to study and learn with their peers. Well-planned congregational structures for Christian education contribute much to the Church's vitality. Parishes that foster strong ministries of teaching for all their members are most likely to grow and to take on meaningful activities of Christian mission. The work of evangelization—reaching out to persons who are not yet baptized or confirmed in the Church—is best undertaken in parishes with strong programs of Christian education.

Christian education is Biblical, theological, historical, liturgical, spiritual, and ethical in content and character. But we do not teach in a setting extracted from the contemporary scene; we are set down in the worlds midst and must learn its language systems in order to communicate and interpret our faith within it. The insights and wisdom of every available discipline devoted to the pursuit of truth about our human situation offer valuable resources for our endeavor.

Members of a congregation, as it gathers for worship and study, bring with them the ways of speaking that are common to their everyday encounters. Teachers in the Church are aware that they must provide bridges between the Word of God (known to us in Jesus Christ, the Bible, and the Church) and the everyday life of learners. Persons who teach are involved in a continual back-and-forth movement between the peculiar language of God's people and the pervasive languages of contemporary society. Toward that end, they are well served by knowledge gained from the social sciences in such areas as these:
- Research and information on patterns of human growth and stages of development that affect how we learn at each age level.
- Theories of group process and behavior that affect the climate of any formal effort to educate persons or to maintain institutions.
- Styles of pedagogy and models for teaching offered as options in schools and classrooms.
- Methods of objective evaluation of the progress of individuals and groups in an educational setting.
- Forms of media used in human communication, with assessment of their relative strengths and weaknesses.

At the very least, the following requisites for a steady program of teaching and learning in the Church will include:

• Committed and prayerful teachers who are dedicated to giving their very best talents and efforts to the enterprise.

• A community of people constantly concerned and willing to support and aid the church's ministry of teaching.

• Appropriately designed material for both teachers and pupils who study the Bible, the Church's story, and the full range of customs and practices of the Anglican and Episcopal traditions in particular.

• Conscious effort on the part of editors, writers, and teachers to relate subject matter to contemporary life issues, in ways appropriate to each age level, with special emphasis on the fostering of individuals' ability to make moral and ethical decisions that reflect their Christian faith.

• Ongoing discussion among teachers (in teams and small groups) concerning the nature of effective Christian education and their own roles.

Effective curriculum resources for Christian education in the Episcopal Church will include the following:

1. Teachers' background material for their personal enrichment as they prepare to teach from the Bible, the Book of Common Prayer, and other sources for interpreting the Church's faith and practice.
2. Helpful discussions of the age-level characteristics of learners.
3. Specific suggestions for teaching procedures.
4. attractive materials to be shared with learners (such as texts and take-home items).

All rights reserved.
Virginia Theological
Seminary, January, 1990

- Notes -

- Notes -

- Notes -

- Notes -

- Notes -

Notes

- Notes -